RELOCATING CULTURAL STUDIES

This collection constitutes a salutary demonstration that Britain no longer serves as the centre for cultural studies. Engaging the critical discourses of feminism, postmodernism and postcolonialism, the contributions explore the renegotiations and changes in cultural studies in the wake of its export from Britain. In particular, the volume shows how the class-dominated issues of earlier practitioners have given way to attempts to understand the lived experiences of marginalized groups, including women and aboriginal peoples in postcolonial states. Questions about the ongoing globalization of capital and culture are linked to constructions of national, local and individual identities.

The alternative relocations of cultural studies offered here manifest two not incommensurate trends: some contributors consider how textual processes of representation articulate with exclusionary practices; others keep alive a sense of politics in respect of institutional and policy debates. The result is an invigorated cultural studies which moves between theory and practice, gives primacy to tensions between extra-local centres of political and economic power and the local, and considers lived experiences within their specific geocultural contexts. It is a collection that can serve as an introduction to cultural studies, a critical re-evaluation of its earlier applications, and a compendium of current theoretical and research interests.

Valda Blundell is Associate Professor in the Department of Sociology and Anthropology, Carleton University, Ottawa; **John Shepherd** is Director, School for Studies in Art and Culture, Carleton University, Ottawa; and **Ian Taylor** is Professor in Sociology, Salford University.

INTERNATIONAL LIBRARY OF SOCIOLOGY

Founded by Karl Mannheim

Edited by John Urry
University of Lancaster

RELOCATING CULTURAL STUDIES

Developments in theory and research

Edited by
Valda Blundell, John Shepherd
and Ian Taylor

London and New York

First published in 1993
by Routledge
11 New Fetter Lane, London EC4P 4EE

Simultaneously published in the USA and Canada
by Routledge
29 West 35th Street, New York, NY 10001

Typeset in Baskerville by Witwell Ltd, Southport
Printed and bound in Great Britain by
TJ Press (Padstow) Ltd, Padstow, Cornwall

British Library Cataloguing in Publication Data
A catalogue record for this book is available from the British Library

Library of Congress Cataloging in Publication Data
Relocating cultural studies: developments in theory and research/
edited by Valda Blundell, John Shepherd, and Ian Taylor.
    p.   cm. – (The International Library of Sociology)
Includes bibliographical references and index.
1. Culture–Study and teaching.   I. Blundell, Valda, 1941– .
II. Shepherd, John, 1947– .   III. Taylor, Ian R.   IV. Series.
        HM101.R425   1993
306′.07–dc20
                                    92-38183
                                    CIP

ISBN 0-415-07548-3
    0-415-07549-1 (pbk)

CONTENTS

v

CONTENTS

CONTRIBUTORS

Tony Bennett is at present Dean in the Division of Humanities at Griffith University where he was also the founding Director of the Institute for Cultural Policy Studies. His publications include *Formalism and Marxism; Bond and Beyond: The Political Hero of a Popular Hero* (with Janet Woollacott) and *Outside Literature*. He is at present completing a study of museums to be published under the title *Show and Tell: The Museum, the Fair and the Exhibition*.

Jody Berland is on the faculty of the Department of Communication Studies, Concordia University, Montreal. She has published widely on music and technology, radio, television, video, and cultural policies. Her most recent paper 'Angels Dancing: Cultural Technologies and the Production of Space' appears in the volume *Cultural Studies*, edited by Lawrence Grossberg, Cary Nelson and Paula Treichler. She is currently researching and writing a series of articles on weather and culture, dealing with issues of technology, politics, gender and representation.

Valda Blundell is Associate Professor of Anthropology at Carleton University in Ottawa. She has carried out ethnographic fieldwork in Australia and Canada, and her interests include the production and consumption of aesthetic forms by or about aboriginal peoples in postcolonial states. Her current research is on cultural tourism in Canada, with particular emphasis on state tourism policies that promote aboriginal cultural forms for touristic consumption. Her papers on Australian aboriginal cultural forms are published in the journals *Culture, Ethnohistory,* and *Mankind,* and those on issues related to First Nations Peoples in Canada in *Anthropologica, Australian* –

Canadian Studies, Inuit Art Quarterly, and *Recherches Amér-indiennes au Québec,* and forthcoming in *Annals of Tourism Research.*

Geraldine Finn is Associate Professor of Cultural Studies at Carleton University in Ottawa. She is a philosopher by training specializing in contemporary feminist and French thought. She has published widely across the disciplines on questions related to science, reason, pornography, fiction, spirituality, music, ethics, politics, and postmodernism. She edited *Feminism: From Pressure to Politics* (with Angela Miles) and *Limited Edition: Voices of Women, Voices of Feminism,* and she is presently working on a book *Feminism and the Politics of Postmodernism.*

Lawrence Grossberg is Professor of Speech Communication, Communications Research, and Criticism and Interpretative Theory at the University of Illinois at Urbana-Champaign. He has published widely on cultural studies, the philosophy of culture, and popular music. He has co-edited several books, including *Marxism and the Interpretation of Culture, Cultural Studies* and *Sound and Vision.* He is the author of *It's a Sin: Essays on Postmodernity, Politics and Culture* and most recently, *We Gotta Get Out of This Place: Popular Conservatism and Postmodern Culture.* He is co-editor of the journal, *Cultural Studies.*

Elspeth Probyn is an Assistant Professor in the Department of Sociology, Université de Montréal, Québec. Her articles on cultural studies and feminism have been published in various journals and anthologies, including *Screen, Hypatia, The Journal of Communication Inquiry, Feminism/Postmodernism,* and *Cultural Studies.* She is the author of *Sexing the Self: Gendered Locations in Cultural Studies* (forthcoming), editor of *Entre le corps et le soi: une sociologie de la subjectivation (Sociologie et Sociétés)* and editor of a new series published by Routledge on feminism, materialism and cultural studies.

John Shepherd is Professor of Music and Sociology at Carleton University, Ottawa, where he is also Director of the School for Studies in Art and Culture. In addition to many articles in the fields of the sociology and aesthetics of music, popular music studies, the sociology of music education, and theory and method in musicology, he is the co-author of *Whose Music? A Sociology* *of Musical Languages*, author of *Tin Pan Alley, La Musica come sapere sociale*, and *Music as Social Text*, editor of *Alternative Musicologies* (a special issue of the *Canadian University Music Review*), and co-editor of *The Music Industry in a Changing World* (a special issue of *Cultural Studies*). Shepherd is currently completing a book with Peter Wicke entitled *The Sound of Music: Meaning and Power in Culture*, which is to be published by Polity in 1993.

Will Straw is Assistant Professor and Program Coordinator of Film Studies within the School for Studies in Art and Culture at Carleton University in Ottawa, Canada. He is a founding member of Carleton's Centre for Research on Culture and Society, and a former chair of the Canadian branch of the International Association for the Study of Popular Music. He has published within the areas of film theory and popular music studies and is on the editorial boards of the journals *Screen* and *Cultural Studies*.

Ian Taylor is Professor of Sociology at the University of Salford, Greater Manchester, England. He is best known for his work in critical criminology, but he has also published a number of papers on current affairs television, 'video nasties', film reviewing, soccer and popular culture in England and the politics of archaeology in Canada. From 1981 to 1989, he was Professor of Sociology at Carleton University in Ottawa and acted for a year as Director of the Centre for Communication and Culture, the predecessor of the present centre for Research on Culture and Society.

Gail Guthrie Valaskakis is a Professor in the Department of Communication Studies and Dean, Faculty of Arts and Science, Concordia University, Montreal. She has researched and written on Northern Native Communications in Canada for two decades, and this work has been widely published. More recently she has written on issues of Indian representation, experience, cultural appropriation and ethnography. This work is published in *Cultural Studies; The Journal of Communications Inquiry; Between Views*, a catalogue of the Walter Phillips Gallery in Banff; and two forthcoming anthologies.

ACKNOWLEDGEMENTS

This book is the result of a collective effort, and therefore we are grateful not only to the contributors whose work appears here but also to the other individuals and institutions who have provided support and encouragement. In particular, we want to thank our colleagues in the Centre for Research on Culture and Society at Carleton University, and also the Deans of Arts and Social Sciences at Carleton for the financial assistance to the Centre which made the initial editing of this volume possible. We give special thanks to Ian Roderick for his painstaking editorial assistance, including the compilation of the book's indexes. Our thanks as well to Wiz Long and Ann Carroll at Carleton University and Sheila Walker at the University of Salford for their help in assembling the final manuscript.

EDITORS' INTRODUCTION

Since the late 1950s there has existed within English-speaking intellectual and cultural life a project which has made a significant impact on academic work within the arts, the humanities and the social sciences. In the 1950s, this project did not have a name. It did not even have a single source. It arose within a particular social and historical context from the work of three individuals with similar but by no means identical concerns. The three individuals (Raymond Williams [Williams 1963], Richard Hoggart [Hoggart 1969], and E. P. Thompson [Thompson 1968]) were concerned in different ways with the question of culture in the class-stratified society of England. In their own way, each author was attempting to understand the role and effect of culture at a critical point in England's own history: a point marked by the end of the Second World War, the inheritance of a class politics of limited endurance in a changed and changing social environment, and the importation or invasion of mass-mediated forms of American culture that made public and highlighted for all the class-ridden character of English cultural life.

It would be misleading to imply that the work of these three authors was in some way co-ordinated. Their work, far from being a *fully fledged* project, was rather a constellation of intellectual and cultural interventions. These interventions were related only by virtue of their authors confronting in their own way similar sets of questions about relations between culture, history and society. Only in retrospect did it become apparent that this work was the beginning of something that later came to be called 'cultural studies'.

1

The name 'cultural studies' derives from the Centre for Contemporary Cultural Studies (CCCS) at the University of Birmingham, and particularly from the 1970s when the Centre was directed by Stuart Hall. 'Birmingham' during this time has taken on a mythological status among cultural studies *aficionados*. It has been graced with the status of a 'school'. However, there were other centres of intellectual activity in Britain at the time (most notably, perhaps, at Leicester and Glasgow) whose work was motivated by similar sets of concerns. Each had its own overall orientation and the scholars who worked there were frequently in dispute with each other and individuals at the Centre in Birmingham. Like Birmingham, they had their own internal differences. Further, there were other foci of intellectual activity such as the New Criminology (associated with the National Deviancy Conferences) and the New Sociology of Education which were informed by concerns similar to those subsequently identified as characteristic of cultural studies. As Hall has recently pointed out (Hall 1990), Birmingham never was a 'school'. It was the location for a set of debates motivated by overlapping and frequently contradictory sets of concerns. This location subsequently became the emblem for ways of thinking about cultural issues symptomatic of a good part of English intellectual life at the time.

It is important to refer to these aspects of the early history of 'cultural studies', not so much to 'put the record straight' or to attempt a precise history as to indicate a fundamental characteristic of the undertaking (or series of undertakings). Unlike established academic disciplines, cultural studies could never aspire to a subject matter capable or deemed capable of being described in terms *abstracted* from the concrete realities it sought to identify and analyse. Cultural studies is not simply about the study of culture. It has never assumed that culture could be identified and analysed in terms independent of the concrete social realities within which it exists and from within which it is manifest. While it would not be totally inappropriate to say that cultural studies has sought to understand relationships between culture and society, it would be to formulate the cultural studies enterprise in one way rather than any other. This formulation would unjustifiably constrain its scope, and would be misleading concerning its motivations and objectives.

Cultural studies has indeed sought to render the relationships between culture and society problematic and to accept that they can never be understood according to the premises of any one theoretical position. However, it has never assumed that there is a phenomenon or set of practices called 'culture' that can be identified separately from any other set of social phenomena or practices. The problem goes further than that of identifying 'culture' and 'society' and attempting to understand the relationships between them. It lies rather in trying to grasp what it feels like to live within particular cultural and social circumstances, and how that feeling or 'structure of feeling' (as Williams referred to it) is embedded within and acts upon wider social practices. If culture is not separable from society then neither, in the conditions of its embeddedness, does it simply reflect the social. Culture is neither distinct from nor reducible to social processes. That, if any, is the character of the cultural studies 'problematic'.

In a strict sense, cultural studies has neither a constantly identifiable subject matter nor theoretical positions that are characteristically its own. A constant in the cultural studies enterprise has, however, been a sense of critical political involvement – in particular, a desire to understand and change structures of dominance in industrial capitalist societies. A sense of this involvement has been present with both cultural studies practitioners and those who view cultural studies from the outside. So a defining characteristic of cultural studies for the majority of its practitioners has been the way in which it has been grounded and politically involved in sets of questions and issues specific to particular social and historical circumstances.

It is important to make these points in a reader dedicated to contemporary developments in cultural studies. These points have been kept general and unspecific because the history of cultural studies has been complex. A knowledge of this history certainly enriches a grasp of contemporary developments. Grossberg's rich and extended opening contribution to this collection serves this purpose. It offers a particular reading of the development of cultural studies from the point of view of an American who spent some time as a graduate student at Birmingham during the late 1960s and who returned to the United States to complete doctoral work and engage in an academic career.

However, while it is helpful to have this kind of perspective on cultural studies in order to understand some of its present concerns, it is not in our view vital to the practice of cultural studies as such. In our view, the purpose of engaging cultural studies is not to learn an intellectual history or a particular set of skills. It is to learn the value of politically engaged intellectual work in understanding how forms of awareness are mediated by and contribute to the social and cultural life in which they occur.

Precisely because it follows its own intellectual nose in terms of what is necessary to understand particular forms of lived awareness, cultural studies does not lend itself easily to the writing of histories or the description of schools. The most that is possible is accounts from various practitioners, each account being informed by the practitioner's own biography and relation to cultural studies. Cultural studies resists being pigeon-holed within the constantly shifting formations of the intellectual map because its concerns are not exclusively or even primarily intellectual. Cultural studies proclaims a concern to understand life as it is lived. This propels cultural studies into an examination of the social, political, cultural and historical forces that are brought to bear on the real complexities of lived experience in particular social formations. But cultural studies is also concerned with the contribution this life makes to the continued trajectories of those forces. Such an enterprise locates its intellectual resources in terms of their appropriateness to the task at hand. These resources have at various times been found within the disciplines of English literature, sociology, communication, anthropology, linguistics and various forms of semiology, film and television studies and, more recently, art history and musicology. Cultural studies takes these resources, interrogates them, adapts them to the task at hand, and interpellates them within its own continuously developing theoretical matrices. These matrices have tended to be complex to match the real complexities of the lived world. And because the majority of cultural studies practitioners have been trained and work within established disciplines, the disciplines that have been touched by cultural studies have been affected significantly by the substance of this theoretical complexity. However, cultural studies itself can never be a 'discipline'. It moves across the intellectual map according to its own motivations and preoccupations, and the directions it takes in its critical negotiations with established disciplinary areas are informed by its political purposes and associated curiosity in respect of theory.

Cultural studies always deals with the everyday world of lived reality, even if only implicitly so. For cultural studies in England, analysis has been focused overwhelmingly on the British working classes. During the 1970s English cultural studies was concerned noticeably with the 'spectacular' styles and behaviour of young working-class men; these styles were then interpreted as a symbolic attempt at 'resistance' on the part of these young working-class males to the facts of their class and age-specific subordination. Later versions of this kind of cultural analysis have broadened the field of vision to include the positions of women and ethnic minorities in a divided society, increasingly feeling the full force of free market policies. Once again, the 'reading' that has been offered of the subcultures of adolescent girls or ethnic minorities is one that searches for signs of resistance and opposition – in the forms of dance hall ritual engaged in by girls or in the Rap music of young West Indians. The tendency, perhaps, has been to read off from these signs the existence of a generalized 'oppositionalism' *vis-à-vis* the dominant culture on the part of women and blacks as a whole.

But if those whom cultural studies analyses have come from the everyday world of lived reality, its analysts have been found in the relatively sequestered world of the academy. While cultural studies has discussed the working classes, visible ethnic minorities, the peoples of the 'Third World', young people, women, gays and lesbians, and – especially in Australian and Canadian work – aboriginal peoples, its academic practitioners have been overwhelmingly white and bourgeois, and predominantly male. This contradiction has been manifest in another way. While the people cultural studies discusses have little trouble grasping the realities of the world in which they live, they would have significant difficulty in understanding many cultural theoretical analyses of them. It is questionable whether the politics and theorizations of cultural studies practitioners always match the political realities of those about whom they write as closely, for example, as the films of Stephen Frears, the popular novels of Hanif Kureishi or the plays of Tomson Highway.

This contradiction, embedded deep in the history and practice of cultural studies, raises the question of who cultural studies is for. Is it for those about whom cultural studies writes? Is it relevant to their lives? Can it make a difference? Or is it for cultural studies practitioners? Does it achieve little but advance the academic careers of those who engage in it? Does it always provide an 'authentic' critique as distinct from a voyeuristic celebration of all that is generated at the level of popular culture? And, at worst, does it function primarily to assuage the political conscience of those (predominantly white, bourgeois and male) who are conscious of difference and differences in power?

These questions are not easy to answer. Neither should they be. The contradiction from which they stem is a contradiction which, in one form or another, continues to fuel cultural studies, to propel it on its various courses in different social and cultural locations. However, what these questions point to is the need to be clear and open on the topic of for whom any intervention is intended. In addressing contemporary developments in theory and research, this volume does not intend to offer a definitive version of the present condition of cultural studies. To do so would be to belie many of the points made already about its character. In so much as the work of cultural studies should be grounded in specific cultural and political moments, so too should critical reflection on cultural studies itself. In the same way that cultural studies cannot bring already existing theoretical and methodological protocols to bear on subject matters that are typically its own, so critical reflection on its theoretical and substantive trajectories has to be grounded in the territory to be examined and the biography of the critic. Such is the case with Lawrence Grossberg's contribution.

The volume is therefore intended to be used rather than studied. It is intended to be a stimulus for students and others in thinking about cultural and political issues in contexts other than those from which the contributions stem. The volume thus attempts the kind of double and dialectical grounding crucial to any cultural studies undertaking: a grounding in the location of the contributions and the biographies of the contributors, as well as a grounding envisioned in the lives and worlds of those for whom the volume is intended.

Critical to this particular grounding is an acceptance that England (or Britain) is no longer *the* locus for cultural studies. With the advent of the Thatcher years cultural studies in England fragmented and was exported to other English-speaking locations, predominantly the United States, Australia and Canada. In these locations the theoretical and substantive concerns that came out of England have had to be not so much inflected as renegotiated. While none of these locations is free of class, the class-dominated concerns of English cultural studies (and particularly its preoccupation with spectacular subcultures) afforded little space for concerns which were not indigenous to English cultural life. It is of interest, for example, that all three locations to which cultural studies was exported have continuing and serious debates about the place of aboriginal peoples in white-dominated societies. These concerns are not present in England, and Europeans in general might have difficulty relating to them.

The fragmentation and export of English cultural studies occurred also at a time when the character of global politics and economics was changing fast. As the 1980s progressed the populist rhetorics of Thatcher and Reagan (in their different ways inclusive, authoritarian and chauvinist) seemed increasingly out of place. Both sets of rhetoric harked back to an era when the political-economic unit of the nation state was important to capital enterprise, and when capital enterprise as a consequence required a substantive ideology, rhetoric or narrative to sustain and reproduce itself. It is significant that while the United States was recently able to wage a war in the Middle East as a way of revitalizing and shoring up its own narrative of self-sufficient individualism and freedom, it was not able to pay for it. In becoming more truly global, transnational capital enterprise needs to transcend the narratives of the national, the regional and the local more than it does reinforce them. There is a sense in which it is no longer important to transnational capital what people buy so long as they do buy. From the point of view of transnational capital, values attached to commodities need no longer serve to sustain ideologies conducive to the reproduction of the national and local structures within which capital operates. Values attached to commodities are, however, important to the formation of tastes which underwrite markets in particular localities.

In this sense it may matter little to capital that values are ascribed 'by consumers' rather than 'by the agents of capital'. If consumers buy what is complexly meaningful to them (complex because meaning is always negotiated, never given or simply ascribed) then the task of capital is to become equally sophisticated in second-guessing not only the particular taste-formations of specific markets, but also the characteristics of

7

commodities that can be interpellated successfully into a wide range of markets with different taste-formations. It is arguable that Michael Jackson's *Thriller* album was successful, not because it contained an inherent set of values or meanings that slavishly hypnotized 40,000,000 consumers across the world, but because it offered up a complex cultural medium in which 40,000,000 consumers could successfully invest meanings that, although complexly negotiated, remained nonetheless distinctively local.

The act of consumption is thus political. However, while it may be important whether a tourist buys a cheap, mass-produced replica of an aboriginal artefact or the artefact itself, the high level of personal investment made by consumers in particular and relatively restricted musical tastes may not. Oppositional meanings and values that once may have appeared to challenge the ground on which capital operated (this was one of the main areas of interest of earlier forms of cultural studies in their interrogations of music and youth culture) may now serve only to constitute that very same ground.

Modernity has thus passed into postmodernity. In parallel fashion, postmodern analyses of culture have become more preoccupied with the consequences of culture's fragmentation and less concerned with the political economy of its production, dissemination and consumption. This fragmentation is variously assumed either to open up possibilities for the political empowerment of consumers or to be symptomatic of the impending dissolution of industrial capitalism as a way of life. As Grossberg indicates, postmodernism represents the most recent area of intellectual endeavour with which cultural studies has intersected in a contentious yet fertile manner.

Given the context of the internationalization of capital and its cultural expressions, students of contemporary culture have been paying increasing attention to questions of identity: identity in relation to the national, the local and the individual. If capital has become increasingly global in its operations, then it has in one sense become further removed from the ground. While it has been increasingly successful in co-opting, recycling and remarketing previous forms of oppositional expression, it has nonetheless afforded more space at the national and local levels within which individuals are frequently able to maintain a degree of autonomy in relation to the transnational. Cultural studies scholarship in the 1980s and 1990s has thus not surprisingly reoriented itself away from the celebration of resistance implicit in much English work of the 1970s. Diversified politically over and above responses to the new geocultural circumstances of the USA, Australia and Canada, it has either become less political, treating textual processes (processes to do with the way in which literate, visual and oral-aural cultural forms signify or 'have meaning') as more aesthetic than political in a postmodernist vein, or alternatively has kept alive a sense of politics in respect, primarily, of institutional and policy debates.

While these two trends may have created a tug of war in reproducing the textual–contextual divide which has characterized much cultural studies work since its inception, they are, as Tony Bennett argues, not incommensurable. Bennett's contribution to this volume moves cultural studies closer to dispensing with a divide which has always been troubling epistemologically. He posits a fundamental challenge to cultural studies' tendency to separate analyses of texts from the examination of practice or policy. In rejecting the 'text' as an aesthetically signifying instrument for changing consciousness (as part of a 'politics of resistance'), Bennett also moves cultural studies closer to a realization that 'textual' processes are *themselves* powerful instrumentally in relation to their governmental, institutional and technological placing. In other words, while the seat of culture's power does not lie in monolithic forces *outside* culture's own processes, culture's power occurs only *in relation to* practices of a policy and institutional order. If the notion that power is both dispersed and 'inherent' remains problematic, then it becomes necessary to theorize cultural effectivity nationally, locally and individually in relation to a great variety of significant centres of extrinsic political economic power.

Questions of identity and of identity's relation to 'centres of power' therefore remain important and necessarily become linked to questions of marginality – to the issue of how experience is lived outside the central locales of political or economic power and influence. The remaining six essays in this volume are concerned in different ways with just these questions. All are by Canadians who contributed (as did Lawrence Grossberg and Tony Bennett) to an international conference on cultural and communications studies held at Carleton University in Ottawa in April 1989. While it would be misleading to overplay the connection between cultural studies as practised in the English-speaking intellectual and artistic communities of Montreal and Ottawa on the one hand and internationally articulated concerns with nationhood, identity and power in postmodern societies on the other, the alliance between location and concerns is hardly coincidental either. It can be argued that there obtain within many of Canada's cultures circumstances which give these questions special significance in Canada – a claim which is also made in much cultural studies work carried out in Australia. Will Straw remarks on this connection in his contribution to this volume. 'At the beginning of the 1990s', he writes, 'I shared with many the sense that, while cultural studies had begun within Great Britain and undergone remarkable expansion within the United States, it promised to become increasingly Canadian and Australian.' He concludes that 'current interrogation of notions of nationhood and cultural identity and the debate over the relationship of cultural theory to questions of public policy and economic development, have at the very least encouraged the migration of theoretical and intellectual work between Canada and Australia'.

As Straw notes, cultural studies in Canada developed historically within communication. This explains a 'long-time tension between the appeal of cultural studies as an ongoing, multi-national project of theoretical revision and [a] commitment to working simultaneously in areas, like those of media policy studies or political economy, which seemed more concretely interventionist'. This explains also the connection to the more policy-oriented work carried out in Australia, work of which Bennett's contribution to this volume is but one example.

The development of communication as a discipline was as heterogeneous in Canada as elsewhere. But, as elsewhere, it too was influenced by the particular intellectual, cultural, policy and topographical environment in which it found itself. Two circumstances in particular have influenced both the development and understanding of communications in Canada: the fact that Canada's relatively small population (smaller than the state of California) is spread along a narrow girth stretching further than is possible in any other country in the world, and the fact that this girth is seldom further than an hour or two's drive from the United States. The concern has therefore been with advanced technology – how to connect a thinly spread, far-flung and culturally diverse population effectively and with specific reference to the 'Canadian experience' – and with how to guarantee the specificity of that experience in juxtaposition to the filling of the airwaves and other media of communication from the South. There has been a concern with the notion of binding a people together across a vast, underpopulated and sometimes hostile territory. However, there has also been an interest in resisting other cultures (particularly as they emanate from the South) as part of the continuing exercise of self-definition.

The exercise remains a difficult and frustrating one. The failure of the Meech Lake accord in the summer of 1990 has effectively left Canada without a workable constitution. Not unrelated to this constitutional uncertainty has been the way in which the dramatic events of the same summer at 'Oka' (explained below) provided a graphic reminder to Canadians of the major and fundamental issues that remain to be resolved between Canada's aboriginal peoples and centres of economic and political power. Finally, the Free Trade Agreement with the United States which came into effect at the beginning of 1989 shows every sign of eroding Canada's economic base and thus making it even more difficult to underwrite cultural identities that are both viable and distinctively Canadian.

The question of English Canadian cultural identity is, however, a long-standing one. While there is a sense in which recognition is afforded internationally to a British cultural identity, an American cultural identity and an Australian cultural identity, English Canadians are acutely conscious that no parallel identity can be exported beyond the country's borders to make a similar impact abroad. Also, while other national identities have at the very least been contested and have provided the ground for cultural theoretical critique (national identities are constructed rather than given, and are markedly less uniform and pervasive than often assumed), there has seemed little in English Canada to contest and critique. The reasons for this are complex and are discussed by John Shepherd in his contribution to the volume. The effect, however, has been central to the way that many English Canadians feel about being Canadian. It is captured powerfully by Jody Berland in a manner which connects back to questions of communication:

While 'Canada' is defined more than ordinarily as a unity bonded by technology, our media more than ordinarily draw us into exterior landscapes. Situated in many places at the same time, tuned in, hooked up, wired into, we know how to see ourselves as part of a global village, and to see its boundarylessness as the essence of who we are. Thus the frequent gender analogies for Canada in relation to the USA: in contemporary feminist analysis, woman is always Other to a dominant power in relation to whom she gains (momentary) advantage through submission, becoming consequently untidy in establishing clear boundaries to her self. It is a state which is intimately related to resentment and to silence and which tends to be articulated, if at all, in a discourse of absence. Thus Canadian culture, manifested in much spoken and unspoken *ressentiment,* a revenge against the present which preserves its own absence by denying its rage . . .

(Berland 1988: 347)

If communication in Canada has ensured a trajectory of cultural studies distinct in its interventionist instincts from the more postmodern and aesthetically textual orientation of cultural studies in the United States, then cultural studies has likewise ensured a form of communication able to sympathize with the overall aims and intentions of successive governments while at the same time illustrating how resulting media policies can belie those very same aims and intentions.

Cultural studies in English Canada distanced itself from communication during the 1980s as that discipline became increasingly professionalized in response to a need on the part of governments and media organizations for graduates from communication programmes. The tension between the international and the local, the theoretical and the interventionist, nonetheless remains. However, the line between the two is difficult to draw, and with good reason. As Straw observes: 'Progressive work within Canadian cultural studies has long held as one of its imperatives the deployment elsewhere of the Canadian example as one with wider applicability, particularly within debates such as those over cultural globalization or postmodernity'. As Straw concludes: 'The project of a "Canadianized" cultural studies . . .

has not confined itself to the adaptation and domestication of theoretical agendas emergent elsewhere'.

Straw's paper provides an important link between the first part of this volume (*Wars of Positions*) and the remaining two parts (*Power and Empowerment* and *Cultural Studies and the Local*). Against the background of Grossberg's critical history and Bennett's invocations for the future, it lays the ground for understanding why concerns of more general current international interest find a particular resonance in English Canada in ways which sometimes evidence distinctive formations. Elspeth Probyn's piece, for example, confronts head-on the issue of who speaks about whom in cultural studies and with what effect. In addressing the 'problem' of autobiography in cultural studies she questions the relation of the subject and the subject's sense of self to experience, the research agenda which may grow out of these biographical processes, and the consequent production of knowledge. It was Angela McRobbie who first connected the 'politics of the personal' and cultural studies' research agenda and so provided cultural studies with its first major feminist intervention (McRobbie 1980). The issues raised in that intervention have hardly been resolved, as Geraldine Finn indicates in her contribution on the 'absence' of women postmodernists. Postmodernism, in her view, is evidence of yet another 'master discourse and discourse of mastery' which continues to operate as a totalizing means of obscuring the self, the subject who is inescapably positioned in one way or another in relation to texts. Finn's feminist critique thus heightens and provides a broader context for other criticisms of postmodernism's influence which have been mounted from within cultural studies.

It is the tradition of post-structuralism which has provided us, as Probyn notes, with 'a more complex view of the subject'. Post-structuralism, however, demonstrated its own totalizing, phallocentric and logocentric biases in precluding significant opportunities for human agency. An assimilation of postmodernism by cultural studies (which has frequently been characterized by its assertions of agency) can nonetheless reassert, as Grossberg argues, the notion of the critical voice. 'As a model of interpretation', he says, 'postmodern conjuncturalism emphasizes its own articulation of the conjuncture which it analyses; it cannot ignore its own reflexive position within it.'

13

Consequently, concludes Grossberg, 'the voice of the critic becomes determining'. It in other words ceases to be spoken for. As well as being influenced by an intellectual movement which lends a mechanism of totalizing silence, therefore, cultural studies itself can provide the critical ground in terms of which it is possible to think of voices with specific identities speaking with consequence to the realities within which they live. As Probyn concludes, 'a feminist cultural studies approach to the autobiographical reveals the voice as strategy'.

While the concerns of Probyn and Finn may not appear distinctively Canadian on the surface (despite the situating of Finn's arguments in certain Canadian intellectual contexts), they are nonetheless concerns which typically resonate, as Berland has indicated, with the lived experiences of English Canadian cultural processes. If Probyn's and Finn's topic, as differently formulated, is the discursive and institutional marginality of women, then it is a form of marginality experienced also by English Canadians in their daily lives. Probyn observes that approaching the voice as strategy 'is not to proclaim its politics as evident truths, but, if worked upon and worked over, these personal voices can be articulated as strategies, as ways of going on theorizing'. This observation may be salutary for the interventionist theorizing of the English Canadian situation.

This situation is nothing if not contradictory. Not the least of these contradictions has been the way in which national, state-sponsored systems of communication (the CBC, Canada Post and other Federal Government agencies) have helped to create and sustain a sense of national identity at the expense of institutionalizing mainstream English and French Canadian cultures as the centres to other margins. Among the many different groups of Canadians excluded from this 'family compact' are aboriginal peoples themselves. Indeed, the extent of this marginalization and exclusion was demonstrated by those events, now signified as 'Oka', which took place on and near two Indian reserves in the province of Quebec during the summer of 1990 in the form of armed confrontations between natives and the Canadian army. The dispute was over land claimed as an Indian reserve by Mohawks of Kanesatake that was being developed as a golf course by residents of the adjacent town of Oka. In sympathy, Mohawks from the nearby Kahnawake reserve blockaded a major bridge between Montreal and its southern suburbs, with angry confrontations resulting between native protesters and non-native Montrealers whose commuting routes to work were blocked off.

As Gail Valaskakis demonstrates in her paper, another particular manifestation of this marginalization and exclusion is the representation of the Indian as an 'artefact' in tourism literature. This is one of many appropriations by non-aboriginal Canadians of aboriginal cultural forms which have the effect (and the affect) of perpetuating myths about aboriginal peoples. As Valaskakis writes: 'these representations conceal the structured subordination of Indians in a country carved out by companies and charters, proclamations and promises'. As recurring references in Canada's political discourses to 'Oka' and 'post-Oka' events reveal, such concerns regarding representational practices occur in the context of a volatile national debate regarding aboriginal rights, as aboriginal peoples seek *both* political and cultural autonomy. Today the agenda of aboriginal 'First Nations' includes not only the settlement of land claims and the establishment of native self-government but also their attainment of greater control over how their cultural products and signs – what they sometimes call 'their stuff' – are to be used, and by whom. As is the case for aboriginal peoples in other postcolonial states, then, cultural forms are an important and increasingly fractious arena of political struggle in Canada, and control over culture is seen by aboriginal peoples as a means of their empowerment.

These questions of power and representation, foreshadowed in the contributions of Probyn and Finn, resurrect themselves in a context other than that of gender. These questions raise other questions to do with power and signification. To what extent does the power to own and place an artefact determine the positions and meanings which flow from it? We are back here with some of the concerns raised by Bennett. In accounting for the absences and silences of English Canadian political cultures and their 'manifestation' in the world of popular music, Shepherd argues that the politics of positioning must still be seen to involve a dialectic. This is crucial to an understanding of value and power in music. Voices will be present, even if their effect can only be a potentially subversive reading and reinscription that is heard only dimly. The fact that voices are always present forces a theorization of the distinction between the presence of

15

texts as material configurations and the opportunities they provide (and do *not* provide) for the construction and investment of various forms of awareness. While material configurations may be easily owned and transferred, therefore, and placed for optimum cultural effect, it does not follow that the effect desired will be the effect achieved. The international currency of the world's music in transnational popular musics provides an interesting case in point. Music operates 'instrumentally' rather than 'aesthetically' in its capacity to structure and position bodies concretely. Yet the 'directness' of its instrumentality is mediated, not only by processes that are governmental, institutional and technological, but by the agency of subject's bodies. Culture, it may be concluded, does not travel quite as easily and quite as innocently as the material grounds and pathways which make its concrete articulation possible.

The power of culture to position is a theme that permeates the concluding contribution to this volume by Jody Berland. Berland's work has of late evidenced a particularly English Canadian trajectory, and her contribution here is no exception to this trend. It is replete, after all, with snow and Mounties. But it is also, and much more importantly, replete with the sense of repression, with the sense of angered silence that characterizes many English Canadian political cultures. A second contradiction of cultural and media policies in Canada has been the way in which their intention to sustain and promote Canadian identity has resulted only in a cultural absence evidenced in the international success of Canadians in styles indistinguishable from those of transnational mainstreams. This sense of a futile cultural silence resonates powerfully, argues Berland, in the way that English Canadians talk only semi-privately yet with hardly a respite about the winter climate, while at the same time tolerating the absence of any meaningful discussion of this climate publicly. English Canadians are not only constrained and controlled by the conditions of their winter climate. They are also constrained, positioned, if not disciplined through the terms of its presentation in the media. It is the absent Other to the warmth and comfort of desires and pleasures structured from elsewhere and a reminder, puritanically and tartly, that English Canadians must always and in a certain sense remain others within that positioning.

16

REFERENCES

Berland, Jody (1988) 'Locating listening: technological space, popular music, Canadian mediations', *Cultural Studies* 2, 3: 343–58.

Hall, Stuart (1990) 'The emergence of cultural studies and the crisis of the humanities', *October* 53: 11–23.

Hoggart, Richard (1969) *The Uses of Literacy*, Harmondsworth: Penguin.

McRobbie, Angela (1980) 'Settling accounts with subcultures: a feminist critique', *Screen Education* 34: 37–49.

Thompson, E. P. (1968) *The Making of the English Working Class*, Harmondsworth: Penguin.

Williams, Raymond (1963) *Culture and Society, 1780–1950*, Harmondsworth: Penguin.

Part I

WARS OF POSITIONS

1

THE FORMATIONS OF CULTURAL STUDIES

An American in Birmingham[1]

Lawrence Grossberg

Any observer of the academic scene in the United States will surely note that there has been a cultural studies 'boom' (Morris 1988a). As Allor (1987) notes, the term itself has become a cultural commodity, apparently free to circulate in the global economy of discourse, ideas, and cultural capital. Five years ago, the term functioned largely as a proper name, referring primarily to a specifically British tradition, extending from the work of Raymond Williams and Richard Hoggart, through the contributions of the various members of the Centre for Contemporary Cultural Studies (CCCS) at the University of Birmingham, to the increasingly dispersed and institutionalized sites of its contemporary practitioners. Additionally – and especially within the field of communication – the term also referenced a uniquely American tradition rooted in the social pragmatism of the Chicago School of Social Thought. However, 'cultural studies' is becoming one of the most ambiguous terms in contemporary theory as it is increasingly used to refer to the entire range and diversity of what had been previously thought of as 'critical theory' (i.e. a range of competing theories of the relation of society and culture, of ideology and art, largely derived from 'high literary theory' and anthropology, with communication and popular culture once again relegated to a secondary position) (Grossberg 1989).

While it is futile to protest against this appropriation of the term, it is important to point to a set of potential dangers: namely, that British cultural studies is reduced to a singular position or a linear history (thus, ignoring its differences) or dispersed into a set of unrelated differences (thus, ignoring its

21

limited. Forms of collective work were celebrated without analysing the ways in which they could disempower as well as empower individuals and groups. Class, gender and race relations institutionalized within the academy remained sites of silence for too long and, despite a real concern for popular culture, the intellectual distanciation from the popular characteristic of the traditional intellectual also remained in place for too long (Fry 1988). Nevertheless, I believe that the Centre (and the formation of cultural studies I am describing) is important, not only intellectually, but also as a model of interdisciplinary, collective and politically engaged research. Finally, I want at least to acknowledge the fact that this formation of cultural studies was produced in the social interactions of real individuals with their own agendas and biographies. A part of the history of the Centre – a part that I will not discuss here – involves the changing histories and relations of those working at the Centre and in cultural studies. Like C. Wright Mills, cultural studies has always embraced the passion of intellectual and political work (even if it rarely theorized passion in its objects of study). Such work is always determined partly by the very real – and in the case of the Centre, enduring – relationships and communities (both positive and negative) that such work produces, even if only through imaginary and retrospective identifications. And the unity-in-difference of cultural studies is partly the result of these very real social and emotional relationships.

A NORMATIVE HISTORY OF CULTURAL STUDIES

Political contexts

Cultural studies emerged in the 1950s at the intersection of a number of complex historical experiences. Sometimes the focus was on 'the Americanization of Britain' and other times on the new forms which modernization was taking after the Second World War. Both descriptions pointed to the appearance of a 'mass culture' made possible through the rationalization, capitalization and technologization of the mass media. Within this new cultural space, for the first time, the vast majority of the population was incorporated into a common audience for cultural products. Of course, the concern for 'mass culture' predated the Second World War. But the obviously central role of American culture and capital to these changes and their increasing reach into British society through popular cultural and communicative forms seemed to make the threat they posed more substantial and specific. This threat was aimed neither at communities nor elites, but rather at class cultures and the possibilities of a democratic cultural formation.[2]

A second historical development was the emergence of the New Left[3] – which counted among its members many of the founding figures of cultural studies – in response, at least in part, to the failure of the traditional marxist left to confront, in both theoretical and political terms, the beginnings of late capitalism, the new forms of economic and political colonialism and imperialism, the existence of racism within the so-called democratic world, the place of culture and ideology in relations of power, and the effects of consumer capitalism upon the working classes and their cultures.

In the 1960s, other concerns impinged upon cultural studies, and while they did not totally displace the earlier concerns, they often gave them new inflections. Here again one can point to two exemplary developments: first, the growing importance of the mass media, not only as forms of entertainment but, inseparably, as what Althusser called 'ideological state apparatuses'. There was in fact, quite explicitly, a significant focus during the 1960s (and through much of the 1970s) on the more overt ideological functions of the media – in the news and documentary programming – where one could see a direct connection to the political sphere. This narrowing of focus was contradicted to some extent by the second development which engaged cultural studies in the 1960s: the emergence of various subcultures which seemed, in various ways, to resist at least some aspects of the dominant structures of power. Yet these subcultures were organized around non-traditional political issues, contradictions, and social positions, and struggled in the uncommon terrain of popular culture. Obviously the rise of various working-class youth cultures and the sustained organization of a middle-class oppositional subculture had an enormous impact on the work of cultural studies.

In the 1970s, we might again identify two significant developments, both of which had immediate and powerful effects on cultural studies. First, the renewed appearance of political and theoretical work around relations of gender and sexual

25

difference. The response to feminism was mediate and sustained, if not always completely sympathetic or adequate. Nevertheless, I think it is fair to say that there is no cultural studies which is not 'post-feminist', not in the sense of having moved beyond it but rather in the sense of having opened itself to the radical critique and implications of feminist theory and politics. The second development was equally powerful, disturbing cultural studies' too-easy identification and celebration of resistance (which rested upon a taken-for-granted analysis of domination and subordination). I am referring to the rise of the New Right as a powerful political and ideological force in Britain (as well as in other advanced capitalist democratic countries), often constructed on top of explicitly racist themes. Additionally, the fortunes of the neoconservatives seemed to be inversely related to the fragmentation, if not the apparent collapse, of organized opposition from the left. As new political agencies and positions emerged on the right, the traditional left seemed incapable of offering coherent strategies and responses.

In the 1980s and early 1990s many of these problems continue to assert themselves, albeit in different and in some cases even more pressing forms. Moreover, there is a return of many of the more apocalyptic concerns that had emerged in the immediate postwar period (global threats to the future and epochal experiences of irrationality, terror and meaninglessness) which appear with great force in both popular media and intellectual discourses. Equally important is the increasing self-consciousness of our own insertion into the construction of domination in our relations to the production of intellectual work and to students and our complex relations to political differences at all levels of the social formation. And finally, the fact that the victory of the right has been secured (at least enough to have allowed Thatcher to undermine significantly the social infrastructure of Britain) can be measured in the left's apparent distance from the majority of the population (not only that between academics and their students) and the inability of the left to secure a new ground from which to organize opposition.

Theoretical development

These political and historical concerns were organized by, responded to with, and mapped onto, a series of theoretical debates and challenges. Sometimes these debates placed cultural studies on one side (e.g. when it firmly opposed what it saw as the abandoning of the materialist problematic by post-structuralist and psychoanalytic discourse theorists). More often, cultural studies places itself between the two extremes, as in Stuart Hall's (1980b) description of the need to locate a space for cultural studies between structuralism and culturalism. In fact, cultural studies seems to slide, almost inevitably, from the former argument to the latter (e.g. Hall [forthcoming] wherein cultural studies is located not in opposition to psychoanalysis but rather in between its extreme reductionist forms and those who would either deny its truth or water down its radical insights). Opposing alternative positions enables it to maintain its own identity and that of its specific problematic and commitments. But mediation allows it to take into account its own inadequacies and the insights which reinflect its problematic and commitments into new historical contexts. Thus, one of the most common rhetorical figures in cultural studies is that which positions its intellectual antagonist as having rightly attempted to avoid one extreme position but having mistakenly gone 'right through to the other extreme'. Within these debates, which often took place within the Centre as well as between the Centre and other institutionalized sites of intellectual activity, we should not be surprised to find that each side necessarily misreads and misrepresents the other side in order to reconstitute its own position.[4]

The beginning of cultural studies is usually located in the debate between the socialist humanism of Williams, Thompson and Hoggart (despite the significant political differences among them) and traditional marxist, literary and historical approaches to contemporary life and politics. The former, including the original New Left group, challenged the economic reductionism of the marxists, arguing for the importance of the creative human actor, of human experience, and of the determining power of cultural production itself. They similarly rejected (to varying degrees) the elitism which was used to justify the erasure of working-class people and culture from the study of history. Such 'culturalists', in their first attempts to define cultural studies, argued that culture was not only the site of struggle but its source and measure as well. Culture was the intersection of textuality and experience, and the task of criticism was to examine how the former represented and misrepresented the latter. They rejected both a theory of dominance (which denied the reality of cultural struggle) and a theory of reflection (which radically separated culture and society, reading society off the meanings of culture even as it was located outside them).

But cultural studies emerges as a disciplinary formation and intellectual position in the confrontation (initially it was often silent) between this humanistic marxism (which Hall calls 'culturalism') and the anti-humanism of Althusser's structural marxism. The latter pointed to the former's reductionist assumption of a series of necessary correspondences between cultural forms, experience and class position. Althusser challenged any appeal to either the subject or experience as the source or measure of history since neither existed outside the processes of historical (and specifically ideological) determination. At the same time, he recognized the power and relative autonomy of the cultural realm. By distancing the 'real' as the determining moment of history (in either the first or last instance), Althusser gave renewed impetus to the project of defining the specificity of the cultural. It is out of this debate that the position which many people identify with Birmingham cultural studies arises. It is a moment in which, to put it emblematically, Williams is 'saved' by rereading him through Althusserian structuralism.

In the mid-1970s, this refined culturalism entered into very explicit (and often heated) debates, not with Althusserianism but with a different appropriation of structural marxism. If cultural studies tempered Williams' humanism with structuralism (and in so doing backed off from Althusser's radical anti-humanism), it opposed those theories which took Althusser into the post-structuralist realm of the necessary lack of correspondence with a new reading of Gramsci, who served to define a different 'middle ground'. Such 'discourse theories' read Althusser's theory of ideology, often in conjunction with Foucault's theory of power, through a Derridean explosion of both signification and subjectification. Moreover, culturalism opposed those who, often from within the Centre, attempted to link Althusser (and perhaps post-structuralism) with a Lacanian psychoanalysis which abandoned any notion of history in favour of a predefined psychoanalytic trajectory constantly traced out upon ideological practices. Both versions of 'post-structural Althusser' ignored the materialist question of the role of ideology in the reproduction of the social formation in favour of what might be described as a discursive social psychology. Cultural studies argued that such theories reduced the question of social identity and its political import to the predetermined repetition of textual and/or libidinal processes. Furthermore, such positions seemed incapable of theorizing even the possibility of resistance except through the production of radically alternative and avant garde discursive forms. Such forms would either necessarily celebrate the infinite plurality of meaning and the endless fragmentation of the subject or they would escape the political terrain entirely by appealing to the ultimate political undecideability of any text.

On the other hand, post-structural appropriations of Althusser argued that cultural studies' continued commitment to humanism (with its concomitant notions of essentialist class identities and experiences) made it impossible to theorize the production of subjectivity and subject-positions as a significant ideological effect which often contradicted the surface content of cultural forms. While cultural studies thought of ideology as a continuous process by which identities, organized at sites of social difference, were given meaning, it was unable to theorize the more fundamental nature of the process by which identities and social differences were themselves produced together as subject-positions. Thus, it was not fortuitous that it would seek out and celebrate the sites of cultural resistance in the working classes but would, at the same time, be incapable of seeing that the forms of such resistances often reinscribed dominant relations of power – especially racism and sexism.

What emerged from this debate, according to the standard history, was a significantly different position which can be seen as either a reading of Gramsci (through Althusser) as a non-structuralist anti-humanist or alternatively, as a rereading of Althusser (through Gramsci, who had of course been a source of Althusser's theorizing) without following the post-structuralists, psychoanalysts and discourse theorists out of the materialist problematic altogether. This Gramscian position defined cultural studies as a non-reductionist marxism which was concerned with understanding specific historical contexts and formations, which assumed the lack of guarantees in history and the reality of struggles by which historical relationships are produced. Such a 'conjuncturalist' theory refuses to assimilate all practices to culture and recognizes the real structuration of power

29

according to relations of domination and subordination. It sees history as actively produced by individuals and social groups as they struggle to make the best they can out of their lives under determinate conditions.

But this position is already entangled in yet another significant debate: its focus on historical and cultural specificity has led it into direct confrontation with the 'postmodernist' theories of Baudrillard, Lyotard, Virilio, and others. While this moment has not yet been incorporated into this linear narrative, the debate between these two narrative opposites is already being constructed as the next chapter of the story. Thus it is already clear that the opposition of cultural studies to the extremism of much of postmodernist theorizing – to its radical critique of the very possibility of any structure, of any meaning, of any subject, and of any politics, and to its reinscription of a form of reductionism in which every text becomes a reflection of our noncontradictory existence within the postmodern condition – is resulting in yet another significant move.

CULTURAL STUDIES: NARRATIVIZING A WAR OF POSITIONS

I do not want to argue against this history so much as to reread it in order to open it up to greater complexities.[5] As far as it goes it is an accurate and important map of cultural studies' shifting position in relation to the larger field of materialist and structuralist theories of ideology and culture. Even more important, it allows us to see that the identity of any theoretical position within this larger terrain is constituted by a series of differences among the range of possible positions. Thus, to a limited extent, this narrative already suggests that cultural studies is constituted through a series of struggles around certain key concepts and critical strategies. For example, the meaning of 'hegemony' within cultural studies cannot be taken for granted. There are significant, and in fact constitutive, differences between its appearance, not only in Williams and Gramsci but in the culturalist and the conjuncturalist positions of the Birmingham group. This normative narrative represents the history as a 'war of manoeuvres' in which a series of closed paradigms, each with its fixed set of assumptions, oppose each other. The narrative represents either a gradual and rational transformation through intellectual dialogue or a series of radically disjunctive and totalized paradigm shifts. In either case, the development of cultural studies *appears* to be linear, progressive, and internally directed. Cultural studies is portrayed as the continuing struggle to realize its own already defined, if imperfectly articulated, project (e.g. an anti-essentialist, anti-reductionist, anti-elitist cultural theory). Although not necessarily teleological, the narrative imagines a series of stages which did not in practice exhibit the necessary conceptual and reflexive capacities with which this project could have been advanced so unproblematically.

Moreover, this narrative ignores the continuous debates within and between the variety of positions offered, not only over time, but at any moment within the Centre and cultural studies. It also ignores the ongoing labour of transformation which has operated on the complex and contradictory terrain of cultural studies. An alternative reading of that history would have to recognize that within the discourses of cultural studies theory proceeds discontinuously and often erratically, that it involves an ongoing struggle to rearrange and redefine the theoretical differences of the terrain itself in response to a particular set of historical questions.

Such a revisionist reading would begin with cultural studies as an historically articulated discursive formation, constantly redefining itself across a range of questions. Rather than assuming an essential and unified harmony, it would begin with diverse sets of conjoint positions in contention with each other at a variety of sites. Rather than offering a rational history of dialectical development, it would constantly destabilize the correspondences between conceptual differences and historical trajectories in order to describe a war of positions, operating over a range of theoretical and political sites. Cultural studies often moves onto terrain it will later have to abandon; and it often abandons some terrain it will later have to reoccupy. Cultural studies, like any critical project, has had its share of false starts which, however necessary, have often taken it down paths it has had to struggle to escape, forcing it at times to retrace its steps and at other times to leap onto paths it had barely imagined. Texts that were read at one point had to be read again; commitments that were articulated had to be re-established at some moments and deconstructed at others.

If we begin to consider the discontinuities as well as the continuities in the various ways cultural studies has occupied and reshaped its own terrain, we need to identify some signposts for the various sites of struggle in this war of positions. Only then can we renarrativize the formation of cultural studies, not merely as one of intellectual influence and progress, but as a continuing struggle, on the one hand, to define the specificity of cultural struggle and, on the other hand, to comprehend the specificity of the historical context of modernity and modernization within and against which contemporary cultural practices function. We might all acknowledge that cultural studies is concerned with describing and intervening in the ways 'texts' and 'discourses' are produced within, inserted into, and operate in the everyday lives of human beings and social formations so as to reproduce, struggle against and perhaps transform the existing structures of power. That is, if people make history but in conditions not of their own making, cultural studies explores the ways this is enacted within and through cultural practices and the place of these practices within specific historical formations. But this description – which underlies the standard narrative – fails to recognize that cultural studies has continuously problematized not only the meaning of 'culture' and 'society' but the historical articulations of the relationships between them.

I shall begin by identifying eight sites of what in contemporary political parlance might be called 'low-intensity warfare', eight theoretical and political issues. They are not all specific to cultural studies but they do enable us to map out some of the directions and tendencies in cultural studies. For the sake of brevity, I will merely list the eight theoretical problematics. They are, I will assume, fairly self-explanatory (and if they are not, they will be explained as the shifts in position are charted):

1 epistemology and interpretation;
2 determination;
3 agency;
4 the structure of the social formation;
5 the structure of the cultural formation;
6 power;
7 the specificity of cultural struggle; and
8 the historical site of modernity.

In what follows, I will not offer a complete and accurate

description of any position (since these are available in other places); instead I want merely to show how the answers to these questions have changed, and often in ways that are neither necessary nor even necessarily consistent across the entire range.

On top of this 'field of dispersion', I want to reinscribe a certain narrative structure of the development of cultural studies. While this revised trajectory will resemble the standard story (the war of manoeuvres), it will allow that narrative to incorporate the fractured and uneven development implicit in the war of positions being fought out along the eight vectors I have identified. I will abstract from the ongoing battles across a wide range of conceptual and strategic differences five temporarily stable forms within the formation of cultural studies (see Table 1.1):

  I the literary humanism (of Hoggart and Williams);
  II the early eclectic effort to define a dialectical sociology;
  III the first distinctly 'Centre position' ('culturalism');
  IV a structural-conjuncturalist position; and
  V a postmodern-conjuncturalist position.

Let me emphasize again the artificiality of my narrative. While these positions may be taken (for the sake of argument) as representing real stages in the history of the Centre or of cultural studies, or as interpretations of particular texts, they are actually abstractions out of the complex terrain of cultural studies meant to suggest something about the multiple sites and vectors along which the war of positions is constantly fought. Individual authors and works constantly moved around the terrain, often sliding back or forward along these idealized vectors. While I will make some effort to point to some of the disjunctions between the intellectual narrative and the real history of this particular formation of the Centre, I do not mean to offer a 'true' historical account. These 'positions' at best represent provisional efforts to occupy particular sites in specific ways and to connect them together into effective responses to the politics of the cultural and social context. Despite the apparent historicality of the narrative, they are offered as a map of the changing state of play in the field of forces that constitute cultural studies, and each of them continues to exist.

I will argue, first, that many of the commitments of cultural studies were defined by the effort to move against the 'literary-humanistic pull' of Hoggart and his conceptualization of its project in opposition to mass communication theory. In this effort, cultural studies increasingly identified its object of study – communication – with a particular conceptual framework (a particular dialectical model of communication). It established a series of correspondences: between culture, ideology, communication, community, experience and inter-subjectivity. It is these assumed relationships which later – conjuncturalist – positions would have to deconstruct. Second, I will argue that the moment of the formation of a 'Centre' position depended upon a limited appropriation of structuralism into the continued framework of the struggle between a literary and sociological pull. This effort was embodied figuratively and historically in the constant return to the texts of Gramsci on the one hand and Althusser/Poulantzas on the other, each time rereading their positions in the light of the effort to rearticulate the historical project of cultural studies.

I A literary humanistic vision of cultural studies

Richard Hoggart was the founder both of the Centre for Contemporary Cultural Studies and of cultural studies as an identifiable analytic/critical project. Through a series of lectures (Hoggart 1967, 1969, 1970), as well as the classic if oddly titled study, *The Uses of Literacy* (1957), he gave cultural studies its first intellectual shape. However great the distance that seems to have been traversed since that early moment, his influence is still strongly present. Hoggart extended and refined Leavis' notion of literary criticism. He argued that art, if read according to the specific practices of 'close reading' that characterized literary criticism ('reading for tone'), revealed something about society that was unavailable in any other way: what he described as 'the felt quality of life' and later, as 'a field of values'. He explicitly located cultural studies in the line of critical concern that Raymond Williams (1958) had constructed as 'the Culture and Society tradition'. Its task was value analysis but its goal was value judgement. The question, defined with a decided literary pull, was not so much what people do with texts but rather the relations between complex cultural texts and 'the imaginative life' of their readers (Hoggart 1969: 18). Cultural studies was to explore the points at which the value laden structures of society

Table 1.1 A reference map of cultural studies via eight theoretical problematics

	Literary humanism	Dialectical sociology	'Culturalism'	Structural-conjunctural	Postmodern-conjunctural
Epistemology	intuitive empiricism	structural empiricism	conventionalism	realism/contextualism	fabrication/apparatus
Determination	atomic essentialism	dialectical essentialism	structural essentialism	articulation as specificity	articulation as effectivity
Agency	humanistic-aesthetic	social humanism	social humanism	social articulation	nomadic articulation
Social Formation	class	class	structure in dominance	fractured totality	fractured totality
Cultural Formation	elite/masses	public/private	centre/margin	dominant/popular	sensibilities
Power	legitimation/value	consent	incorporation/resistance	domination/subordination	empowerment/disempowerment
Specificity of Cultural Struggle	culture/society as structure of feeling	ideology as world view	ideology as experience	civil society	the popular
Site of Modernity	mass media	mass media	consumption	hegemony	the masses

intersect and interact with the psychic life of individuals as represented in cultural texts (Hoggart 1969: 19). Although Hoggart's ultimate concern was always centred on the normative dimension of the structures of meaning, he argued forcefully for the complex, multidimensionality of cultural existence. One could not understand the impact of cultural changes apart from the dense, sensuous, everyday life of the people:

> Only art re-creates life in all its dimensions – so that a particular choice is bound up with space, people and habits. Only here do we at one and the same time see ourselves existentially and vulnerably; and also as creatures who can move outside the time-bound texture of daily experience. The two make up, in Auden's phrase, 'the real world of theology and horses'.

> (Hoggart 1970: 249)

Similarly, Raymond Williams (1965) had argued that any cultural text could only be understood in the context of the entire social formation, of the relations among all the elements in a whole way of life. And this totality was not reducible to a semantic abstraction divorced from the lived experience of individuals. Williams argued that the significance of any cultural text was always mediated by its relationship (which he assumed to be that of a structural homology) to the 'structure of feeling'. Hall's early (n.d.) model of the labour of cultural studies clearly demonstrates the distance between the Centre's project and that of the more socially based disciplines of communication studies: first, to obtain 'as full a "reading" of the material as is possible, using critical analysis both of content and structure, and of attitudes and assumptions, latent as well as manifest values'. Second, 'to consider its effect upon society, the nature of its appeal and popularity'. And third, to 'place' the material 'in its social and cultural setting' and to interpret it, 'as far as is possible, for its cultural meaning and significance' (p. 2).

At the same time, the Centre was seeking to find models of collective, interdisciplinary work which would enable it to carry out the project. Hoggart emphasized that the requirements of knowledge and competence would demand a methodology that was fractured across disciplines. His model of interdisciplinary research was 'divide and unite': literary studies on one side, sociologists and anthropologists on the other. They were to be brought together, to educate, enlighten and help one another, but they remained separated; literary analysis was a difficult task which took a sophisticated education, and sociology was a discipline too far removed from it. Of course, the ultimate task was for the two disciplines to bring their insights together, to be able to offer new and important insights into the relationship between culture and society. Hall, on the other hand, focused on the need to work through and unite the three moments of cultural studies: 'The analysis would not, of course, be split up into three separate phases: but it would not be complete until all three phases were carried through and related together' (p. 3).

Hoggart's position was built upon a number of commitments and assumptions. Epistemologically, it followed the path of Leavis' intuitive empiricism: close reading revealed the meaning of a text. This was obviously linked through its strong literary pull (not only in its sense of method but of value as well) to a rather simple theory of determination which might be described as 'atomic essentialism'. Both texts and cultures were self-identical and their relations could be read through an assumed necessary correspondence. Behind this correspondence was the (imaginative and creative) individual as the agency of history or at least of that province which was the concern of cultural studies.

Moreover, behind the historical changes which *The Uses of Literacy* seemed to be tracing was a rather nostalgic sense of an 'authentic' working-class experience. If its model of the social formation was that of class struggle, it was especially defined in the specific terms of culture in a decidedly non-marxist way: the people caught between an artistic and a media elite. Power is necessarily expressed in terms of a struggle for legitimation and exposure, as the colonization of one way of life by the communicative 'field of values' of a dominant elite rather than the expression and critique of a way of life by an artistic elite. And cultural struggle involved a war of legitimacy and cultural status. Finally, the specific site of modernity which concerned Hoggart was the mass media. *The Uses of Literacy* was taken to be a study in the ways in which the new cultural forms of mass media and Americanization were 'colonizing' the working class. It was read 'such were the imperatives of the moment – essentially as a text about the mass media' (CCCS 1969-71: 2). Consequently,

37

cultural studies was often framed as a literary-based alternative to the existing work on mass communication. 'The notion that the Centre, in directing its attention to the critical study of "contemporary culture" was, essentially, to be a centre for the study of television, the mass media and popular arts . . . though never meeting our sense of the situation . . . nevertheless, came by default, to define us and our work' (CCCS 1969–71: 2).

It was in this complex set of positions that the specificity of cultural studies was initially constituted: it studied the relationship between culture and society at a particular point of intersection, a point at which one had moved from texts and social structures to the whole way of life, to the 'structure of feeling'. Here one was operating between the two realms, or perhaps more accurately, in their overlap. There was, however, even in its earliest stages, a certain dissatisfaction with the position and the way cultural studies was constructed within it. Thus, at the same moment – in fact, as early as 1966 – an alternative if undeveloped model of cultural studies was taking shape, one built upon a different reading of *The Uses of Literacy*:

> Its graphic portrayal of the extremely complex ways in which the 'springs of action' of a subordinate class might be 'unbent' by a dominant culture intent, with the new means of communication at its disposal, of winning consent precisely in that class – the link, that is, indissoluble as it turned out, between the 'first' and the 'second' halves of 'The Uses of Literacy'.
>
> (CCCS 1969–71: 2)

Furthermore, Hall was increasingly drawn to the project of locating this argument within a marxist theory of 'mediations', a discursive image which was to increasingly dominate the work of the Centre and to displace the literary concerns of Hoggart:

> Certainly, where the critic moves from the text 'in itself' to its relation to society and culture, the 'mediations' between the two need to be as clearly established as is possible, given the nature of the material studied and the complexity of relations which it is possible to discover.
>
> (Hall n.d.: 2)

II The formation of dialectical sociology

In recent histories of the Birmingham Centre the 'second phase' of the Centre's work, which proceeded from the late 1960s into the early 1970s, often disappears. There are at least two significant reasons for this: first, on the surface, it is more difficult to describe because it often involved an eclectic and uncomfortable exploration of alternative positions and methods. Second, its texts are difficult to locate; they appeared in the Centre's Working Papers and later in its journal – which was and still is largely unavailable outside England – and only some of this work has been reprinted subsequently in various collections. The result is that the different positions embodied within them have been glossed over as they are assimilated into later, more explicit positions. Yet this was a crucial period for, although many of its early theoretical formulations were soon abandoned, it did open up new spaces and shifted the grounds of cultural studies in ways which have continued to be influential. It won important new positions even if, occasionally, it also gave up some positions that would have to be reappropriated later in different forms. Moreover, it was during this phase that the Centre began to explore truly collective forms of research; the first such effort was an attempt in 1969 to read a short story, 'Cure for Marriage', from a 'woman's magazine'.

Moving from questions of the actual history of the Centre, the position which emerged can be seen as a retheorization of the work of Raymond Williams. Two significant developments mark this early formation, and they roughly correspond to Williams' two major conceptualizations of culture: the 'structure of feeling' (as the object of interpretation and the content of community) and the 'community of process' (as the social process of community and communication). Thus, on the one hand, there was an attempt to find broader and more 'scientifically' grounded or at least methodologically rigorous procedures for literary and cultural readings. Stylistic analysis, rhetoric and semiotics/structuralism were all added onto the agenda of cultural studies as alternatives to the empiricism, elitism and verbal bias of traditional literary studies. It was, in the final instance, semiotics and structuralism which had an enduring impact not only methodologically but theoretically as well. On the other hand, reading in sociology and anthropology led the

39

Centre increasingly into phenomenological sociology not in its individualist forms but rather as a dialectical theory of inter-subjectivity: 'The question is . . . how subjective meanings and intentions come, under certain determinate conditions, to create and inform the "structures" of social life? And how, in turn, the structures of social life shape and inform the interior spaces of individual consciousness' (Hall 1971: 98). By refusing to identify public and subjective meanings, cultural studies avoided the mechanism of traditional marxism; by refusing to identify situ-ated social meanings and culture, it avoided the idealism of phenomenology and existential sociology. The question of cultural studies had to be understood dialectically: how people fill the void between inadequate collective representations and imperfect private meanings. '[B]y what "mediations" do the subjective meanings of actors, who share a common social world, become expressed or "objectivated" in cultural artifacts, in social gesture and interactions' (CCCS 1966–67: 29). Inter-subjectivity was the key mediating term between individual experiences and social structures. The problem for cultural studies was to find an adequate model of the processes of mediation by which 'structures of meaning' came to move within the spaces of cultural texts, understood increasingly on a model of commu-nication as the inter-subjective construction of meaning (see e.g. Hall 1972; Smith 1975). The focus on a theoretically constituted process of communication helped to dismantle the privileging of art so common in Williams and Hoggart.

Despite the eclecticism of this period, the terrain of cultural studies was radically reorganized.[6] While much of the inter-pretive work was still based in an empiricist epistemology, it was increasingly a structural (or semiotic) empiricism grounded in the reading of the structures and systems by which meanings are organized. It also moved beyond Hoggart's essentialism which seemed to postulate a direct correspondence between culture and society. This first 'Centre position' emphasized the necessary mediations between culture and society, the complex dialectic between the individual and society. That dialectic was given shape as the process of communication – an inherently 'social form of praxis' – as relations between public and private mean-ings, or between personal and collective realities (the latter defined as 'publicly routinized social existence').

Perhaps most importantly this dialectical sociology took the emphasis away from the agency of the individual and increasingly located historical agency within the realm of inter-subjective meaning, of the socially positioned subject. This does not mean that it abandoned a notion of an essentially creative human subject. But it did transform the structure of its humanism, increasingly defined less by the literary pull of Hoggart than by a 'sociological' pull (Allor 1987). If the model of the social formation it offered continued to be defined as a class structure, this was given an increasingly marxist reading. But the cultural formation was significantly re-envisioned, not as a structure of the conflict between the people and the dominant elite, but as a processual totality produced through the ongoing processes and structures of social communication. Thus, while it continued to locate modernity within the mass media (and to offer itself as an alternative to mass communication theory), it significantly rethought the site of cultural power and struggle. The specificity of cultural studies was located in the realm of inter-subjective meaning (which mediated between culture and society) or, in what became the increasingly common term, ideology. Even in its earliest formations the Centre argued against reflectionist and reductionist notions of ideology in favour of an effort to understand it as the construction of a consensual world view: cultural power as consent, cultural struggle as the opposition of competing, sociologically locatable structures of meaning.

In this way a cultural theory of communication was transformed into a communicational theory of culture which redirected the focus of cultural studies onto questions of shared meanings, participation within a community, and the ideological mediations between social position, the production of meaning and experience. If culture was bifurcated into the relations between texts and lived reality, the former was defined by inter-subjective meanings, the latter by socially determined experience. But this recognition of cultural complexity and competition (which in many ways reproduced aspects of Williams' work) did not provide cultural studies with the grounds for theorizing the notion of struggle or even resistance. For it moved from a real recognition of complexity (or what Hall would later call difference) to notions of competing interests, overlapping structures of meaning, and negotiated compromises.

If this position as I have described it was dominated by the phenomenological reconceptualization of culture and

41

communication, the increasing interest in semiotics and structuralism pointed in a radically different direction. For semiotics presented a different model of culture; in the work of Eco and Barthes, the Centre was drawn into a discourse which thought of communication as a formal process rather than a sociological one. The semiotic notions of encoding and decoding (Hall 1980a) as two points in a purely signifying structure increasingly forced cultural studies to recognize the implications of a concept of difference; it challenged the assumption of inter-subjectivity (and the assumed existence of shared codes). An increasing attention to the texts of Marx (especially the *Grundrisse* and the 'Notes on Method' [Hall 1974]) and the beginnings of the Centre's efforts to read and argue with Althusser reinforced the possibility of a semiotic theory of culture which, by denying any unified consensus, would provide the theoretical grounds for the possibility of resistance.

III The culturalist formation

The position most commonly identified with the Centre emerged in the mid-1970s through the interaction of two fairly coherent and isolated bodies of work. The first focused on the study of youth subcultures; the second offered a model of media communication built upon the disjunction between encoding and decoding. It is important, however, to recognize the historical developments through which these researches were brought together into a theory of the complex relations between power and resistance. The theory of resistance in media developed from the purely semiotic theory of resistant decoding positionalities. While this formal theory had recognized that such positions were related to institutional and social determinants (drawing upon the work of Parkin and Mann), the positions themselves remained abstract possibilities in the relations of power rather than interpretive positions. But when these positions were assigned sociological embodiments – that is, correlated with empirically identifiable audiences and social groups that could be characterized sociologically (Morley 1980) – the Centre was able to justify theoretically its argument that the working class had not been fully incorporated into the dominant culture.

Subcultural theory, which is often taken as the primary example of the Centre's theory of resistance, actually began as part of the Centre's effort to define a phenomenological theory of society and culture. Using ethnography, this body of work opposed the 'labelling theory' of the sociology of deviance with the argument that style was an ideological discourse (Willis 1978). It attempted to place the question of meaning – and the construction of deviant identities – into the broader context of specific social and cultural formations. The theory of resistance, so brilliantly articulated in the first chapter of *Resistance Through Rituals* (Clarke *et al.* 1975) was, in fact, written after the actual work of the 'subculture group'. However, we must at least acknowledge the diversity which existed within each of these traditions; not only across different authors but over time (as new ideas were engaged) positions differed (e.g. there are significant differences between the subcultural work of Clarke, Willis, Jefferson, and Hebdige).

It was Hall's (1980b) article which partly helped to cement these two bodies of work into an apparently consistent theoretical space, located between Williams' culturalism and Althusser's structuralism. Hall's article can be read as a retrospective effort to reinterpret the debate between humanism and structuralism from the perspective of a third cultural studies position which already saw itself as inhabiting the space between them. It was less a call than a self-representation. Hall argued that Williams' theory assumed too harmonious and well structured a social totality in which everything fitted together. While it allowed for resistance located in the human subject, it had difficulty accounting for domination. And, most important, it explained ideology (and its mystificatory effects) by measuring it against reality understood experientially. Experience was available apart from ideology and the struggle over ideology was then how those experiences were interpreted.

Structuralism, on the other hand, in the work of Althusser (and his followers) assumed a structure built upon difference, but the differences too easily became autonomous as the relations amongst the different levels were deferred into a mystical last instance which never came. While it explained domination (in its theory of social reproduction), it offered no space for resistance (not as a result of its anti-humanism but in its failure to explore the connections between the socio-economic and cultural relations of ideology – embodied in the gap between the two halves of 'the ISA's essay') (Althusser 1971). And, finally, structuralism

43

explained experience as the product of ideology. There was no reality outside ideology to which one could refer it - except of course for the possibility of a discourse (a science) which is not ideological. Ideology, then, is not false consciousness; it is rather a necessary mystification which represents 'the way in which we live our imaginary relations to our real conditions of existence' (Althusser 1971: 162). The struggle is not over the interpretation of experiences but rather over the systems of representation which construct the experiences. Moreover, the most important (if not in the end, the only) process by which ideology works is that of interpellation: ideological practices, by positioning the individual within discourse, define their subjectivity.

Thus, what has often been taken as a *theory of ideological resistance* was, in many ways, an attempt to *reinsert ideology* into a broader, albeit historically specific, cultural formation and that, in turn, into the real social, economic and historical relations within which both subcultures and audiences were located. I want to focus briefly on how the Centre's position negotiated between culturalism and structuralism. The Centre maintained a basically humanistic conception of culture as 'the way social categories and meanings mediate social processes between individuals and groups' (CCCS 1972–74: 3):

> We understand the word 'culture' to refer to that level at which social groups develop distinct patterns of life, and give *expressive form* to their social and material life-experience. Culture is the way, the forms, in which groups 'handle' the raw material of their social and material existence . . . The 'culture' of a group or class is the peculiar and distinctive 'way of life' . . . Culture is the distinctive shapes in which this material and social organization of life expresses itself.
>
> (Clarke *et al.* 1975: 10)

Yet, while locating ideology within culture, the Centre gave it a decidedly Althusserian reading, recognizing that 'men live, in ideology, an "imaginary relation" to the real conditions of their existence' (Clarke *et al.* 1975: 33). Ideology could serve as a form of resistance, not because of some authentic 'experience' behind it but precisely because it offered 'ways of expressing and realizing in their culture their subordinate position and experiences' (Clarke *et al.* 1975: 12). Their experience is constructed as the dominant ideology's imaginary relations, and at the same time, that very production of subordinate experiences opens up the possibility of expressions which resist the dominant ideology. The notion of consensus provided a common ground between the two positions: ideological domination (or 'hegemony') 'prescribes . . . the *limits* within which ideas and conflicts move and are resolved' (Clarke *et al.* 1975: 39). But the ideological construction of identity was rehumanized: ideology constructs identities by giving meanings to the various social differences and roles which are a part of our real conditions.

This view of the relationship between culture and ideology was itself located in a decidedly Althusserian image of the social formation within which cultures and ideologies are 'relatively autonomous': 'subcultures represent a necessary . . . but *intermediary* level of analysis. Any attempt to relate subcultures to the "socio-cultural formation as a whole" must grasp its complex unity by way of these necessary differentiations' (Clarke *et al.* 1975: 15). Thus, culture was 'doubly articulated' (CCCS 1972–74: 2), first to its own specificity and second to 'the inextricable interconnections of culture with social structures, historical trends, social relationships between groups and classes, institutions'. Not only did this position incorporate images of the structured complexity and historical specificity of social and cultural formations, it also emphasized the complex processes of over-determination through which possibilities for resistance were enabled because the correspondences between the various levels of any formation were never guaranteed or predetermined. And yet at the same time that it appropriated 'Althusserian' ways of talking about ideology and the social formation, its description of culture and experience remained decidedly humanistic, emphasizing their mediating role between social position and cultural interpretations, resources and competencies.

It is this gap which defined the particular view the Centre took of the possibilities and forms of resistance. In both its studies of subcultures and the encoding/decoding of mass media, a specific social group was isolated, its identity defined by its place within an objective set of social relations. These real relations were seen to correspond, on the one hand, to a social identity constructed around socially defined differences and, on the other hand, to a set of experiences. It was this identity which largely defined the site of ideological struggle, in the ways these differential experiences were themselves constructed within the ideological imaginary and hence experienced. That is, the identity of any group was doubly connected to experience or rather the meaning of 'experience' itself slides between two senses: that which is immediately and objectively determined by social position and that which, through ideological interpretation, describes how people live those relations. For example, when subculturalists talk about style as a 'magical response' to the lived contradictions of a particular over-determined social group, that contradiction is always ambiguously located both in the real relations and in lived experience. The style has to appear as a 'magical' solution because it is, at least in the first instance, clearly within the lived (the imaginary) and has no necessary (and certainly no direct) connection to the real relations. It is a form of resistance precisely because the identity it constructs is 'forbidden', outside the hegemonic limits of the dominant ideology. The connection between its resistance and its 'responsiveness' to the lived contradictions, like that between the two senses of experience, depends upon the assumption of a structural correspondence – or homology – between the various levels of the subculture's existence. The contradictions acted out in a subcultural style are always determined elsewhere. Thus the correspondence between position, identity and experience is not, at least theoretically, necessarily given. Yet, in practice, whether homologies were understood as repeated commitments and images, structures of meaning or signifying practices, they were always delivered in advance. The correspondence between the two levels of experience had to be assumed if experience were to mediate effectively between the larger terrains of culture and society.

The account I have offered of this crucial moment in the formation of cultural studies focuses on the Centre's continued engagement with Althusser and the various post-Althusserians (Hall 1985) through an increasing appropriation of Gramscian formulations. Cultural studies' concern for the specificity of ideological practices (operating within hegemonic relations of consensus and incorporation) was explicitly opposed to the structuralist concern for the specificity of signifying practices. The Centre sought to study the *relative* autonomy of culture within historically specific social formations as an alternative to the structuralist tendency to give cultural practices an absolute autonomy and to ground them in universal textual and psychoanalytical processes. If, for structuralists, subjectivity is constitutive of ideology, cultural studies argued that ideology constitutes subjects. Rather than looking at how subjects are positioned within the discursive production of meaning, cultural studies raised the question of social identity as part of the larger social struggle over meanings. The subject was assumed to exist outside any specific ideological event, defined by its place within systems of social differences. The question is where the lines of difference are located and how people and meanings are assigned to them. The subject comes to ideology, already positioned (outside of discourse), as a potential site of struggle and as the active source of meaning production.

Let me briefly summarize the various positions which the Centre tried to occupy and unite within the terrain of cultural studies during this phase. Its interpretive position had become increasingly structuralist and conventionalist. Not only were cultures to be read formally (not only in terms of shared structures but also in terms of such formal notions as modes of address and ideological problematics), but such formal mediations were always operative, even in the critical act itself. There was no science of ideology critique and no guaranteed political position outside the processes of ideological maps of meanings. Thus, through a detour into structuralism, cultural studies reaffirmed a conventionalism which dominated much of humanistic marxism. Its theory of determination was, as I have already suggested, more the result of an uncomfortable tension. While its Althusserian theory of relative autonomy and over-determination placed an increasing emphasis on difference, on the lack of necessary correspondences, its desire to escape the extreme denials of any historical correspondences, and its theory of homologies, reinscribed a systemic essentialism of structural correspondences which were always guaranteed in practice. It continued the sociological pull of the earlier theory but challenged its easy assumption of social totality, favouring Althusser's notion of a structure-in-dominance, coupled with Williams' (1973) distinction between 'residual', 'emergent' and 'dominant' formations (the former two could exist in harmonious, negotiated or oppositional relations to the latter).

The increasing possibilities of constructing social difference (through decoding and appropriation) suggested, however, a different model of the cultural formation, one built upon the

47

radical separation, however temporary, between the centre and the margins. Thus, while it was able to locate moments of resistance (however fragmented and imaginary), the resistance of difference (in subcultural theory) was always linked to a moment of authenticity which was threatened by a hegemonic incorporation of the margins into the centre, a process which apparently guaranteed the co-optation of resistance. By locating the site of resistance within consumption, this position transformed the problem of modernity into one of consumption itself: on the one hand, the new possibilities that consumption appeared to offer, and on the other, the rapidly increasing rate at which cultural practices and social groups were incorporated into the hegemonic formation. Finally, the Centre's position, despite its distinction between culture and ideology, continued and even furthered the identification of the problematic of cultural studies with that of ideology; ideology however no longer referred directly to a coherent world view but rather to the production of social identity and experience around real sociological differences.

But this view of the Centre's position, accurate as it may be, underplays the growing importance of Gramsci throughout this phase of the formation. Gramsci was continuously reread, first as a humanist, then as an alternative form of engaging with Althusser's theoreticism (in his theorization of historical specificity, relative autonomy, and hegemony) and Poulantzas (on the state, class, and mode of production). His influence was felt, not only in the broad theory of ideology and social formations, but in the emerging working groups on the state, race relations, etc. The first real sign of the increasing pull of Gramsci was the collective work which led to the publication of *Policing the Crisis* (Hall *et al.* 1978) which, although still decidedly Althusserian in its view of ideology and the social formation, began to offer a different view of the relationship of culture to the historical conjuncture. While not yet able to theorize the conjuncture – *Policing the Crisis* began with the conjuncture already defined by the collapse of social democracy – it represented an important shift away from the communicational or transactional model of culture (defined either semiotically or inter-subjectively) to a more historical and 'structural' (not structuralist) theory:

There are, we argue, clear historical and structural forces at work in this period, shaping, so to speak, from the outside, the immediate transactions on the ground between 'muggers', potential muggers, their victims and their apprehenders. In many comparable studies, these larger and wider forces are merely noted and cited; their direct and indirect bearing on the phenomenon analysed is, however, left vague and abstract – part of 'the background'. In our case, we believe that these so-called 'background issues' are, indeed, exactly the critical forces which *produce* 'mugging' in the specific form in which it appears . . . It is to this shaping context, therefore, that we turn: attempting to make precise, without simplification or reduction, the other contradictory connections between specific events of a criminal-and-control kind, and the historical conjuncture in which they appear.

(Hall *et al.* 1978: 185)

While *Policing the Crisis* continued the focus on social identity through the construction of the meaning of social differences, it recognized that identity itself is structured in contradictions. As it began to move away from the subjective interpretations of texts and the experiential dimension of ideology, it placed a greater emphasis on popular languages and common sense, on the construction of a field of meanings and differences which is linked, on the one hand, to hegemonic projects and, on the other, to certain conditions of possibility. Although in many ways it remained with the cultural studies position that I have described, it represented an important vector pointing to other possibilities.

IV A structural-conjuncturalist formation[7]

While the normative history of cultural studies sees Gramsci as offering a new and different way of occupying the middle ground, of limiting the tendencies of structuralism without falling back into humanism, I want to suggest that the (re)turn to Gramsci significantly rearticulated the commitments of cultural studies and shifted the very problematic which constituted its identity. Rather than occupying a middle ground, the position changes the rules of the game; it shifts the discourse of cultural studies in fundamental ways, opening it up to new questions of differences. Obviously, Gramsci's impact cannot be understood in isolation: there were historical and political pressures (both from within and from outside the Centre) and there were other significant intellectual forces, including Foucault. Most especially, feminism challenged many of the intellectual assumptions of cultural studies. It offered, among other things, its own radical critique of essentialism and its own theory of difference even while it placed the problem of identity back onto the cultural studies agenda.

Perhaps the simplest way to present the radical implications of the theoretical shift into a 'conjuncturalist' cultural studies is to describe the particular ways in which it responds to the eight questions that summarily structured my presentation of earlier moments in the formation of cultural studies in the Birmingham Centre. 'Conjuncturalism' can be seen as a model of 'determinateness' which attempts to avoid the twin errors of essentialist theories of determination: necessary correspondences and necessary non-correspondences. Both of these alternatives are reductionist: they assume that history is guaranteed, even if it is only its indifference or indeterminacy that is guaranteed. Conjuncturalism argues that while there are no necessary correspondences (relations), there are always real (effective) correspondences. The meaning, effects and politics of particular social events, texts, practices, and structures (what we in fact mean by their 'identity') are never guaranteed, either causally (by their origins, however deferred) or through inscription (as if they were self-determined). Thus, while conjuncturalism follows the post-structuralist emphasis on difference and the need to deconstruct identity (so as to deny its essentiality and necessity), it follows feminist theory in arguing for the additional critical task of reconstructing the historical context within which the production of a particular identity has been accomplished. Only in this dual task can one understand both the reality of such productions and the possibilities for change. In conjuncturalism, the anti-essentialism of a theory of difference is not defined by its opposition to a theory of identity but rather by its reinterpretation of the latter as a theory of specificity. The specificity of any conjuncture, at whatever level of abstraction, is always produced, determinate.

The theory of agency in this version of cultural theory can be condensed into the notion of 'articulation' as an interpretation of Marx's statement that 'people make history but in conditions not of their own making'. The links that seem to give a particular text (or set of texts) a particular effective meaning, that connect it with a particular social group and political position, are forged by people operating within the limits of their real conditions and the historically articulated 'tendential lines of force'. Articulation refers to the ongoing construction of unstable (to varying degrees) relations between practices and structures. It involves the production of contexts, the ongoing effort by which particular practices are removed from and inserted into different structures of relationships, the construction of one set of relations out of another, the continuous struggle to reposition practices within a shifting field of forces. Yet neither the elements nor the context can be adequately described outside the relations; neither can be taken to pre-exist the other. Texts are not added onto already existing contexts (inter-texts); rather, texts and contexts are articulated to each other, each inserted into the other as it were. In fact, the difference between a text and its context, or a practice and a structure, is only a product of the level of abstraction at which one is operating and often the history of common sense (e.g. the fact that a narrative, or an author's name, or at another level, the binding, is often taken to delimit a 'text' is a deeply rooted part of our taken-for-granted assumptions).

A theory of articulation denies an essential human subject without giving up the active individual who is never entirely and simply 'stitched' into its place in social organizations of power. Individuals and social groups can and do make history, not because of some essential creativity (or impulse to resistance) nor because they are determined by their historical, social, and cultural positions. Positions are won and lost, occupied and evacuated. There is always a multiplicity of positions, not only available but occupied, and a multiplicity of ways in which different meanings, experiences, powers, interests, and identities can be articulated together. The historical individual is itself the site of ongoing struggles and articulations. Still, this is always a socially defined individual, constituted by its location within already inscribed systems of difference. It begins with the givenness of sociological difference, around which articulations are organized. But perhaps its most important implication is its anti-elitism. It says that people are always active; we cannot predict or prejudge where their practices will operate in some way against particular historical tendencies. Nor can we predict, in those situations where there is a struggle between competing articulations, who will win or what such a victory will ultimately signify. While it is *au courant* to affirm that 'people are not (cultural) dopes', its radical implications, both politically and analytically, are rarely taken seriously.[8]

While conjuncturalism seems to describe the social formation, following Althusser, as a 'structure-in-dominance', it demands that the very concept, as well as any specific conjuncture, be historicized and therefore problematized. Not only does it reject that the structural totality is guaranteed, in either the first or last instances (as if somehow, the economic always comes through for us), it also rejects the model of levels, each of whose specificity (relative autonomy) can be located outside specific conjunctures. Of course, critics often do – and must – operate on different levels of abstraction, but specificity is always historically articulated. Furthermore, there are no guarantees concerning what levels, or even how many, are active in what ways at any moment. Any level (e.g. the political, the ideological, the economic) – to the extent that it is a useful concept – must be seen as both internally and externally articulated, full of differences and contradictions. Thus, rather than a totality in difference, we might talk instead about a fractured or articulated totality in order to emphasize that how the totality breaks up – where its lines of fissure are, where it is stitched together, how its 'teeth gritting harmony' is constructed – is unpredictable in advance, never guaranteed, even though our theories might like it better the other way.

The conjuncturalist theory of the cultural formation significantly relocates both the problematic of cultural studies and the line between culture and society. Because it recognizes the complexity of the terrain of culture, models of elite/mass, public/private and even centre/margin are seen as specific historical – and politically inflected – descriptions. It is necessary then to turn to a more abstract description: dominant and popular, where the popular is always defined by and as its difference from, its subordination to, the dominant culture; this, in some sense, guarantees to the popular at least the possibility of resistance. But the abstractness of this structure is only a result of its decontextualized appearance here; specific relations will always demand a recognition of the different ways in which relations of dominant and popular cultures are constructed.

Conjuncturalism describes cultural relations within a discourse of power – a discourse of domination and subordination which sees people living in complex and changing networks of social relations. Consequently, they are implicated, often in contradictory ways, in differential and hierarchical relations of power. Even at its most concrete, relations of power are always multiple and contradictory. Wherever people and practices are organized around particular contradictions, there are multiple, differential relations of power involved. State power, economic power, sexual and gender power, racial power, class power, national power, ethnic power, age power, etc. – all are potentially active at various points in the social formation as a 'unity-in-difference' and, at any point, they may operate in different relations to each other as well. If there are no guarantees that the elimination of class domination and exploitation will eliminate sexual and gender domination and exploitation, there is also no guarantee that the latter will carry the former with it. A conjunctural theory of power is not claiming, however, that all such relations of power are equal, equally determining, or equally liveable; these are questions that depend upon the analysis of the specific, concrete conjuncture. This theory of power has a number of consequences: first, the form of such cultural relations must always be analysed conjuncturally; second, to be in either a dominant or subordinate position – whether at a specific historical site or within a more dispersed (but still articulated) social structure – involves a complex and determinate set of relations which are often contradictory, not only internally but also in their relations with other social positions and structures; and third, both domination and subordination are always actively lived. And the active practice of living one's subordinate position need not always merely reproduce, or even accept, the dominant articulations of that positioning. Thus conjuncturalism makes explicit what remained implicit in earlier forms of cultural studies: that there are multiple forms of resistance as well as of power.

Before turning to how this conjuncturalist version of cultural studies understands the specificity of the cultural and of its historical conjuncture, let me (re)turn to the question of its epistemology and interpretive practice. Conjuncturalism eschews the conventionalism of culturalism in favour of a revised realism. Hall's (1976) re-invocation of Benjamin's image of the materialist – as a surgeon cutting into the real – as opposed to the empiricist – as a magician laying hands upon the surface – indicates a renewed effort to take seriously the constraint of historically and materially constituted realities (at least in the form of tendential forces, which are not the same as discursive 'realisms'): there is a world that has to be made to mean! The fact that one can only make the real intelligible through ideological forms need not negate their difference, nor the effectivity of the real. Ideologies articulate real practices, positions, and relations; they do not invent them, nor do they render them irrelevant or undecidable. There is, as well, a particular and distinctive new interpretive strategy operating. The task is a contextualist one: not merely to try to identify the objective context into which a particular text is inserted, but to (re-)construct the context – which can never be centred around any single text or practice – of a particular (e.g. ideological) field, in terms of how it is articulated, both internally and externally, into specific relations. That construction is always the site of contradiction and struggle. Interpretation involves mapping out the determinations which, to varying degrees, are actively producing the context, defining its specificity. But this can only be accomplished if the critic is constantly aware of the different 'levels of abstraction' – the distances from the specific context in which one is interested – on which determinations are operating. For example, Marx's description of the structure of capitalism in *Das Kapital* describes real historical determinations, but they are located at a high level of abstraction, far removed from the specificity of late capitalism in the 1990s. Within such a contextualist practice, the 'depth' of the context is understood largely in epistemological terms. And consequently, there always remains some distance between the political and the epistemological measures of competing theories and articulations.

We are now in a position to understand the 'double articulation' of ideology as a way of moving beyond the methodological opposition which structured previous forms of cultural studies – between encoding and decoding, or between a textualist-idealist problematic (its literary pull) and a social-materialist problematic (its sociological pull). Within conjuncturalism, the question of ideology is how a particular text articulates a specific signifier as part of common sense and the production of experience. Ideology, as discourse, first involves an internal articulation: what meaning is produced depends upon where and how

particular discursive practices and forms are inserted into larger
'intertextual' relations. Power is already operating here since
struggles over how texts are interpreted can always be located
within such competing articulations. Texts must not only be
made to mean but there must be recognition of the struggles to
achieve, maintain and change the common-sense alignments and
formations of discourse. Within the plane of signifying effects,
other effects are produced and struggled over as well: particular
subject-positions are offered, but these do not come in already
guaranteed relations to either signifying practices or particular
structures of meaning. The ways in which meanings and subject-
positions are linked are yet another site of articulation. Further,
neither meaning nor subject-positions, once produced, guarantee
how such articulations will themselves be articulated to other
practices – in particular, to the real conditions of existence. If
reality is not textual, it has to be 'represented' as well as signified.
Thus, ideological struggles involve a second articulation, a
second plane of effects, in which meanings are articulated to real
social practices, relations and conditions. Differences, which may
be constructed elsewhere (e.g. in textual, psychoanalytic or
economic relations) are linked, through meanings, to social
positions and to socially empowered systems of connotation. If
such articulations are to be put into place, the connections have
to be made apparent, real, natural, inevitable. Only in that way
can they become 'common sense' and only through that double
articulation do ideological articulations come to constitute the
ways we live our relations to the real (i.e. to produce experience).
Difference, interpellation, connotation – wherever they are
actively produced – are articulated together around the ideological production of representational effects. Cultural studies now
looks at how it is that particular texts, practices, identities
already appear to be interpreted, their politics predefined, while
acknowledging that this appearance is always in part illusory
because it is never guaranteed. People are always struggling
against the preconstructed articulations (both internal and
external, both signifying and representational), looking for the
openings, the weak links, which allow them to bend texts and
practices into their own lives. Of course, the points at which this
double articulation is successful – at which an ideology is offered
and potentially becomes dominant – can themselves come to
define tendential forces. The victories, however temporary and

contradictory, leave their traces upon the social and cultural formations, contributing to the real historical tendencies which define the conditions under which further articulation is both necessary and possible.

There is a common misreading of the conjuncturalist form of cultural studies (e.g. by Johnson 1986–87) which assumes that it continues to define the problematic of cultural studies within the ideological. This ignores the fact that the project of cultural specificity must be located within the demand for historical specificity. Cultural studies is concerned with the intersection of discourse (the place of the articulation of meaning and representation and subjectivity), power and civil society as discussed by Gramsci. It is the historical appearance of civil society – as the domain within which notions of freedom, privacy, the absence of force are assumed – that defines the specificity of cultural studies. It is in this context that Hall's (1986) theory of hegemony makes sense within cultural studies: hegemony is more than a matter of ideology and is not reducible to the process of the production of consensus; it also involves the ways in which a specific alliance of class fractions is able to assume the position of economic and political leadership. One cannot analyse hegemony, on this model, in purely ideological terms, for although it is constructed partly through ideological work it is also connected to economic and political struggles (although these have to be represented in ideology); it may even implicate forms of repressive force at moments. A hegemonic project or victory does *not* necessarily demand the production of a consensus (for common sense is often contradictory and fragmentary) or a process of incorporation (for hegemony produces its own positions of both subordination and resistance). It does operate through the production of a certain convergence of interests through which subordination and resistance are contained. But containment is not the same as incorporation (although this may be a local strategy in specific struggles) since it involves a negotiation with subordinate and resistant fractions which may restructure the dominant as well as the subordinate interests. Hegemony seeks to win a position of leadership; it demands consent and need only contain (not eliminate) opposition. It must articulate itself, in particular ways, to both the common sense of the people and the political, economic, and ideological institutions of the society. A hegemonic bloc only needs to win popular assent to its position, to its conception of a crisis which demands a far-ranging solution, not to its specific ideological representations; it can allow for complex differences in what ideological articulations are taken up and how. Moreover, the struggle to construct hegemony is never a simple and singular one; it requires a national project which is articulated across the broad range of activities and institutions that make up civil society.

But I do not mean to argue that hegemony defines the specificity of cultural studies. For while there is a tendency to equate hegemony with the ongoing and omnipresent struggle for power within civil society, I want to follow Hall in restricting it to a description of a particular historically constructed structure of power. In that sense, hegemony defines not the specificity of cultural studies but rather a conjuncturalist conception of the locus of historical specificity. On this reading, it has been argued that Gramsci was concerned with the question of Italian hegemony because Italy had yet to achieve it (and the closest it had come was the moment of fascism). Hegemony is a historically emergent struggle for power called into existence by the appearance of the masses on the political and cultural scene of civil society. The masses are not identifiable with any of the usual divisions of power in society; they cut across class, gender, race, age, etc. They are in fact only defined by their place within civil society and within the hegemonic struggle to win a position of leadership in the contemporary world of advanced capitalist, democratic societies.

V A postmodern conjuncturalism[9]

Hegemony is one possible response to the historical context of modernity, to the broader historical conditions of the appearance of the masses as, in the first instance, a new form of cultural agency which is articulated into various political and economic positions (Hall and Jacques 1989). The close connection between the emergence of contemporary forms of mass cultural dissemination and the complex (re)articulation of historical agency (in which the masses are both the subject and object of the contemporary forms of power of late capitalism) is precisely the point at which a conjuncturalist form of cultural studies intersects with the postmodern turn (for cultural studies, it is a return) to the problematic of mass communication. Thus, to conclude

57

my survey of the different forms within this specifically marxist formation, I want to point to the emergence of another position – one which is more difficult to define because it is a relatively recent and as yet unsystematized position and because there are significant differences amongst its proponents. For example, Hebdige (1987, 1988) and Chambers (1986) pull it back into its previous position, while Chambers simultaneously propels it into a postmodern position; McRobbie (1986) and Morris (1988a, b) link it in important ways to developments in feminism; while both Ross (1989) and I (Grossberg 1988, 1992) tend to emphasize its relation to the American political context. Consequently, my attempt to present the commitments of this version of cultural studies will be more self-consciously an attempt to 'fabricate' the position, following its own project of negating the epistemological concern: truth is itself an effect of power and history. The key difference between the two versions of conjuncturalism is that the postmodern form refuses to privilege difference, to assume its reality or effectivity. On this view, it is possible for differences not to make a difference; their existence (i.e. their effectivity) is itself the historical product of their articulation. Rather than confronting continuously self-reproducing discourses of otherness, postmodern cultural studies attempts to rearticulate the increasingly transnational context of (post)modernity.

As a model of interpretation, postmodern conjuncturalism emphasizes its own articulation of the conjuncture which it analyses; it cannot ignore its own reflexive position within it. Consequently, the voice of the critic becomes determining (e.g. the emergence of first-person ethnographies in which the researcher, as a member of the culture, becomes their own native informant). We can draw upon Foucault's (1980) notion of 'apparatuses' as heterogeneous ensembles of practices or events to describe the object of such postmodern cultural studies:

> It is not a question of putting everything on a certain plane, that of the event, but of seeing clearly that there exist a whole series of levels of different types of events, which do not have the same range, nor the same chronological breadth, nor the same capacity to produce effects. The problem is to both distinguish the events, differentiate the networks and levels to which they belong, and to recon-

stitute the threads which connect them and make them give
rise to one another.

(Foucault 1979: 33)

Reality here is not defined as a metaphysical or even an historical
origin but rather as an interested mapping of the lines of concrete
effects. Reality is not 'outside' any apparatus, merely represented
within the discourses comprising it. This assumed difference
between discourse and reality gives rise to the epistemological
problem. But if reality is always articulated through our own
fabrication of it, one cannot define the specificity (the difference)
of any practice or conjuncture apart from its ongoing articulation within the history of our constructions. Reality is always a
construction of and out of the complex intersections and
interdeterminations among specific conjunctural effects. Reality
in whatever form – as matter, as history or as experience – is not a
privileged referent but the ongoing (in Deleuze and Guattari's
[1981] term 'rhizomatic') production or articulation of apparatuses. And the only grounds for deciding, in Benjamin's terms,
how deeply and precisely one has cut into the body of the real are
political and historical.

This model of articulation as the production of the real
implies a slightly different theory of determination as well. For
the construction of an apparatus can never remain within, nor
locate the specificity of a particular practice within, some small
set of planes of effects. If reality is always constituted by the
multiplicity of effects (e.g. the production and distribution of
meanings, desires, representations, money, labour, capital,
pleasures, moods, emotions, force, etc.), then one cannot, for very
long, maintain any separation between the so-called levels of the
social formation. Ideology (the double articulation of meaning
and representational effects) is always in determinate relations
with political and economic practices, but also with desiring-
effects, mood effects, etc. These other planes of effects cannot be
bracketed out for they determine whether and how meanings and
subject-positions are taken up, occupied, invested in, and
possessed. There are no guarantees of which practices are
effectively determinate. For example, the commodification of
discourse may have less of an effect on contemporary ideological
struggles than on other economic events and practices. While
(structural-)conjuncturalism continues to define culture (and

discourse) through its articulation of meaning-effects (and secondarily, representational effects), discourse can, in particular apparatuses and to varying degrees, be articulated to other effects. In fact, its most powerful determinations within an apparatus may not even entail meanings or representations. Postmodern conjuncturalism opens up the fields of effects within which cultural studies operates. It does not begin by assuming that the question of the intersection of power and culture is defined by the ways in which texts articulate specific meanings and relations; instead, it seeks to understand the text as and within a conjunctural assemblage determined by and determining its effectivity. That is, interpretation is always con-structural, (re)producing the ways in which practices are positioned within and articulate a 'unity-in-difference'. This can be seen as a theoretical solution to a very real practical problem in contemporary cultural studies: what do you do when every event is potentially evidence, potentially determining and at the same time changing too quickly to allow the comfortable leisure of academic criticism? It is also at least partially responsible for a new sense of interdisciplinarity which is slowly emerging in cultural studies.

The theory of articulation and affectivity undermines as well our ability to assume the differences within which subjectivity and identity are constituted. It challenges the sociological pull of cultural studies which has located the subject within multiple social differences and their ideological articulations. The subject – as actor, audience, communicator or agent – is itself a construction, the articulated and articulating movement within and between apparatuses. In postmodern cultural studies, agency is always articulated through and depending upon specific effects. For example, the ideologically articulated subject has no necessary relationship to political agency. Such links have themselves to be constructed and taken up. Moreover, the agent of articulation is always anonymous although articulation is carried out by real individuals and groups. This is merely to restate Marx's claim that while we make history, we are not in control of it. It is not merely a matter of unintended consequences for that eliminates any question of agency; it is rather that practices are always actively contested, rearticulated, hijacked, detoured, etc., that the relations between practices and effects do not follow preconstituted lines. Furthermore, as the above argument suggests, there is no necessary completeness of the subject which is required by the demands of agency: subjects can, in particular instances, be partial; on one level, the subject may be effective as a body (without consciousness) or even as a partial body; on another level, the complicitous subject may be defined in affective rather than ideological or material terms, and on still another level, whether, where and how their gender identity is determinative within a particular apparatus (and not merely how that gender difference is articulated) is part of the active reality of the apparatus itself. This vision of 'nomadic subjectivity' existing only within the movement of and between apparatuses rejects both the existential subject who has a single, unified identity and the deconstructed, permanently fragmented subject. Moreover, it refuses to reduce the subject to either a psychoanalytic or a social-textual (ideological) production. The nomadic subject is constantly remade, reshaped as a mobile situated set of vectors in a fluid context. The subject remains the agent of articulation, the site of struggle within in its own history, but the shape and effective nature of that subject is never guaranteed. The nomadic subject is amoeba-like, struggling to win some space for itself in particular apparatuses (as historical formations). While its shape is always determined by its articulations, it always has an effective shape. Thus, the possibilities of articulation depend in part on where and how the nomadic subject occupies its place(s) within a specific apparatus. Additionally, it always inhabits numerous apparatuses simultaneously which are themselves articulated to one another.

While the theory of the social formation remains the same in the two versions of conjuncturalism, their theories of power differ significantly. According to postmodern cultural studies, history is always the product of struggles which empower and disempower different practices and social positions in different ways. While the very articulation of relations and structures is the site of power, it is also the necessary shape of history. To deny structure is merely a utopian dream of anarchy. Power is real and operates at every level of our lives, located in the limited production and unequal distribution of capital, money, meanings, identities, desires, emotions, etc. It shapes relations, structures differences, draws boundaries, delimits complexity, reduces contradictions to claims of unity, coherence and homogeneity, organizes the multiplicity of concrete practices and effects into identities, unities, hierarchies, and apparent necessities (which ideologies seek to predefine, by closure and naturalization, retroactively). At its most concrete, power is the enablement of particular practices within specific relations; power is always empowering (one need not actively use power to be in an empowered position) and disempowering. Thus the notion of empowerment suggests the complexity of the empowering effects operating within any conjuncture. A practice not only may have multiple and even contradictory effects within a single (e.g. ideological) register but across a range of different registers as well. Thus a particular articulation can be both empowering and disempowering; people can win something and lose something. Power can only be analysed in its specific, conjuncturally articulated, forms. This model of power is opposed to the various versions of postmodern resistance: it refuses to celebrate any local resistance as if it were desirable in itself; it refuses to accept that only the oppressed can speak or struggle for themselves; it refuses to see the aim of resistance as the reflexive production of the self (as if all power were 'technologies of the self'); and it refuses to valorize hyperconformity as radical resistance. Instead, it argues that resistance is produced out of people's ongoing activities within specific conjunctures, activities that may be motivated by and directed toward very disparate effects. But resistance itself is never sufficient; it must be articulated into opposition which is effective and progressive within specific formations of power.

Finally, I want to consider the last three questions – the cultural formation, the specificity of cultural struggle, and the site of modernity – together, for they constitute a postmodern conjuncturalist conception of the specificity of cultural studies. Let me begin by returning to the notion of hegemony as a particular structuration of social power which operates within civil society to place an alliance of class fractions in the leading position. The masses then need not consent to the particular values and directions of those occupying the leading position: they must merely be articulated into the position of willing followers. A part of this articulation obviously involves ideological work on what Gramsci called 'common sense'. Sometimes it involves the work of everyday cultural apparatuses – the sites of relaxation, privacy, pleasure, tastes, and enjoyments. But this suggests that there is a second vector within the production of hegemony, a vector which Gramsci described as the production of a 'national popular'. It is this determination of 'the popular', the articulation of *the popularity* of particular discourses that defines the focus of postmodern cultural studies. The repressed of cultural studies (and it is still being repressed in the contemporary appropriation of the term), that which needs to be placed back on the agenda, is the specificity of, and struggles around, the popular. The denigration of popular discourses has a long history and it has been accomplished through a variety of strategies (e.g. from Plato, Augustine and the Enlightenment to marxism and the neoconservatives); the popular is generally granted status only when it can be reclaimed to the operations of 'art' or perhaps ideology.

At the same time, it is important to avoid locating the popular as if it were somehow always the other of a dominant (e.g. elite or central) culture, always the source of oppositional impulses. The dominant culture has its own forms of popularity, as do all class formations. The popular is historically articulated; it might be understood, initially at least, as those discursive forms and practices which necessarily (although only in part) function outside the signifying web. The popular is that which is always inscribed upon the body: tears, laughter, spine-chilling, screams, fright, erections, etc. These visceral responses – which often seem beyond our conscious control – are the mark of the affective and libidinal work of the popular: it is 'sentimental', 'emotional', 'moody', 'exciting', 'prurient', 'carnivalesque', etc. These do not define some essential property of the popular, either formal-textual or responsive. Rather, they describe the articulation of specific sorts of effects, the historically specific ways in which some practices are inserted into the apparatuses of everyday life. The popular, then, describes concrete, historically located 'sensibilities' (Bourdieu 1984); it is a matter of the affectivity-determined ways in which 'popular objects' are taken up, invested in, and articulated.

Civil society, then, cannot be understood merely in terms of ideological articulations. It demands as well an acknowledgement of what cultural studies has *always* perceived: that the increasing power of the mass media is reshaping and redistributing the forms and positions of the popular (and consequently, of the masses) within contemporary life. It is here that we can locate the point at which cultural studies intersects not only the theory of ideology and social power but also mass communication theory and the various theories of postmodernity. Postmodern cultural studies returns to the questions that animated the original passion of cultural studies: what is the 'modern' world? How do we locate ourselves as subjects within that world? How do our investments in that world provide the possibilities for regaining some sense of its possible futures?

NOTES

1 An earlier version of this paper was published in *Strategies* 2 (Fall 1989), pp. 114-48. I would like to thank Stuart Hall, Martin Allor, Jennifer Daryl Slack, James Hay, Elspeth Probyn, Jon Crane, Julian Halliday and Charles Acland for their comments and criticisms. For an overview of the Centre's work, see Hall *et al.* (1980). For an overview of contemporary work, see Grossberg *et al.* (1991).
2 There is of course a history, yet to be written, of the postwar American response to mass culture which has its own similarities and differences to the British response. See Ross (1989).
3 For a discussion of the British New Left, see Oxford University Socialist Discussion Group (1989).
4 See, e.g. Coward (1977) and Chambers *et al.* (1978).
5 Stuart Hall has recently offered a different narrative of the development of cultural studies. See Hall (1991).
6 See Grossberg (1988) for a more detailed analysis of the historical conditions and theoretical logic of this system of identifications.
7 For a discussion of Hall's Gramscian position, see the special issue of the *Journal of Communication Inquiry* 10 (Summer, 1986). See also Hall (1989). Hall's recent work (1987) explicitly addresses questions of identity and subjectivity.
8 The fact that people cannot be treated as cultural dopes does not mean, however, that they are not often duped.
9 For an expanded discussion of such a postmodern conjunctural theory of cultural studies, see Grossberg (1992). Note also that there are significant differences not only between the Deleuze and Foucault-influenced work of both Morris and Grossberg, and the more marxist-feminist work of Chambers, Hebdige and McRobbie, but also within each of these groups.

REFERENCES

Allor, M. (1987) 'Projective readings: cultural studies from here', *Canadian Journal of Political and Social Theory* 11: 134-8.
Althusser, L. (1971) 'Ideology and ideological state apparatuses', in *Lenin and Philosophy and Other Essays*, trans. B. Brewster, London: Verso.

Bourdieu, P. (1984) *Distinction: A Social Critique of the Judgement of Taste*, trans. R. Nice, Cambridge: Harvard University Press.

CCCS (Centre for Contemporary Cultural Studies) (1966-67; 1969-71; 1972-74) *Centre Reports*, University of Birmingham.

Chambers, I. (1986) *Popular Culture: The Metropolitan Experience*, London: Methuen.

Chambers, I., Clarke, J., Connell, I., Curti, L., Hall, S. and Jefferson, T. (1978) 'Marxism and culture', *Screen* 19: 109-19.

Clarke, J., Hall, S., Jefferson, T. and Roberts, B. (1975) 'Subcultures, culture and class: a theoretical overview', *Working Papers in Cultural Studies* 7/8: 9-74.

Coward, R. (1977) 'Class, "culture", and the social formation', *Screen* 18: 75-105.

Deleuze, G. and Guattari, F. (1981) 'Rhizome', *I & C* 8: 49-71.

Foucault, M. (1979) 'Truth and power', in M. Morris and P. Patton (eds) *Michel Foucault: Power, Truth, Strategy*, Sydney: Feral Publications.

—— (1980) *Power/Knowledge*, C. Gordon (ed.), New York: Pantheon Books.

Fry, T. (1988) 'From (sun)light to sin', in L. Grossberg (ed.) (1988).

Grossberg, L. (ed.) (1988) *It's a Sin: Essays on Postmodernism, Politics and Culture*, Sydney: Power Publications.

—— (1989) 'The circulation of cultural studies', *Critical Studies in Mass Communication* 6: 413-20.

—— (1992) *We Gotta Get Out Of This Place: Popular Conservatism and Postmodern Culture*, New York: Routledge.

Grossberg, L., Nelson, C. and Treichler, P. (eds) (1991) *Cultural Studies*, New York: Routledge.

Hall, S. (n.d.) 'Cultural analysis', CCCS publication.

—— (1971) 'Response to people and culture', *Working Papers in Cultural Studies* 1.

—— (1972) 'The social eye of Picture Post', *Working Papers in Cultural Studies* 2.

—— (1974) 'Marx's notes on method', *Working Papers in Cultural Studies* 6.

—— (1976) 'Introduction' to D. Selbourne, *An Eye on China*, London: Black Liberation Press.

—— (1980a) 'Encoding/decoding', in S. Hall *et al.* (eds) *Culture, Media, Language*, London: Hutchinson.

—— (1980b) 'Cultural studies: two paradigms', *Media, Culture and Society* 2: 57-72.

—— (1985) 'Signification, representation, ideology: Althusser and the post-structuralist debates', *Critical Studies in Mass Communication* 2: 91-114.

—— (1986) 'Gramsci's relevance for the study of race and ethnicity', *Journal of Communication Inquiry* 10: 5-27.

—— (1987) 'Minimal selves', ICA Document 6 (*Identity: The Real Me*), London: Institute of Contemporary Arts.

—— (1989) *The Road to Renewal*, London: Verso.

—— (1991) 'Cultural studies and its theoretical legacies', in L.

Grossberg, C. Nelson and P. Treichler (eds) *Cultural Studies*, New York: Routledge.

—— (forthcoming) 'Cultural studies and psychoanalysis'.

Hall, S. and Jacques, M. (eds) (1989) *New Times: The Changing Face of Politics in the 1990s*, London: Lawrence and Wishart.

Hall, S., Critcher, C., Jefferson, T., Clarke, J. and Roberts, B. (1978) *Policing the Crisis: Mugging, the State, and Law and Order*, New York: Holmes and Meier.

Hall, S., Hobson, D., Lowe, A. and Willis, P. (eds) (1980) *Culture, Media, Language*, London: Hutchinson.

Hall, S., Grossberg, L. and Slack, J. D. (forthcoming) *Cultural Studies*.

Hebdige, D. (1987) 'Digging for Britain: an excavation in seven parts', *The British Edge*, Boston: ICA.

—— (1988) *Hiding in the Light*, London: Routledge.

Hoggart, R. (1957) *The Uses of Literacy*, London: Essential Books.

—— (1967) 'The literary imagination and the study of society', CCCS Occasional Paper.

—— (1969) 'Contemporary cultural studies', CCCS Occasional Paper.

—— (1970) *Speaking to Each Other* (2 volumes), New York: Oxford University Press.

Johnson, R. (1986–87) 'What is cultural studies anyway?' *Social Text* 16: 38–80.

McRobbie, A. (1986) 'Dance and social fantasy', in A. McRobbie and M. Nava (eds) *Gender and Generation*, London: Methuen.

Morley, D. (1980) *The 'Nationwide' Audience*, London: BFI.

Morris, M. (1988a) 'At Henry Parkes Motel', *Cultural Studies* 2: 1–47.

—— (1988b) 'Banality in cultural studies', *Discourse* 10: 3–29.

Oxford University Socialist Discussion Group (1989) *Out of Apathy*, London: Verso.

Ross, A. (1989) *No Respect: American Intellectuals and Culture*, New York: Routledge.

Smith, A. C. H. (1975) *Paper Voices: The Popular Press and Social Change*, London: Chatto and Windus.

Williams, R. (1958) *Culture and Society 1780–1950*, New York: Harper and Row.

—— (1965) *The Long Revolution*, Middlesex: Penguin.

—— (1973) 'Base and superstructure in marxist theory', *New Left Review* 82: 3–16.

Willis, P. (1978) *Profane Culture*, London: Routledge and Kegan Paul.

2

USEFUL CULTURE

Tony Bennett

> To work with a government implies neither subjection nor
> global acceptance. One can simultaneously work and be
> restive. I even think that the two go together.
>
> (Foucault, cited in Burchell *et al.* 1991: 48)

It is useful, in the context of the so-called 'policy debate' in
cultural studies, to call to mind Foucault's contention, as
summarized by Colin Gordon, that a governmental logic of and
for the left ought to be possible 'involving a way for the governed
to work with government, without any assumption of com-
pliance or complicity, on actual and common problems'
(Gordon 1991: 48). For, predictably enough, the mere mention of
terms like 'government' and 'policy' in connection with cultural
studies sparks off in some a yearning for a moment of pure
politics – a return to 1968 – in whose name any traffic with the
domain of government can be written off as a sell-out. Something
of this was evident in Helen Grace's review of the Australian
Cultural Studies conference held at the University of Western
Sydney in December 1990, and especially in the oppositions
which organize the discursive strategy of that review in, on the
one hand, linking the turn to policy with pragmatically driven
research and a yearning for money and power while, on the
other, ranging against these an uncontaminated holy trinity of
theory, scholarship and textual analysis (Grace 1991).

My principal concern here, then, is to suggest that viewing 'the
policy debate' through the prism of such oppositions runs the
risk of distorting the issues that are at stake in that debate.[1] These,
I want to argue, do not take the form of a generalized choice
between theory on the one hand and policy on the other, or

between textual analysis and pragmatically oriented research. Rather, they take the form of a choice between *different* bodies and styles of theory, between *different* ways of construing the relations between theoretical and pragmatic concerns, and between *different* kinds of textual analysis and their associated estimations of the issues at stake in the conduct of such analysis.

This is not intended, however, as a way of pulling the policy punch, or of seeking to legitimize policy work by claiming that it, too, can lay claim to a stock of theoretical credentials of its own. Nor is it intended as a pluralist argument for relations of peaceful coexistence with other styles, paradigms or tendencies within cultural studies. This is not to suggest that all work within cultural studies (however we might want to define it) should or need be directly concerned with policy matters. What it is to suggest is that all such work is indirectly affected by policy issues and horizons. This being so, my contention is that recognition of this would, and should, make a considerable difference to the manner in which the concerns of cultural studies are broached and conceptualized as well as to the political styles and dispositions governing the ways in which work in the field is conducted and the constituencies to which it is addressed.

In these respects, my presentation takes its bearings from Stuart Cunningham's contention that the incorporation of an adequate and thoroughgoing policy orientation into cultural studies would see a shift in its 'command metaphors away from rhetorics of resistance, progressiveness, and anti-commercialism on the one hand, and populism on the other, toward those of access, equity, empowerment and the divination of opportunities to exercise appropriate cultural leadership'.[2] Such a project, Cunningham argues, enjoins a far-reaching theoretical revisionism that 'would necessitate rethinking the component parts of the field from the ground up' (Cunningham 1991: 21). It is to this task that I wish to contribute here by reviewing – and suggesting alternatives to – the concepts of culture which have subtended the cultural studies enterprise.[3]

HISTORIES OF CULTURE

This is a timely undertaking. In *Politics and Letters*, Williams claimed that his motives in writing *Culture and Society* were mainly oppositional. His aim, he wrote, was 'to counter the appropriation of a long-line of thinking about culture to what were by now decisively reactionary positions' rather than 'to found a new position' (Williams 1979: 97–8). There can be little doubt that this work proved to be decisively enabling for the subsequent development of cultural studies in the new views and definitions of culture it helped establish. The limitations of the new definitional horizons Williams thus opened up, however, are becoming increasingly apparent.

The respects in which Williams' concept of culture as a 'whole way of life' is connected to a Romantic conception of the historical process as one destined to restore us to the communal ways of living from which it has allegedly rent us asunder have already been subject to comment elsewhere (see Hunter 1988). So, too, have the respects in which his enthusiasm for the historical restitution of community rests on an over-sentimental attachment to the patriarchal forms of Welsh working-class culture (see Jardine and Swindells 1989). Here, then, I shall seek to add to these perspectives by focusing on the limitations of the kind of historical account Williams offers of the evolution of the range of meanings associated with 'culture' in its modern usage.

These limitations are not ones of error; rather, they are ones of implication. I do not, that is to say, wish to question Williams' reading of the line of descent from Coleridge and Newman to Arnold and thence to Leavis. What I do want to question, however, is the assumption – largely taken on trust in cultural studies – that an adequate definition of culture can be derived from such an analysis. In tracing the emergence of the selective definition of culture, understood as a standard of achieved perfection, Williams offers an account of its functioning as a key term in modern forms of social critique and commentary. Important though this is, there are limits to the conclusions that can be derived from such a history. In particular, there are no good reasons to suppose that such semantic shifts can be regarded as anything but symptomatic of the concurrent changes affecting the organization and social functioning of those practices which fall within the category of culture so defined. Or, to put this another way: the changing definitional contours of 'culture' comprise merely a part of the changing set of relations in which, in the period since the late eighteenth century, cultural forms and activities have come to be implicated. Viewed in this light, I want to suggest, the transformations to which we should pay attention concern less the changing semantic fortunes of 'culture', particularly as manifested in its development into a standard of achieved perfection, than the role which such developments played in relation to the emergence of the wider domain of 'the cultural' as a field of social management.

This, then, is the nature of the revisionism I wish to propose, one in which the distinctiveness of culture – in its modern forms – is sought less in the specificity of its practices than in the specificity of the governmental tasks and programmes in which those practices come to be inscribed. By 'governmental' here, I should stress, I do not mean 'of or pertaining to the state'. Rather, I have in mind the much broader conception of the governmentalization of social relations – that is, the management of populations by means of specific knowledges, programmes and technologies – which, according to Foucault, most clearly distinguishes modern forms of social regulation from their predecessors. An adequate genealogy of modern culture, I want to suggest, needs to take more account of its practical deployment within such governmental processes than previous accounts have been wont to.

The perspectives I shall draw on in support of this argument are derived from work-in-progress on the early history of the public museum and, in the British context, the rational recreations movement. These provide some rough and ready coordinates for a history of culture which focuses on the manner in which the practices that are so described have come to be rendered useful by being harnessed to governmental programmes aimed at transforming the attributes – mental and behavioural – of extended populations. Such a history would, of course, be quite different from the more familiar ones within cultural studies in that it would take its bearings from the changing forms and contexts of culture's governmental and administrative utilization rather than from its shifting semantic horizons. It is a history, moreover, written in the institutional arrangements and programmes developed by cultural administrators like Henry Cole – the architect of the Great Exhibition and of London's South Kensington museum complex – rather than, as Williams proposed, one contained in the texts of cultural critics. And it is a history, finally, in which policy – which, in its broad sense, I define as the governmental utilization of culture for specific ends – would appear not as an optional add-on but as central to the definition and constitution of culture and so also, therefore, equally central to the concerns of cultural studies.

There is not space, here, to do more than sketch the contours of such a history. In doing so, however, I shall try to demonstrate how the arguments advanced so far undermine the intelligibility of a polarity between, on the one hand, theory, politics and textual analysis and, on the other, an unprincipled, policy-oriented pragmatism. I shall do so by means of three provocations. First, I shall seek to show how a stress on the governmental utilization of culture can suggest new approaches to some of the perennial theoretical problems and concerns of cultural studies. My contention in this regard will be that the emergence of the modern relations between high and popular culture can be viewed as an artefact of government in view of the degree to which the former was – and still is – subjected to a governmental technologization or instrumentalization in order to render it useful as a means of social management. Second, I shall endeavour to show how acknowledging the intrinsically governmental constitution of modern culture undermines the logic of a cultural politics of resistance or opposition to some generalized source of cultural domination. I shall suggest that, on the contrary, modern forms of cultural politics often have their origins and *raison d'être* in the governmentalization of culture: that is, that the objectives to which they are committed are a by-product of the governmental uses to which specific forms of culture have been put just as those objectives can only be met via modifications to existing governmental programmes or the development of new ones. My third provocation will be to suggest that the ends toward which textual analysis is directed, the means by which such analysis is conducted and the political issues which hinge on its pursuit are an effect of the ways in which specific regions of culture (literature, art) have been instrumentalized via their inscription within particular governmental cultural technologies or apparatuses.

CULTURE AND POWER

As good a way as any of broaching these various issues is to suggest that cultural studies might usefully review its understanding of the relations between culture and power in the light of Foucault's critique of juridico-discursive conceptions of power. The main burden of Foucault's critique, it will be recalled, is that western political thought, up to and including marxist theories of the state, has proved incapable of recognizing the capillary network of power relations associated with the development of modern forms of government because it still envisages power, on the model of its monarchical form, as emanating from a single source. The primary concern of political theory has accordingly been to specify how limits might be placed on the exercise of such power or to identify sources external to it from which it might be opposed. To cut off the king's head in political theory, Foucault argues, means

> . . . that we should direct our researches on the nature of power not towards the juridical edifice of sovereignty, the State apparatuses and the ideologies which accompany them, but towards domination and the material operators of power, towards forms of subjection and the inflections and utilizations of their localized systems, and towards strategic apparatuses.
>
> (Foucault 1980: 102)

It also means, he argues, that we should forsake looking for a source outside power from which it might be opposed and seek instead to identify the differentiated forms of resistance which the exercise of power – through multiple and dispersed networks of relations – itself generates.

Many of the views regarding the relations between culture and power still current within cultural studies suggest that an equivalent cutting off of the king's head has yet to take place. While the dominant ideology thesis has few remaining supporters, the perspective of cultural hegemony which – by and large – has replaced that thesis remains committed to a juridico-discursive conception of power in its deployment of what Foucault calls a descending analysis of power which, in positing a centre of and for power, then aims to trace the means by which that power percolates down through the social structure so as to reproduce itself in its molecular elements. It is true that, in its more sophisticated variants, this perspective stresses the negotiated nature of this process: that is, that power is never exercised without encountering sources of opposition to which it is obliged to make concessions so that what is consented to is always a power that has been modified in the course of its exercise. Nonetheless, it remains the case that the field of culture is thought of as structured by the descending flows of hegemonic ideologies, transmitted from the centres of bourgeois cultural power, as they reach into and reorganize the everyday culture of the subordinate classes. As a consequence, analysis is then often concerned to ascertain how far and how deeply such ideologies have reached into the lives of the subordinate classes or, *per contra*, to determine the extent to which their downward transmission has been successfully resisted. It is thus that studies of the mid-nineteenth century advocacy of rational recreations are usually preoccupied with assessing the degree to which bourgeois cultural and ideological values succeeded in reorganizing working-class thought and feeling, and especially with determining how far down the class structure their influence reached: only so far as the upper reaches of the labour aristocracy or more deeply into the 'respectable' sections of the working class?[4]

While not wishing to gainsay the importance of such concerns, the focus they embody is, at best, one-eyed. For the assumption that the advocacy of rational recreations was premised on their anticipated success in transforming working-class ideology and consciousness is a questionable one, and especially so if it is supposed that such a transformation was expected to result from the simple exposure of the working class to the purely mental influence of such recreations. Rather, cultural reformers were often less concerned with questions of consciousness than with the field of habits and manners. Moreover, in so far as they did anticipate any changes in the former, it was thought that this would only come about as a result of transformations in habitual norms and codes of conduct that contact with rational recreations would effect.

Such contact, however, was not envisaged as exclusively or even mainly mental in form. Rather, if access to the world of rational recreations was expected to result in changed forms of behaviour and habits of conduct, this was because that contact was planned to take place in a technologized environment – the museum or the concert hall, for example – in which the desired behavioural effect was to result not from contact with 'culture' in itself but rather from the deployment of cultural objects within a specific field of social and technological relations. Thomas Greenwood's staunch advocacy of the civilizing virtues of science museums thus rested less on the intrinsic properties of the objects displayed than on the manner of their display within the specialized classificatory environment of the museum.

> The working man or agricultural labourer who spends his holiday in a walk through any well-arranged Museum cannot fail to come away with a deeply-rooted and reverential sense of the extent of knowledge possessed by his fellow-men. It is not the objects themselves that he sees there, and wonders at, that cause this impression, so much as the order and evident science which he cannot but recognise in the manner in which they are grouped and arranged. He learns that there is a meaning and value in every object, however insignificant, and that there is a way of looking, at things common and rare, distinct from the regarding them as useless, useful, or merely curious.
>
> (Greenwood 1888: 26)

Similarly, the specific knowledge acquired in the course of such a visit is less important than the new habits to which it gives rise – ideally, a self-activating desire for the pursuit of knowledge that will serve as an antidote to less civilizing habits. Greenwood thus continues:

> After a holiday spent in a Museum the working man goes home and cons over what he has seen at his leisure, and very probably on the next summer holiday, or a Sunday afternoon walk with his wife and little ones, he discovers that he has acquired a new interest in the common things he sees around him. He begins to discover that the stones, the flowers, the creatures of all kinds that throng around him are not, after all, so very commonplace as he had previously thought them. He looks at them with a pleasure not before experienced, and talks of them to his children with sundry references to things like them which he saw in the Museum. He has gained a new sense, a craving for natural knowledge, and such a craving may, possibly, in course of time, quench another and lower craving which may at one time have held him bondage – that for intoxicants or vicious excitement of one description or another.
>
> (Greenwood 1888: 26–7)

The behavioural changes which might result from the exposure of the working class to art in art galleries were similarly often expected to derive from the opportunities for mingling with middle-class exemplars which visiting art galleries afforded as much as from the qualities of the art displayed.[5] Indeed, the quality of the art displayed was often viewed as quite incidental to the prospective technological effects of art galleries in these regards. When quizzed before the 1867 Select Committee on the Paris Exhibition, for example, Henry Cole could not be budged from the view that, once placed in the environment of a museum, *any* art was imbued with a civilizing potential which made it preferable to no art at all:

> . . . and I understand you to state that you consider that the gift of indifferent pictures to the museum would be productive of unmitigated good; is that your opinion? – Certainly; but it is a vague term to say indifferent pictures. I could go through the National Gallery where there are many pictures which in one sense are indifferent pictures; there they are, and people go there to see them; you cannot say it is evil and not good. I say it is an unmitigated good . . .
>
> Do you think it is desirable that the standard of taste should be maintained in this country at its present level, at which you say that a picture like the 'Derby Day' would beat any Raphael hollow? – I presume to say I do not know what is the standard of taste.
>
> I understand you to say, that if the 'Derby Day', by Mr Frith, and a Raphael were exhibited in this country, the 'Derby Day' would beat the Raphael hollow in its appreciation by the people of this country; do you think that state of things is desirable? – No; but I think it is desirable that people should be taught to look at the pictures, and to take pleasure in them.
>
> Either good or bad? – Either good or bad, unless they are indecent or bloodthirsty; but I think a picture which is harmless in its morality is a work of art; and I think if it attracts anybody to look at it, that is something gained to the cause of civilisation. I had much sooner that a man looked at an inferior picture than that he went to the public-house.
>
> Why do we try to purchase good works of art, if it is desirable to have bad ones? – Just in the same sense that a

glass of table beer is better than nothing, but you would prefer sherry, perhaps, if you could get it.

(Report on Paris Exhibition 1867: 920–4)

In the nineteenth-century advocacy of rational recreation, then, as well as in the development of public art galleries, museums and concert halls, we can see the development of a new orientation *vis-à-vis* culture, one in which specific forms and arrangements of culture are judged capable of being harnessed to governmental programmes aimed at the transformation of popular morals and manners. This envisaged effect, however, is anticipated in view of the way in which specific forms of culture are instrumentalized – fashioned into useful vehicles for governing – rather than from their intrinsic properties even though, as I shall argue shortly, this inscription of culture into governmental programmes both supplies the conditions for and is assisted by the development of essentializing aesthetic discourses.

I am suggesting, then, that an understanding of the relations between culture and power in modern societies needs to take account of the instrumentalization of culture which accompanies its enlistment for governmental purposes. For the culture/power articulation which results from these developments is quite distinct from the organization of such relations in earlier societies. Within the absolutist regimes of early modern Europe, for example, culture certainly formed part of the strategies of rule and statecraft. It thus formed part of a sphere of elite display through which, in pre-revolutionary France, the aristocracy could be bound to, and rendered dependent on, the world of the court. Equally, so far as the relations between state and people were concerned, it formed part of a politics of spectacle through which the might and majesty of royal power was dramatized via its symbolic display.[6]

Of course, there remains a symbolic aspect to the relations between culture and power in modern societies; the 'politics of spectacle' did not die out with the *ancien régime* or Old Corruption.[7] However, this aspect no longer exhausts such relations or even accounts for their most distinctive qualities. Rather, these are to be found in the respects in which culture comes to be imbricated within governmental programmes directed at transforming the mental, spiritual and behavioural attributes of the population. If culture is the servant of power within absolutist regimes, the power it serves is – if not a singular one – certainly a power which augments its own effects in being *represented* as singular just as it is a power whose interest in the generality of the population is limited to the need to impress it into obedience. In the early nineteenth century, by contrast, we see the sphere of culture being, quite literally, refashioned – retooled for a new task – as it comes to be inscribed within governmental strategies which aim less at exacting popular obedience to a sovereign authority than at producing in a population a capacity for new forms of thought, feeling and behaviour.

Both relations of culture and power, of course, are productive; but their productiveness belongs to different modalities. They aim at producing different kinds of persons, organized in different relations to power, and they proceed by means of different mechanisms for distributing the effects of culture through the social body: the representational and symbolic versus the governmental and technological. If we are to write an adequate history of culture in the modern period, it is to the changing contours of its instrumental refashioning in the context of new and developing cultural and governmental technologies that we must look. This is not to say that the changing co-ordinates of 'culture's' semantic destinies are unimportant. However, it is to suggest that these derive their significance from their relations to culture's governmental and technological refashioning. Some pointers as to the directions which such a revisionist history might take can be indicated by briefly developing the three provocations I mentioned earlier.

CULTURE AND ITS DISCONTENTS

The differences between high and popular culture, Geoffrey Nowell-Smith has argued, are becoming increasingly blurred in view of two considerations. First, the fact that virtually all forms of modern culture are capitalist means that different realms of culture can no longer easily be distinguished in terms of their relations of production while, second, modern culture tends increasingly to comprise a 'single, intertextual field whose signifying elements are perpetually being recombined and played off against each other' (Nowell-Smith 1987: 87). There is, however, a third reason. For it is also true that virtually all forms of

77

culture are now capable of being fashioned into vehicles for governmental programmes of one sort or another – for AIDS education programmes, for example, or, as popular literary texts come to be incorporated into the literature lesson, as textual props for ethical or civic trainings of various kinds. It is, indeed, precisely these kinds of changes which form part of the material and institutional conditions of existence which have supported the development of cultural studies.

In these various ways, then, the co-ordinates of the discursive field in which the modern concept of culture first emerged – a field characterized by the antinomy between the high and the popular – are being weakened. Yet these discursive co-ordinates were also practical ones in that it was precisely the production of a vertical relation between the high and the popular which established the gradient down which the 'improving' force of culture could flow in order to help 'lift' the general cultural level of the population. The point I'm after here is that it was precisely the aestheticization of high culture which provided the enabling conditions for the production of such a gradient. There is not, that is to say, any opposition between culture's aestheticization and its being rendered useful as an instrument for governmental programmes of social and cultural management. On the contrary, it was only the development of aesthetic conceptions of culture which allowed the establishment of those discursive co-ordinates in which elite cultural practices could be detached from their earlier functions – of dazzling spectacle, for example – and then come to be connected to civilizing programmes in which they could function as instruments of cultural 'improvement' directed toward the population at large.

If, today, the discursive co-ordinates which supported such conceptions and strategies are mutating, this is partly because of a tendency toward self-undoing that is inherent within them. An important characteristic of the relations between culture and power developed in the nineteenth century consisted in the degree to which forms of culture needed to be valorized as embodiments of universal norms of civilization or humanity in order to be rendered governmentally useful. Yet this process has also served to generate alternative demands and oppositions from the zones of exclusion and margins which it itself establishes. It is in this respect, to come to my second provocation, that many modern forms of cultural politics can be viewed as by-products of culture's governmentalization rather than as arising autochthonously out of relations of repression. Foucault has argued that the government of sexuality has given rise to a new sphere of biopolitics in which new kinds of counter-politics have been generated in view of the 'strategic reversibility of power relations' through which, as Colin Gordon puts it, 'the terms of governmental practices can be turned around into focuses of resistance' (Gordon 1991: 5). We need also to be alert to the ways in which the utilization of culture as an instrument of government has exhibited a similar capacity to generate its own fields of counter-politics.

Demands that representational parity be given to women's art in art galleries or to the histories of subordinate social strata in history museums are thus ones which are generated out of, and fuelled by, the norms of universal representativity embodied in the rhetorics of public art galleries and museums. Earlier collections of valued objects seem not to have given rise to any similar demands – partly, no doubt, because of the limited influence of democratic and egalitarian philosophies but also because the principles of curiosity and wonder which governed the constitution of such collections meant that no general political value could be attached to the question of what was included within, or excluded from, such collections. For, where objects were collected for their curiosity value, it was their singularity that mattered, not their representativeness.[8] Only the refashioning of the semiotic frames of reference of collecting institutions such that cultural objects came to be displayed and classified in terms of their representativeness of general norms of humanity lent any cogency or purpose to the view that the histories and cultures of different social groups should be accorded equal representational rights and weight. The first organized campaigns for more attention to be paid to women's history and culture in collecting institutions thus took the form of a demand that such matters be accorded representational parity within the universalizing project of modernity as exemplified by the international exposition.[9]

Many aspects of modern cultural politics, then, are effects of the ways in which specific fields of cultural practice have been governmentally deployed. The same is true of many aspects and forms of cultural analysis. Moreover, this is so in ways which render the opposition between textual analysis and policy analysis quite disabling. For the text which analysis encounters and which must be engaged with, theoretically and politically, is never simply given to analysis. Rather, what a text is, and what is at stake in its analysis, depends on the specific uses for which it has been instrumentalized in particular institutional and discursive contexts – some of which, of course, will be governmentally constructed and organized. This being so, the development of politically self-reflexive forms of textual analysis depends precisely on adopting a policy perspective – that is, on recognizing how the textual regime in question functions as part of a technological apparatus with a view to considering the kinds of reading activities and relations through which that regime might be redeployed for new purposes.

Take the modern art museum. Clearly, many forms of textual analysis – art history, for example, in its commitment to tracing intertextual relations within the archive of the museum text – are dependent on the assemblage of art within museums and on the systems that have been developed for recording, collating and exchanging information between museums. However, it can also be argued that, in view of its functioning as an institution of social differentiation, the modern art museum has fashioned a distinctive textuality for the modern art object, one which organizes social relations of inclusion – which, of course, are also always ones of exclusion – by producing an invisible depth within the artwork (the depth, precisely, of its intertextuality) such that a line can be drawn between those who can, and those who cannot, see its 'hidden' significances. Questions of textual analysis – and of how to approach them – thus cannot, in this view, be posed independently of their implications for the positions and practices they make available in relation to this specific, socially and historically produced form of textuality. Indeed, political debates within the art museum are, in essence, debates about how (if at all) this distinctive textuality of the art object might be re-technologized and for what purpose – questions whose axes are simultaneously policy and textual ones.

FROM CRITICS TO TECHNICIANS

Government, then, is not the *vis-à-vis* of cultural politics. It is not an abstraction to be opposed in the name of a cultural politics which imaginarily draws its nourishment from a ground outside the governmental domain: the purely economic conditions of existence of a class, say, or the somatic resistances of the body. Rather, the relations between government and modern forms of cultural politics are ones of mutual dependency. How cultural forms and activities are politicized and the manner in which their politicization is expressed and pursued: these are matters which emerge from, and have their conditions of existence within, the ways in which those forms and activities have been instrumentally fashioned as a consequence of their governmental deployment for specific social, cultural or political ends.

Clearly, perspectives of this kind sit ill at ease with what have come to be regarded as the central paradigms of cultural studies. For if cultural studies is defined by its concerns – theoretical and practical – with the relations between culture and power, it has largely envisaged such relations negatively in its critiques of dominant cultures as instruments of an oppressive power. The position argued here, by contrast, attributes a certain productivity to power in contending that the modern forms of culture's politicization are historical outcomes of the specific relations between culture and power that have been embodied in culture's fashioning as an instrument of government. This theoretical dissonance, moreover, has far-reaching practical consequences in suggesting that cultural studies needs to devise different ways of intervening within the fields of cultural politics it identifies as relevant to its concerns.

The issues that are at stake in many fields of modern cultural politics, I have thus argued, are a historical result of the ways in which cultural forms have been technologically adapted in order to be rendered governmentally useful. However, if this is so, then it follows that making a difference to how culture works – altering the fields of uses and effects within which specific forms of culture are inscribed and which they help to support – is also a technological matter requiring that close attention be paid to the nuts-and-bolts mechanisms which condition the governmental uses of specific cultural practices in the framework of particular cultural technologies or apparatuses. Take the manifold political issues associated with the relations between nation, culture and identity. It is clear that this nexus of relations has been shaped into being by the activities of modern governments concerned to endow their citizens with specific sets of nationalized traits and attributes. It is also equally clear that, whatever their present

81

configuration, there can be no reorganization of the relations between nation, culture and identity without intruding policy – and so a shift in culture's governmental deployment – into that trinity. Such an intrusion might take different forms: the regulation of broadcast content by bodies like the Australian Broadcasting Tribunal, for example, or the monitoring of the cultural resources available to minority ethnic groups of a kind undertaken by the Office for Multicultural Affairs. It might equally take the form of new protocols of reading which, in allowing literary or film texts to be technologized in new ways by providing readers with different exercises to undertake in relation to them, allow those texts to play a role in the refashioning of national identities.

Cultural change – or, perhaps better, changing what culture does – thus emerges as a largely technical matter; not, however, in the sense that it is something to be left to specialists but rather in the sense (the good Brechtian sense) that it results from tinkering with practical arrangements rather than from an epic struggle for consciousness. For cultural studies this would mean not merely a shift in its command metaphors of the kind proposed by Cunningham (away from rhetorics of resistance, progressiveness, etc., and toward those of access, equity, and empowerment). It would also entail a shift in its conception of the kind of enterprise it envisages itself as committed to and of the means by which that enterprise might be realized.

The style of intellectual work – and the associated rhetorics, modes of address, styles of pedagogy and forms of training – cultural studies sees itself as concerned to promote is of crucial significance in this respect. The model of the cultural critic – of the intellectual engaged in the struggle for consciousness by means of techniques of cultural commentary – has not been the only model of the intellectual informing the history of cultural studies. It has, however, been an influential one, and it is one that is deeply written into the tradition – at least in its British versions – given its historical affiliations with literary criticism. It is, moreover, a model of the intellectual that is now being significantly re-inscribed into cultural studies as – in one of the more influential of the many guises in which it now appears within the academy – it is increasingly cast in the role of heir and successor to English. This unfortunately means that it also often takes on the moral mantle of English in supplying an institutional and discursive context in which the trainee cultural critic can become adept in using a range of moralized enunciative positions. As an alternative, then, cultural studies might envisage its role as consisting of the training of cultural technicians: that is, of intellectual workers less committed to cultural critique as an instrument for changing consciousness than to modifying the functioning of culture by means of technical adjustments to its governmental deployment.

NOTES

This paper has also been published in *Cultural Studies* (1992).

1 Especially as there are signs that this version of the 'policy debate' will prove an influential one within Australian cultural studies. Grace's antinomic constructions are thus echoed by Deborah Chambers in her editorial for the June/July 1991 issue of the Australian Cultural Studies Association Newsletter.
2 Cunningham's use of the term 'leadership' here is, perhaps, misleading. My sense, from the context of his discussion, is that the concept of 'cultural facilitation' would have better suited his purposes given, on the one hand, the elitist associations of traditional conceptions of cultural leadership or, on the other, their association with Gramsci's conception of the role of intellectuals in providing moral and cultural leadership for social classes and allied social movements. Clearly, neither of these meanings accords well with Cunningham's sense that intellectuals should play more of a technical and co-ordinating role in enhancing the range of available cultural resources and facilitating more equitable patterns of access to those resources.
3 For a complementary discussion of related issues, see Bennett (1991).
4 See, for example, the discussions of Bailey (1987) and Gray (1976).
5 See Arscott (1988) for a fascinating discussion of the influence of such views in the development of art galleries and exhibitions in mid to late nineteenth-century Leeds.
6 Even though the text (and not just the reception) of such spectacles was often more ambiguous than has usually been supposed. See Laqueur (1989).
7 However, the rhetorical strategies of the politics of spectacle were significantly transformed in the nineteenth century. See Bennett (1988) for a discussion of these transformations in the case of museums and exhibitions.
8 See Breckenridge (1989) for an excellent discussion of the contrast between the focus on the singularity of objects in premodern collecting institutions and the concern with the representativeness of objects evinced by modern public museums and exhibitions. For a detailed example of the premodern concern with the singularity of objects, see MacGregor (1983).

9 For a full account of the most influential of these campaigns and its influence on American feminism, see Weimann (1981).

REFERENCES

Arscott, C. (1988) ' "Without distinction of party": The Polytechnic Exhibitions in Leeds, 1839–45', in J. Wolff and J. Seed (eds) *The Culture of Capital: Art, Power and the Nineteenth Century Middle Class*, Manchester: Manchester University Press.

Bailey, P. (1987) *Leisure and Class in Victorian England: Rational Recreation and the Contest for Control, 1830–1885*, London: Methuen.

Bennett, T. (1988) 'The exhibitionary complex', *New Formations* 4: 73–102.

—— (1991) 'Putting policy into cultural studies', in L. Grossberg, C. Nelson and P. Treichler (eds) *Cultural Studies*, New York: Routledge.

Breckenridge, C. (1989) 'The aesthetics and politics of colonial collecting: India at World Fairs', *Comparative Studies in Society and History* 31, 2: 195–216.

Burchell, G., Gordon, C. and Miller, P. (1991) *The Foucault Effect: Studies in Governmentality*, London: Harvester/Wheatsheaf.

Cunningham, S. (1991) 'A policy calculus for media studies', Paper presented to the Fourth International Television Studies Conference, London.

Foucault, M. (1980) 'Two lectures', in C. Gordon (ed.) *Power/Knowledge: Selected Interviews and Other Writings 1972–1977*, New York: Pantheon Books.

Gordon, C. (1991) 'Governmental rationality: an introduction', in G. Burchell, C. Gordon and P. Miller (eds) *The Foucault Effect: Studies in Governmentality*, London: Harvester Wheatsheaf.

Grace, H. (1991) 'Eating the curate's egg: cultural studies for the nineties', *West* 3, 1: 46–9.

Gray, R. (1976) *The Labour Aristocracy in Victorian Edinburgh*, Oxford: Clarendon Press.

Greenwood, T. (1888) *Museums and Art Galleries*, London: Simpkin, Marshall & Co.

Hunter, I. (1988) *Culture and Government: The Emergence of Literary Education*, London: Macmillan.

Jardine, L. and Swindells, J. (1989) 'Homage to Orwell: the dream of a common culture, and other minefields', in T. Eagleton (ed.) *Raymond Williams: Critical Perspectives*, Cambridge: Polity Press.

Laqueur, T. W. (1989) 'Crowds, carnival and the state in English executions, 1604–1868', in A. L. Beier, D. Cannadine and M. R. James (eds) *The First Modern Society: Essays in English History in Honour of Lawrence Stone*, Cambridge: Cambridge University Press.

MacGregor, A. (1983) *Tradescant's Rarities: Essays on the Foundation of the Ashmolean Museum, 1683, with a Catalogue of the Early Collection*, Oxford: Clarendon Press.

Nowell-Smith, G. (1987) 'Popular culture', *New Formations* 2: 79–90.

Select Parliamentary Committee Report on the Paris Exhibition, 1867
(1971) *British Parliamentary Papers*, Shannon: Irish University Press.
Weimann, J. (1981) *The Fair Women*, Chicago: Academy Press.
Williams, R. (1979) *Politics and Letters*, London: New Left Books.

3

SHIFTING BOUNDARIES, LINES OF DESCENT
Cultural studies and institutional realignments[1]

Will Straw

As an intellectual project, cultural studies is intimately connected to notions of dialogue or exchange within intellectual life. These notions are, obviously, at the heart of the appeal of this project, and central to the political claims made in its name. At the same time, however, one is likely to live cultural studies as a set of ongoing tensions and disputes, and as the source of perpetual anxieties over the relationships of one's own place of work (whether this be defined in geographical or disciplinary terms, or as the set of socio-cultural identities which one occupies) to a variety of intellectual communities. My concern, in this paper, is with mapping out certain of these tensions and anxieties as they have shaped the ongoing development of a cultural studies project in English Canada. The value and legitimacy which I ascribe to this project itself is largely unstated here, and I would hope that the analysis which follows is not seen simply as a cynical recounting of localized struggles for prestige and influence. Nevertheless, if one accepts that the terrain of cultural studies is one which will forever be marked by disputes and jurisdictional battles, and that the final dissolution of these is neither imminent nor possible, then an analysis which seeks to specify their effects within a context such as that of English Canada serves to clarify the conditions under which cultural studies communities take shape.

GEOGRAPHICAL REALIGNMENTS

By the mid-to-late 1980s, one could reasonably claim that cultural studies (from which the qualifying 'British' had now detached itself) was flourishing most visibly within the academic culture of the United States. In part, this repeated the predictable itinerary of recent projects of theoretical revision; like psycho-analytic film theory or literary deconstruction, cultural studies had crossed the Atlantic and settled into the elephantine infra-structure of the US academy. More accurately, perhaps, cultural studies in the United States represented the turn within a number of disciplines in the humanities to concerns and methods which one might risk calling sociological – towards, for example, the ethnography of audiences in media studies, the study of intellectual formations and institutional power in literary history, or accounts of the construction of social space in a variety of cultural forms. In many cases, as well, disciplines such as film or English studies which had lived through their post-structuralist moments found themselves newly authorized by a politics of social identity to investigate the representational status of cultural artefacts. Media or cultural texts were increas-ingly examined in terms of their role as sites for the figuring of social identities, from perspectives which remained cognizant of the specificities of particular textual forms but no longer obsessively insistent upon them.

More so than has been the case elsewhere, I would argue, cultural studies within the United States has been marked by the minor role played within it by the established social sciences. The sociological turn described above has been produced within the humanities, as part of a larger transformation by which a politics of cultural identity (of race, gender and sexuality) has come to dominate the wider space of oppositional politics generally, within and outside the academy. The symptomatic development here is not merely the cohering of most opposi-tional politics under the sign of the cultural, but the extent to which the humanities (and the discipline of anthropology, which has moved to embrace them) have come to authorize within their boundaries the discussion of virtually any question of socio-cultural interest. (Communications studies, situated conceptually and institutionally at the boundary between the humanities and social sciences, may be seen to function as a bulwark between the two, as far as the migration of cultural studies is concerned.) In this respect, the situation is an inversion of that observable in the 1960s, when sociology and neighbour-ing disciplines within the social sciences opened their doors to embrace most of the resonant questions of the period.

At the beginning of the 1990s, I shared with many the sense that, while cultural studies had begun within Great Britain and undergone remarkable expansion within the United States, it promised to become increasingly Canadian and Australian. Discounting those biases rooted in my own geographical location, one can see in the evolving agenda of cultural studies the emergent centrality of questions with a particular relevance to these two countries. The current interrogation of notions of nationhood and cultural identity, and the debate over the relationship of cultural theory to questions of public policy and economic development, have at the very least encouraged the migration of theoretical and intellectual work between Canada and Australia. For those working in these countries, I suspect, this development has partially resolved a long-time tension between the appeal of cultural studies as an ongoing, multinational project of theoretical revision and our commitment to working simultaneously in areas, like those of media policy studies or political economy, which seemed more concretely interventionist. Within media analysis in Canada, the turn towards 'thick policy' studies, to work which is not simply a chronicling of victimization or dependency but a rethinking of the terms of cultural identity, has been nourished in part by the larger shift in cultural studies within the Anglo-American world.

INSTITUTIONAL REORDERINGS

Whether or not it has succeeded in producing a significant transformation in the substance of particular domains of knowledge, cultural studies has noticeably reordered the contexts and frames of reference within which intellectual work in a variety of fields is undertaken. Tony Bennett's call for an analysis of the 'institutional conditions of cultural studies' (Bennett 1992: 23) invites attention to the ways in which cultural studies has produced new relationships between individual intellectual activity and a variety of communities of interest whose scale, geographical location and institutional position vary widely. In this respect, Ellen Rooney's appealing definition of cultural studies – as 'an anti-disciplinary practice defined by the repeated, indeed, endless rejection of the logic of the disciplines' (Rooney 1990: 21) – demands a measure of qualification. As a collective conversation, cultural studies has not threatened the boundaries

88

between disciplines so much as it has altered the terms under which change within them occurs. By continuously redefining the priorities and procedures of cultural analysis, cultural studies has produced and perpetuated the sense of there being a 'centre' within cultural research. It has, however, simultaneously ensured that the location of this centre, relative to the place of different disciplines and currents of intellectual work, will shift over time.[2]

In my own institution, for example, the emergent appeal of a social geography has, in minor but observable ways, diminished the prominence of film theory, whose centring of questions of gender and ideology around issues of spectatorship once proved more resonant across a number of disciplines and constituencies. The relationship of individual or disciplinary intellectual projects to cultural studies is partly a function of the extent to which currents within these projects are tied to the latter's trajectories of change. It is an effect, as well, of the degree to which shifts in the relative prominence of different disciplines within cultural studies will alter the range of questions about which such disciplines feel authorized and compelled to speak. It would do an injustice to those working within cultural studies to see the institutional politics which surround it as driven exclusively by struggles for prestige and influence, but the administrative accommodation of this work is often one response to the trivialization with which disciplines in the humanities have, for many years now, been marked.

The recent history of comparative literature is revealing in this respect. In the 1970s, comparative literature programs were among the principal sites for the dissemination of continental and post-structuralist theoretical currents within Canadian universities. The embracing of this work represented, in many cases, a turn away from an older *comparatiste* conception of the discipline whose appeal had waned. As these perspectives made their way into a variety of other disciplines within the humanities, several comparative literature programs have undertaken major projects of redefinition, redefining their object as that of 'social discourse' in a broadly defined sense, or moving to concerns, like that of the relationships between literary production and technology, for which claims of relevance may be easily made.

In this respect, decisions by disciplines to embrace many of the concerns of cultural studies are often made in response to a perceived diminishing of their status and influence within intellectual culture, and are not inevitably or exclusively the result of projects of radical transformation. Crises of purpose within literature, music or anthropology departments, for example, which one might read as evidence of their historical decline, often result in processes of disciplinary rejuvenation which maintain these disciplines' intellectual and institutional hegemony. The most common response to these crises is the observation that these disciplines are becoming interesting again, as their own processes of internal critique come to be monitored by those working in a variety of adjacent disciplines. To take the most prominent recent example, the demonstration that forms of ethnographic or anthropological writing are ultimately 'literary' constructions, whose inseparability from regimes of geopolitical power is now evident (e.g. Clifford and Marcus 1986), has served to invigorate and recentre the discipline of anthropology as much as it has produced calls for its disappearance. In important ways, obviously, these internal changes are welcome, and their effects on pedagogical substance and faculty composition are not negligible. At the same time, however, by invoking their past importance and power to justify the urgency and prioritizing of their own projects of internal transformation, these disciplines are often able to maintain their institutional privilege.

The risk of an engagement with cultural studies is that of participation in an intellectual field in which, as a feminist film theorist described it recently, race has displaced gender, or in which a rethinking of nationhood has taken over from a preoccupation with questions of subjectivity. In one sense, cultural studies exists only to the extent that we can identify certain collective shifts of interest or movements of theoretical development across a broad intellectual terrain. Arguably, then, cultural studies may not be defined in substantive terms, but functions as the name given to a relatively unitary enterprise of theoretical revision, in which ideas are scrutinized and debated while their usefulness to ongoing and long-term disciplinary and political projects is determined. The advantage of ongoing theoretical revision over time is that, like most enterprises which produce temporary orthodoxies, it can forge a sense of collective purpose among those participant in it. The well-intentioned claim that work within cultural studies responds directly to contextual political imperatives, and that fashions and orthodoxies constitute distractions from these, misses the extent to which the emergence and gravitational pull of points of reference serve to perpetuate exchange between otherwise disparate projects. The danger, of course, is that the regular displacement of one set of theoretical questions by another may be taken as evidence that political and quotidian realities are themselves necessarily changing.

In English Canada (as in Great Britain) the emergence of a cultural studies has been marked by a more persistent enterprise of dialogue between the humanities and social sciences. 'Culture' has continued to be a question of sociological importance within Canada, at the centre of ongoing political tensions and disputes over regional and linguistic diversity, so that attempts to demarcate those academic boundaries within which it will be studied have not usually succeeded. While historical borders between domains of intellectual practice in Canada have thus been less rigid than in many other contexts, it would be misleading to claim that they have been dissolved or transcended. One effect of the circulation of 'cultural studies' (as, simultaneously, a term, a project and a set of theoretical legacies) has been the institution of an almost permanent unease with prevailing institutional definitions of intellectual work. At one level, this unease contains an implicit teleology positing that moment when these definitions will disappear. At the same time, however, one of its concrete effects has been a preoccupation with the relative influence of particular centres and currents of intellectual activity. Cultural studies is characterized (and its development driven) by the contradiction between its self-conception as the institutor of permanent dialogue and its status as a field marked by shifting agendas. This contradiction has given rise to a significant paradox within the politics of intellectual communities. While, on the one hand, cultural studies has created a space for transdisciplinary dialogue – a dialogue institutionalized within interdisciplinary programs, cross-disciplinary research groups and academic conferences – this space has also become the vantage point from which the relative value of different traditions and sites of cultural analysis may be newly observed and measured. In particular, it has magnified long-standing tensions between those who call regularly for work

91

which is 'grounded' in political or economic realities and others for whom the style appropriate to cultural analysis is to be an interpretive or broadly speculative one.

In this respect, debates over the theoretical and political substance of cultural studies often elide the function of the term itself within academic and intellectual culture. 'Cultural studies', in the English Canadian context, has come to designate a space to be occupied and claimed as much as it has named a substantive theoretical heritage to be perpetuated and adapted. The simple existence of the term, it might be argued, has called forth this space as the stake and pretext underlying new forms of interaction between intellectual domains. Increasingly, the only agreement concerning cultural studies in English Canada resides in the implicit assumption that it will serve to circumscribe a certain unifying impulse in cultural research, but the nature and purpose of this unification elicit ongoing disagreement, as does the question of who will dominate it. Thus, for certain currents within English Canadian academic culture, 'cultural studies' designates the pulling together and scrutinizing of a variety of dispersed writings on Canadian culture, many of which predate or have been untouched by the legacy of British cultural studies. In this sense, the term has encouraged – and been affixed to – the retrospective construction of a tradition which might sustain and renew long-standing debates over the character of English Canadian culture. For others, cultural studies represents participation in the ongoing, multinational project of theoretical revision and debate discussed above, in which political priorities and theoretical agendas constantly succeed and displace each other. The unity of cultural studies, defined in this way, has less to do with the persistence of shared concerns than with collective commitment to an unfolding dialogue whose points of reference, orthodoxies and pertinence to the Canadian situation are constantly changing.

Tensions over these very different conceptions of 'cultural studies' manifest themselves regularly in familiar, even gossipy disagreements over the long-term value or momentary trendiness of particular positions. In this respect, analogies between cultural studies and punk music (which arrived in Canada at approximately the same time) are not entirely frivolous and occasionally invoked. The communities which took shape around each in Canada have been marked by contradictions between an avowed, even platitudinous, commitment to the local and a cosmopolitan investment in criteria of authentication and expertise elaborated elsewhere. Extending this analogy, one might note the prevalence in both communities of recurrent anxieties over fashionability, institutionalization and celebrity. These concerns are obviously common within subcultures self-defined as those of opposition or resistance. They are magnified, nevertheless, in the Canadian case, by the long-standing suspicion that status or currency are ultimately validated within centres of power and legitimation located somewhere else.

This is a well-known quality of Canadian intellectual life, concisely expressed in Michael Dorland's account of the prominence of *ressentiment* as a political impulse (Dorland 1988). In the debate over intellectual cosmopolitanism, however, lines of political demarcation are not easily drawn between those whose context of intervention is locally circumscribed and others whose work circulates elsewhere. Progressive work within Canadian cultural studies has long held as one of its imperatives the deployment elsewhere of the Canadian example as one with wider applicability, particularly within debates such as those over cultural globalization or postmodernity. The project of a 'Canadianized' cultural studies, therefore, has not confined itself to the adaptation and domestication of theoretical agendas emergent elsewhere. It has often promised, as well, the insinuation of Canadian preoccupations and theoretical insights into the larger agenda of cultural studies internationally.

What follows is one personal account of the institutional situation and development of cultural studies within English Canada. This account draws on my own intellectual and professional trajectory, and is inevitably distorted by the institutional contexts and generational solidarities which have shaped my experience and understanding of cultural studies. It privileges, as well, the place of communications studies as a discipline within this development, and there are no doubt alternative points of departure from which this history could be written. I would argue, nevertheless, that the elusive character of cultural studies within English Canadian intellectual culture is best grasped, at least initially, in the unfolding and intersection of such individual trajectories.

THE COMMUNICATIONS CONTEXT

In the fall of 1978, I arrived in Montreal to begin a Master's degree in McGill University's Graduate Program in Communications. My Bachelor's degree had been in film studies, but the absence of postgraduate film studies programs in Canada meant I could not continue within that discipline without going to the US or Great Britain. I chose, for financial and personal reasons, to remain in Canada, reassured by those familiar with McGill's program that I could 'do film' and virtually anything else I wished within its boundaries. (I stayed on, in 1980, to do a PhD.) The Graduate Program in Communications had grown out of McGill's English department; personal ties and intellectual sympathies linked it, in its early years, to the figure of Marshall McLuhan. The project of a McLuhanist communications studies encouraged approaches to the study of media which were speculative, humanistic and explicitly rooted within English Canadian intellectual traditions. Prominent among these were an interest in the historical role of communications technologies in processes of nation-building (which drew on the work of the historian Harold Innis) and a concern (part of the legacy of John Grierson and the National Film Board) with the role of documentary media forms in the construction of a national imaginary. However marginal these influences might become in subsequent years, they could be invoked thereafter to support claims that communications studies in Canada need not be tied inevitably to models enshrined elsewhere.

These interests would persist within communications studies in Canada, but the symptomatic development over the next five years, in my view, was the consolidation of two very different poles of attraction to graduate students within the discipline. One of these poles was that of media policy studies, the chronicling of economic dependence and governmental complicity in the development of the Canadian broadcasting and cultural industries. By this historical point, the Canadian Broadcasting Act of 1968 (with its institution of Canadian content quotas for radio and television) and governmental support of the film industry had been in place for a decade or so. Their effects, and the historical conditions which had led up to them, were scrutinized in a number of theses and publications. In a very different trajectory, other graduate students (myself among them) were drawn further into the project of monitoring and becoming conversant with critical and cultural theory, refining our own positions (and policing those of others) in the debates over western marxism and theories of subjectivity. In the context of McGill, both directions led away from the English department, and from the combination of humanistic and nationalist impulses which had been present at the program's founding.

Communications programs in Canada, as elsewhere, are commonly marked by divisions between those students or faculty with interests rooted in the humanities and others educated within the social sciences. While the background and student recruitment practices of the McGill Program in the early 1980s appeared to favour the humanities, the national growth of the discipline as a whole coincided with the rise to prominence of media-related questions within public policy, and with a widespread concern with the effects upon Canada of emergent new communications technologies. I remember this period in part for the abundance of contract research projects employing students, and for the sincerity with which many of us believed that unfolding theoretical developments (such as the refinement of the encoding/decoding model for audience research) might prove useful within these projects.

It was often within these collective enterprises that divisions rooted in the disparity of academic backgrounds were most obvious. The significant differences here were not simply those, long standing within the discipline, between qualitative and quantitative methodologies, or textual and sociological forms of analysis. They manifest themselves more fundamentally in what might be regarded as differences of intellectual taste or disposition. In the contexts in which I worked, the most typical of these emerged between those whose approaches were marked by a privileging of specificity or complexity (of textual structures or practices of reading) and others whose work required the finality of political or sociological characterization. These differences were often homologous to those between the anglophone and francophone scholarly communities, in the context of a city with two prominent communications programs in each language. While the graduate student culture of anglophone departments was often marked by personal, geographical displacement and an implicitly bohemian conception of intellectual work, that of the francophone institutions offered a more readily available connection to state and media institutions and to collaborative projects which sought to study or transform them. In this respect, the peculiar role of 'French Theory' within Canadian intellectual life (and in highlighting the divisions just mentioned) deserves comment. With their stronger ties to the humanities, anglophone communications programs within Quebec and English Canada included large numbers of people participant in the long winding down of French marxist, psychoanalytic and semiological perspectives which dominated Anglo-American critical theory through the 1970s and 1980s. For many francophones involved in communications studies, this seemed little more than an anachronistic attachment to paradigms, works and conceptions of intellectual politics which they had studied and left behind in their undergraduate years. It stood, as well, as evidence of an unfamiliarity with more recent developments within French theory (such as the emergent sociologies of cultural production or postmodern culture), whose gravitational centre was closer to the social sciences, and whose presence within Anglo-American cultural studies had not yet been felt.

The role of communications as a discipline in nurturing the growth of cultural studies in the United States has been noted elsewhere (Nelson, Treichler and Grossberg 1992: 16). At the beginning of the 1980s the field seemed, to many of us at McGill and elsewhere, the most appropriate context for an articulation of British cultural studies with the legacies of the Chicago School of Sociology and the McLuhan–Innis tradition of Canadian research. Informal links between Canadian departments and others within the United States (most notably, that at the University of Illinois – Champaign–Urbana) took shape around such an enterprise, and the contemporary work of James Carey was an important and shared point of reference. If this project stalled or was postponed, it was in large measure because ongoing developments within critical and cultural theory pulled many individuals in other directions. Lines of fracture appeared between those for whom the theoretical unity of communications studies was to grow from an ongoing refinement of the marxist or culture-and-nation traditions (in particular, those of Williams and Innis), and others for whom that same unity required participation in a larger, international enterprise of theoretical movement which threatened (rightly or wrongly) to leave those traditions behind. Feminist theory, in particular, circulated within and between intellectual communities whose solidarities and frameworks of reference exceeded the national and the disciplinary. The increased velocity of change within Anglo-American cultural theory – itself rooted in the expansion of an infrastructure of conferences, academic units, books and journals – produced cleavages within departments and interpersonal networks based in part on differences in levels of investment and involvement in this change. My own reading of developments in the early-to-mid 1980s suggests that 'cultural studies', during this period, came to function less and less as a project for the redefinition of communications studies as a discipline. Increasingly, it designated a subculture which was highly visible within the discipline but involved in a variety of ways with communities outside it.

In Canada, where cultural studies established its initial presence largely within communications studies, it did so in a disciplinary space which had no 'logic' to speak of. While the McLuhanist legacy implicitly authorized a non-positivist approach to communications-related research within Canada, the close links between regulatory or media institutions and the academy have encouraged (and often underwritten) an ongoing tradition of what Todd Gitlin has designated as 'administrative' research (Gitlin 1978). Inasmuch as each of these conceptions of the discipline has been able to claim for itself a nationalist and progressive purpose, lines of political demarcation between them are not easily drawn. (The distinction between 'administrative' and 'critical' work, elaborated within the United States, has proved much less appropriate in characterizing Canadian research.) The failure of either tradition to establish absolute hegemony within processes of disciplinary formation and consolidation allowed cultural studies to enter the mix with relative ease. The subsequent development of cultural studies within Canada, nevertheless, was shaped by the growing importance of an intellectual space whose disciplinary and institutional boundaries were less concretely defined.

EVOLVING SPACES

Over the course of the 1980s, the outlines of a broader Canadian cultural studies 'scene' – which included currents within communications studies, but encompassed a variety of other intellectual communities – would become apparent. To a degree determined in no small way by the academic hiring crisis of the late 1970s and early 1980s, conferences had assumed a central role in the dissemination of new intellectual work, and in the forging of interpersonal networks between graduate students.[3] Most Canadian academic associations meet concurrently, in a nod to economies of scale, at an annual event known as the Learned Societies Conference. (Its title usually offers an irresistible target to editorial cartoonists in the host cities.) By 1983, panels on 'cultural studies', sometimes offered jointly by the communications and sociology/anthropology associations, were regular events at these conferences. These panels attracted a wide range of constituencies: faculty from the only cultural studies program in Canada (the undergraduate unit at Trent University in Peterborough, Ontario), sociologists associated with the traditions of continental critical theory, and, influentially, those working within feminist theory and women's studies. Links between graduate students, which would later be formalized within publishing projects or collegial collaborations, were initiated at these events, and transdisciplinary communities of interest (such as that around popular music) often took shape.

With the rise to prominence of postmodernist currents within cultural studies, around the middle of the decade, these cross-disciplinary events were themselves displaced by one-day mini-conferences on cultural theory, sponsored by the *Canadian Journal of Social and Political Theory* and organized by Arthur and Marilouise Kroker. These occasions, and the discourses which circulated within them, would intensify ongoing debate over the appropriate stakes and styles of cultural analysis within Canada. At one level, differences in the response to postmodernist theory within Canada perpetuated tensions which had surrounded cultural theory generally, though these were frequently magnified within the observable giddiness and perceived urgency of the moment. For a number of constituencies, the rhetorical forms of postmodernist writing exemplified and confirmed the cosmopolitanism and detachment from a locally or nationally constituted politics with which the cultural studies project had long been tainted. Briefly, these tensions organized themselves around a Montreal–Toronto rivalry, wherein those affiliated with the Toronto-based Ontario Institute for Studies in Education claimed for their work a more highly interventionist purpose seen to be lacking within that of the *Canadian Journal of Political and Social Theory* and those within its orbit. Within communications studies, as well, one could perceive moves towards disciplinary retrenchment, as many for whom cultural studies had meant a revitalized sociology of popular culture or developmental phase within marxist media theory balked at its new association with questions derived from the visual arts or philosophy. In an important sense, however, this moment was marked as well by the intermittent sense that the substance and style of postmodern theories – broadly speculative and diagnostic as they often were – might authorize a new realignment of Canadian cultural studies with an indigenous tradition (that of McLuhan, Innis and the philosopher George Grant) which had earlier articulated similar concerns. From quite distinct points of departure, those works constituting this tradition had investigated the relationships between technological change and culturally specific forms of subjectivity, and in the work of Kroker, for example, the attempt to give these works a distinctly postmodernist turn is evident (Kroker 1986). As a result, the lines of demarcation which emerged in response to postmodernist theory in Canada were not entirely coterminous with those produced earlier by post-structuralism and related developments in theory. Currents within the study of Canadian literature or the visual arts, and others involved within the institutional space of Canadian studies, frequently found within the terms of postmodernist writing the bases for a new or reformulated account of Canadian distinctiveness (e.g. Hutcheon 1988).

More so than in the United States, many Canadian universities accommodating interdisciplinary work in the humanities are located in large centres of political and economic power, such as Montreal, Toronto, Vancouver and Edmonton. One effect of this, generally unacknowledged, has been the geographical proximity of academic programs offering an interdisciplinary grounding in cultural theory to the informally organized artistic scenes which are a feature of these cities.[4] This proximity has shaped the political economy and theoretical preoccupations of cultural studies in important ways, which I can enumerate only briefly here.

The growing centrality of cultural theory within artistic and intellectual communities has made passage through an academic program in which that theory is disseminated common within the personal trajectories of those involved in such communities. Large numbers of students typically emerge from undergraduate programs in literature, art history or film studies – or from local artistic scenes – with a keen interest in broadening and pursuing newly acquired theoretical interests. Inasmuch as graduate departments within the relevant specialized disciplines in Canada are often non-existent or unsympathetic to theoretical work, programs in communications studies – and, in particular, those at McGill and Concordia Universities in Montreal – have emerged as major poles of attraction. Pressures upon such programs to admit students from a diversity of disciplinary backgrounds, and to meet their demands for a curriculum which completes or extends their grounding in the broad range of contemporary cultural theories, are increasingly felt. In many cases, these pressures conflict with the ongoing research agendas or pedagogical imperatives of the faculty members most likely to encounter them.

The advantage, of course, is that pressures from these constituencies work against impulses towards disciplinary retrenchment. In this respect, the significant current shifts within cultural studies in Canada are not exclusively those towards an accommodation with the traditions and preoccupations of cultural policy analysis. The growing weight and allure of cultural theory within artistic practices, and in the scenes which surround them, has produced another gravitational pole which has proved equally compelling. As publishing, and the organizing of public talks or symposia have become central activities within these scenes, the forms of entrepreneurship and collaboration which they involve have altered the ways in which cultural studies work in Canada is supported. The new prominence of cultural theory within artistic scenes has produced a host of problems for these scenes which cannot be discussed here,[5] but, from the perspective of an academic, it has noticeably and positively expanded the ways in which intellectual work is supported. It has, as well, worked to slow the institutional ossification of cultural studies within the Canadian university.

In claiming this, I am hopefully not evoking those fantasies of extra-institutional intervention of which I am normally highly suspicious. Nevertheless, it has become increasingly clear in recent years that cultural studies in Canada is sustained as much in the spaces between institutions as it is within those institutions themselves. This is not merely (if at all) the result of a wilful marginality, and the role of universities in the unifying and indirect subsidization of these spaces should not be underestimated. To a considerable extent, nevertheless, the recent liveliness of intellectual life in Canada has been nourished by traditions of public support for an infrastructure of publishing and exhibition ventures or curatorial and critical activities wherein the influence of cultural studies has been evident (traditions increasingly threatened within the current financial and political climate).

The influential magazines within English Canadian cultural studies – *Public, Parallelogram, CinéAction, Borderlines* and many others – have grown within the overlapping spaces of graduate student cultures, editorial collectives and the parallel gallery system, and have not, for the most part, been attached to university or commercial publishers. While the initial concerns of most of these publications took shape around specific artistic media or relatively coherent political projects, most have moved, in the course of their histories, to participation in a broader and more diverse intellectual dialogue. In this respect, and to return to a link evoked near the beginning of this essay, the Canadian scene has come more and more to resemble another which proved highly attractive to many of us during the 1980s: that of Australia. Distance and a high level of publishing activity may very often disguise fragile and marginalized conditions for intellectual work, as many who made the pilgrimage to Birmingham in the 1980s would discover. Nevertheless, the range of publications, sense of sustained dialogue and presence of shared concerns which seemed to many Canadians to characterize cultural studies in Australia has offered a more appealing and viable model than those of either Great Britain or the United States.

NOTES

1 Ongoing conversations with Martin Allor, Maged El Komos, Jody Berland, Paul Attallah and many others over the last decade have nourished my sense of the place and history of cultural studies in Canada. They are in no way responsible for its biases or errors.

2 This aspect of cultural studies is taken up in greater detail, and with

somewhat different conclusions, in Nelson, Treichler and Grossberg (1992), which I read only after this section of my essay was written.
3 I owe this reading of the role of conferences to David Galbraith.
4 Communications studies programs, to a considerable extent, sustain this interdisciplinary work in Montreal and Vancouver. In Toronto, the Social and Political Thought program at York University and Ontario Institute for Studies in Education have been important centres of activity within cultural studies.
5 These problems were the focus of the conference 'Art and Theory/ Theory as Art', organized by Jody Berland, David Tomas and myself, and held at the University of Ottawa from 29 November to 1 December 1991.

REFERENCES

Bennett, T. (1992) 'Putting policy into cultural studies', in L. Grossberg, C. Nelson and P. Treichler (eds) *Cultural Studies*, London: Routledge.

Clifford, J. and Marcus, G. E. (1986) *Writing Culture: The Poetics and Politics of Ethnography*, Berkeley: The University of California Press.

Dorland, M. (1988) 'A thoroughly hidden country: ressentiment, Canadian nationalism, Canadian culture', *Canadian Journal of Political and Social Theory* 12, 1–2: 130–64.

Gitlin, T. (1978) 'Media sociology: the dominant paradigm', *Theory and Society* 6: 205–53.

Hutcheon, L. (1988) *The Canadian Postmodern: A Study of Contemporary English-Canadian Fiction*, Toronto: Oxford University Press.

Kroker, A. (1986) *Technology and the Canadian Mind: Innis, McLuhan, Grant*, Montreal: New World Perspectives.

Nelson, C., Treichler, P. and Grossberg, L. (1992) 'Cultural studies: An introduction', in L. Grossberg, C. Nelson and P. Treichler (eds), *Cultural Studies*, London: Routledge.

Rooney, Ellen (1990) 'Discipline and vanish: feminism, the resistance to theory, and the politics of cultural studies', *Differences* 2, 5: 14–28.

Part II

POWER AND EMPOWERMENT

4

TRUE VOICES AND REAL PEOPLE

The 'problem' of the autobiographical in cultural studies

Elspeth Probyn

It is incontestable that autobiography is difficult. As Paul de Man put it, '. . . the theory of autobiography is plagued by a recurrent series of questions and approaches that are not simply false . . . but that are confining, in that they take for granted assumptions about autobiographical discourse that are in fact highly problematic' (de Man 1979: 919). And if the theory of autobiography is problematic, the use of the autobiographical, or what I will call a personal voice, within cultural theory highlights some crucial epistemological questions now facing the human sciences. As Lawrence Grossberg recently observed, the autobiographical voice is often understood as an individual's search for identity rather than a critical strategy in cultural interpretation.[1] However, I will argue here that the use of the autobiographical can be made to question implicitly the relation of self to experience, researcher to researched, and the production of knowledge itself. Therefore, I will reframe his reservations as a series of questions: does the autobiographical voice presuppose an unmediated subject? What conception of subjectivity is inscribed in autobiography? And, what is the nature of the truth produced through autobiography? As autobiography is 'discovered' by more and more theorists – from Paul Smith's critical turn (Smith 1988: 100) to the self-reflexive move within ethnography – it is increasingly important to articulate these questions, and ask about their political import.

Indeed, this discovery of autobiography should be more aptly described as a re-emergence. While my own hesitancy about autobiography stems in part from its overnight popularity amongst some male theorists, I also feel a sense of deja-vu. I mean have not we gone through this before, raised our consciousness as to the importance of everyday histories and lived the personal as political? The memory of being excluded on the grounds that the realm of the personal is not social scientific knowledge lingers. The very male voice that is now being rendered 'personal' served, in part, to exclude feminist work from critical discourse. While this is not to guard the personal jealously within the terrain of feminist thought, it is to remember important feminist articulations of the autobiographical voice. In the midst of all the critical acceptance and appropriation of self-reflexivity, the recognition of previous articulations requires that we question why this particular discursive formation, at this specific time, has gained favour. After all, not so very long ago de Man characterized autobiography as a 'disreputable and self-indulgent form' (de Man 1979: 919). Thus rather than taking autobiography's reappearance as a sign of 'progress' on the part of male theorists, I want to ask why now? Some thirty years ago, Richard Hoggart noted that 'almost all autobiographical writing today is strikingly attuned to readers in a particular literary-social-cultural mood'. No fan of autobiography, Hoggart went on to characterize the readers of the 1960s as 'particularly undiscriminating' (Hoggart 1963: 73). Now whether or not readers are once again 'undiscriminating' is a moot point, but an investigation of the conditions that allow for the re-emergence of autobiographical writing may tell us something about the theoretical and political mood we live in.

At first glance, the popularity of the autobiographical in cultural theory is surprising. Its claims to truth, its clear ontological assumptions, appear overly sincere and straightforward for our cynical and postmodern times. Against the sophistication of Lacanian thought, the complexity of post-structuralism, the rigour of feminist-marxist critiques, and the Nietzschean gloom of some postmodern thought, an autobiographical voice seems so positive, so straightforward in its appeals.

While autobiography raises a myriad of interesting issues,[2] I will construct a problematic of the autobiographical voice in cultural theory around the following key words: ontology, epistemology, and gender. The concept of the personal voice that I propose is in part theoretically bounded by: feminist rearticulations of the literary canon and the influence of Elaine Showalter's work on 'gynocritique'; critiques of the relation of the subject to experience as exemplified in Paul Smith's recent reworking of post-structuralism; and the articulation of the autobiographical voice within theory as practised by some feminists influenced by cultural studies. As a very rough frame, I see Showalter's work as mainly ontological in its approach and aims, Smith's as epistemological, and the work of Valerie Walkerdine and Carolyn Steedman, among others, as moments of ontological and epistemological integration. Simply put, the autobiographical can be seen to operate on (at least) three intercalated levels: as a mode of writing and reading; as a way of speaking; and as a theoretical practice.

FOUND VOICES

Jacqueline Rose recently pointed out that 'Literature served as a type of reference point for feminism, as if it were at least partly through literature that feminism could recognise and theorise itself' (Rose 1987: 10). She further argues that 'precisely because of that historically attested link between writing and the domain of the personal, feminism risks at that same moment the aestheticisation and the liberalisation of its own politics' (p. 10). Rose's discussion of the institutionalization of feminist literary criticism is important; however, at this point I want to look at her leading premise: the construction of an 'Anglo-American account of literary selfhood' (p. 12). As Rose herself points out, it is quite common in some circles to dismiss early American (let us forget this grossly generalizing Anglo-American bit) feminist criticism as unsophisticated archival work. Indeed, the very appellation, 'Images of Women', lends itself to accusations of naivety – that representations of women were discrete entities to be found and reproduced as banners. Rose's argument, however, raises the historical link between feminist politics and literary criticism through the figure of the 'literary selfhood'. This historical articulation cannot (or should not) be overlooked because it bears witness to the grounded beginnings of feminist literary criticism. In Elaine Showalter's words: 'The interest in women's writing . . . that is crucial to gynocritics preceded theoretical formulations and came initially from the feminist critic's own experience and from her identification with the anxieties and conflicts women writers faced in patriarchal culture' (Showalter 1987: 39).

In her subjective history of feminist criticism Showalter

distinguishes between gynocriticism and gynesis, and identifies the former as 'historical in orientation; it looks at women's writing as it actually occurred and tries to define its specific characteristics of language, genre, and literary influence, within a cultural network that includes variables of race, class, and nationality' (p. 37). Gynesis, coined by Alice Jardine, 'seeks instead to understand the space granted to the feminine in the symbolic contract' (p. 37). The latter has, of course, gained great cachet from its connection with 'French feminism' and is taken as the more theoretically elegant of the two. However, for my purposes, gynocriticism is the more interesting. And in Showalter's words 'the theoretical complexity of gynocritical analyses . . . were never as innocent or unselfconscious as later arrivals have complained' (p. 40). While her point could be slightly qualified (some were/are quite innocent, but what is wrong with a bit of innocence?) Showalter points us to a crucial moment in the movement of feminist literary criticism. Writing in an autobiographical voice, Showalter remembers '. . . a generation of women who liked books . . . whose avid, devoted, socially-reinforced identifications with fictional heroines were coming into conflict with the sexist realities they encountered every day' (p. 35).

Now this quote is not quite as innocent as it seems. From Showalter's own account, we are dealing here with 'faculty wives, highly educated products of the academic expansion of the 1960s' (p. 35); we are in the realm of the American white middle class. Seen as the dupes of a system that silenced others in more spectacular ways, Showalter's bookworms do not command much sympathy. Middle-class women's reading habits, after all, are not highly valorized; the resistance is harder to find. However, Showalter makes us aware of the isolation of those readers, of what Catherine Stimpson calls 'the lack of a history that might have bonded women to each other' (Stimpson 1987: 1). Thus what Showalter raises is the paradoxical roots of American liberal feminist criticism: through literature individual women came to recognize the sexist structure of their collective everyday lives. This move from an isolated individual experience to a wider theoretical account seems to be especially endemic to the white middle-classness of liberal feminism (think of Betty Friedan's account of the suburban 'problem that had no name' [1963]). As Barbara Christian writes of her Afro-Caribbean background, '. . . the women I grew up around, continuously speculated about the nature of life through pithy language that unmasked the power relations of their world' (Christian 1988: 68). For Christian, the patriarchal structure of her world was revealed through the words and actions of other women around her. While I do not want to romanticize and pull this example out of shape, it does contrast sharply with the image of women looking up from their books in dismay at the 'real' world.[3] Moreover, this difference in socio-historical speaking is crucial to a very different construction of selfhood. As Judith Fetterley has said of (white) women reading American (mainstream and male) fiction:

> In such fictions the female reader is co-opted into participation in an experience from which she is explicitly excluded; she is asked to identify with a selfhood that defines itself in opposition to her; she is required to identify against herself.
>
> (cited in Suleiman 1986: 125)

Thus for Fetterley, the female reader necessarily is aware of the contradiction between representation and self, to the point that she reads 'against herself'. This notion of inhabiting an impossible position as a female reader is, of course, congruent with the psychoanalytic concept of masquerade.[4] Within gynocriticism, however, the textual representations are seen to articulate more fluidly with the reader's experience. As Showalter says, gynocritics focus on 'the specificity of women's writing' as opposed to 'the French exploration of the textual representations of sexual difference' (Showalter 1987: 37). It would be wrong to conclude from this dichotomy that there is no distinction between representation and self within gynocriticism. What is clear, however, is that gynocritique constructs a particular ontology between the written self and the reading, experiencing self.

The particular ontology that gynocritics supposes can be more clearly seen if contrasted with the ontological underpinnings revealed in Christian's observation. For Christian, the world and one's position in it is revealed through talking and listening to one's friends, mothers, and neighbours. Their experience and being tells of your own. On the other hand, when we consider Showalter's depiction of the early stirring of gynocritics, we see that a sense of being is constructed in relation to textual

109

representations (or, in other words, the book's hero or heroine). Thus a literary selfhood is quite literally created that stands apart from the actual reader. While I am unconcerned here with which (if any) is more 'authentic', the differences are important when considering the place of autobiographical voices. Keeping in mind the particular relationship and conflation that gynocritique establishes between the reader, her sense of self, and literary representation, we can understand the generalizing tones of much current writing on autobiography. In good liberal parlance, we can hear where they are coming from. For instance, Domna Stanton argues that 'creating the subject, an autograph gave the female "I" substance through the inscription of an interior and anterior' (Stanton 1984: 15). The articulation of self and representation here is quite explicit. Furthermore, the idea that the self becomes more substantial as it is tied into the literary autograph, becomes the basis, within this discourse, for auto-biography's political positivity. The reading self directly corresponds with the representation, creating an ontological literary self. In a more forceful way, Sidonie Smith simply states that, '. . . women have taken their own voices as the source of autobiographical truth' (Smith 1987: 175).

And indeed, why should not women hold their own voices as true? Given the ways in which we have been represented and written off, not to mention siderailed into the oblivion of history, whose story can we trust if not our own? But, of course, the nagging question of whose story, along whose lines, raises its head. This question, unfortunately, is not mere academic quibbling, but one which covers over a lot of pain and violence. When Elizabeth Fox-Genovese writes of the autobiographies of Afro-American women, she states that '. . . each word invites a theoretical and practical battle' (Fox-Genovese 1987: 161). In her article, the battle is waged primarily against the post-structuralist edit of the 'author's death': 'To categorize autobiographies according to the race and gender of those who write them is to acknowledge some relation, however problematical, between the text and its author and, more, between the text and its author's experience' (p. 161). While Fox-Genovese's wrath against the dismissal, if not exclusion, of autobiographies is justified, it is unfortunate that Foucault's and Barthes' arguments against the epistemic power of the (male) creator should once again serve as straw men. It is more important that the difference (both in enunciation and reception) of the marginal autobiographical voice be raised and investigated. Indeed, Fox-Genovese later does question the suitability, and the ideological imprint, of certain interpretative strategies: '. . . the reading of black women's autobiography forcefully exposes the extent to which the tools of criticism are shaped by the politics that guide them' (p. 163). While of course post-structuralism has a lot to answer for in the ways in which 'it' or some post-structuralists write off experience altogether, liberal humanism has never exactly aided women in speaking their specificity. Thus, it is strange that Fox-Genovese seems to opt for the latter: 'These days, taking the autobiographical text on its merits is further taken to expose as "romanticism" and "humanism" any concern with the "self" as, in some way, prior to the text' (p. 163). However, when she describes the difficulty of autobiography, she precisely does it in ways that would undermine humanist notions of the transparency of 'writing the self':

> To write the account of one's self is to inscribe it in a culture that for each one of us is only partially our own. For black women autobiographers, the gap between the self and language in which it is inscribed looms especially large and remains fraught with struggle.
>
> (Fox-Genovese 1987: 177)

While the project of gynocritique is responsible for raising the profile of women writers, one of the consequences of its literary self is that the interaction between text and reader is given an ontological weight. The distinctions between the reader's experience of the text, the reader's own various subjectivities, and the textual representation of others' experiences implode. The reading experience is thus constructed as a 'special order of reality' which James Olney has attributed to autobiography (Olney 1980: 237). Gynocritique thus supposes an ontological moment when the reader's self and the represented subject are transubstantiated into one being. The gynocritical point is thus akin to what Olney calls 'ta onta': 'all things existing in a concrete, dense moment of time that is the phenomenological present' (p. 238). Now, while there is nothing particularly wrong with this (there is nothing better than 'being lost in a good read'), it does have political implications. If we all are equally lost in a literary self, what happens to the experiences of others, to difference, when this

111

ontological moment takes over? Responding that we are all women anyway is hardly adequate. In fact it may be part of the problem, as Fox-Genovese says of black women autobiographers, 'in complex ways, their self-perceptions retain a characteristic-ally uneasy relation to the wrappings of gender' (Fox-Genovese 1987: 177). While the project of gynocritique remains inestimable in its search for 'lost' voices, we should be careful that the quest to identify (with) them does not obviate a demand for respecting difference. The influence of gynocritique in the recent move to the autobiographical must be acknowledged, along with some of its liabilities. As Showalter writes, it certainly was a definitive moment when 'the difference or specificity of women's writing was conceptualized as the focus of feminist criticism' (Showalter 1987: 39). This movement also inaugurated a new mode of writing and reading. In thinking about the personal voice as an elaboration of that mode, we should keep in mind the commit-ment to women's writing that gynocritique represents while we challenge the effects of its ontological pull.

'I AM NOT WHAT I WAS'

The present tense of the verb 'to be' refers only to the present; but nevertheless, with the first person singular in front of it, it absorbs the past which is inseparable from the pronoun. 'I am' includes all that has made me so. It is more than a statement of immediate fact: it is already an explana-tion, a justification, a demand – it is already autobiograph-ical.

(Berger 1980: 46–7)

In his typically lyrical way, John Berger here personalizes some of the difficulties that immediately confront the potential meet-ing of post-structuralism and the autobiographical. Another way of putting Berger's observation might be that, 'wherever the "I" speaks, a knowledge is spoken; wherever a knowledge speaks, an "I" is spoken' (Smith 1988: 100). However, where Berger cele-brates his perfectly articulated subjectivities, Paul Smith finds the autobiographical 'I' inevitable and rocky. Smith's project is, of course, of a different order from Berger's; he wants to confront 'the "tactical reasons" for wanting to break open "the enunciatory abyss", and for underscoring the mediating gap between the "knowledgeable subject" and the "I" that speaks . . . in the discourses of the human sciences' (p. 100). Smith identifies three 'I's. Calling on de Man's deconstructionist and post-structuralist project, he critiques a binary organization of the subject: 'the subject of the enunciation' and 'the subject of the enounced'. As Smith explains, ' "I" does not talk about or correspond to "I": rather "I" talks about "me" ' (p. 105). Smith sees de Man's position as fundamentally apolitical (or 'morally and politically blind'): 'For de Man, there is "subject" and there is object, and never the twain shall meet, since the "subject of enunciation" can never stand in the place of the other except by the illusion of the mirror' (p. 100). Smith's third 'I', however, 'is the cerned and complete individual which will be called upon to hold in place the circuit of guarantees obtaining between "subject" and knowledge' (p. 100). This third 'I' is therefore the ideological and legal subject that Julien Henriques *et al.* (1984) critique so thoroughly. This unitary subject is constructed by the symbolic and interpellated ways in which we are positioned in everyday life by state apparatuses. What Smith adds to this work is the idea that the ideological 'I' is also epistemological; it operates the placement of the subject in relation to knowledge, it 'guarantees' certain forms of knowledge. Smith uses 'traditional' forms of autobiography as an illustration of this mechanism: 'autobiography itself cannot be underestimated as a privileged form of ideological text wherein the demand that we should consist as coherent and recognizable "subjects" in relation to a particular knowledge appears to be rationalized' (p. 105–6).

Another, and more understandable way of talking about this manoeuvre would be Stuart Hall's theory of articulation and the production of 'common sense'. It would, indeed, be commonsensical to say that the writer of an autobiography knows what he or she is talking about. Though most people are probably a bit sceptical of Lee Iaccoca or Donald Regan's motives in writing their autobiographies, the information contained within them may be taken as more or less true. Of course, *Iaccoca* is ideological on several levels. In Smith's sense, out of the 'I' writing 'me' emerges the ideological and unitary subject of the autobiography.

Smith distinguishes between this type of traditional autobiography and the writings of Barthes (principally *Roland Barthes par lui-meme* and *La Chambre claire*). For Smith, it is with Barthes that the political possibilities of autobiography appear. Barthes, then, jostles 'the cohesion and the propriety of that moral construct', the third 'I' (Smith 1988: 106). Taking from the epistemological break inaugurated by photography, Barthes describes the effects of the shift from the specularity of the mirror to the fictionality of the photograph: 'my "me" . . . won't coincide with my image' (p. 106). Thus we can see 'the tensions between the ideological demand that we be one "cerned" subject and the actual experience of a subjective history which consists in a mobility, an unfixed repertoire of many subject-positions' (pp. 106–7). The model of autobiography that this suggests cannot proffer a simple story of 'I', and it may counter the ideological stitching together of the subject:

> There is no referent to be 'historicized' (if I may refloat an archaic verb which means to relate as history, to narrate), but there is a continual process of 'historicization', the ever renewable representation of instances of subjectivity and situation across time.
>
> (Smith 1988: 111)

The political import of this form of 'récit' lies in its refusal to present, in Smith's words, a 'cerned' or bounded subject. In Barthes' celebration of jostled subjectivities we find a refusal to see the subject as unitary and fixed. This is, of course, coupled with the impossibility of full voluntarism. The epistemological value of this position lies in the recognition of how subjects are placed in relation to forms of knowledge; notably, of who they 'really' are. Against the ontology of gynocritique, there can be no presumption of seizing representations as evidence of one's being. Gynocritique's liability, discussed previously, is that it constructs a model of reading that works against the political possibilities of autobiography. That is, in privileging the textual mediation between reader and represented experience, difference disappears. What we can take from Smith's critique and reworking of post-structuralism is that the text is only a semblance of the writer's life, and that the reader is not a unitary soul. In Augustine's words, 'I'm not what I was' (cited in Smith 1988: 105). She, as the writer, is a jostled amalgam of various subjectivities. The goal, then, of this mode is an autobiographical voice that 'imposes a state of loss, discomfits . . . unsettles the reader's historical, cultural, psychological certainties, the

114

consistency of tastes, values, memories, and throws the relationship to language into crisis' (Barthes, cited in Smith 1988: 113). It follows that the autobiographical voice can be used to upset stable notions of the subject. That voice can tell not only of the past but of the difficulties that fragment and unsettle the narrative flow. And against Smith's rather generalized account of the problems inherent in speaking, the autobiographical voice may yield specific instances of struggle against the ideological centring of the subject.

'ENOUGH ABOUT YOU, LET'S TALK ABOUT ME'[5]

If gynocritique privileges an ontological moment in reading autobiographies, and Smith, taking from Barthes, focuses on the epistemological construction the self, some British feminist work attempts to articulate the two. Thus the agenda becomes one of how to textualize one's own experience through writing while maintaining the notion of a mediated subject. In other words, how do you speak the autobiographic without rendering it transparent and unproblematic? Can the autobiographical voice be used as a theoretical strategy, integrating both ontology and epistemology without privileging either? The type of work exemplified in the writings of Carolyn Steedman and Valerie Walkerdine, and others, is quite definitely British in nature, articulating as it does the traditions of marxism, psychoanalysis, British feminism and British cultural studies. While it would be ridiculous to suppose that these theories are unique to Britain, this theoretical mixture produces a particular personal voice. It would also be reductive to intimate that recent autobiographical writings share a unified theoretical agenda; it would, however, be safe to say that a consciousness of class and gender differentiates British work from gynocritique or Barthesian analyses. Class, therefore, problematizes gynocritique's undifferentiated notion of the ontological selfhood – one cannot freely read outside a consciousness of one's class position. The emphasis on gender, on the other hand, rearticulates as it goes beyond Smith's epistemological construct of the subject: through various social technologies of gender, the subject becomes 'me' in all of my 'I's. An insistence on the material nature of experience also ensures an historical specificity. The wish to come to grips with a particular moment of history is clear in Liz Heron's edited book, *Truth, Dare or Promise*: 'the end of the Second

World War marked the start of a new era, of a new period whose initial character shaped the way we live now' (Heron 1985: 1).[6] Heron's project here is to understand 'the fifties', not only because she and other noted feminists were born into them but also in order to map the birth and conflict of new social discourses. Thus a common thread of this collection is that: 'The women writing here were all born in Britain between 1943 and 1951 . . . We all have different stories to tell, stories that in their singularity and uneven reflections of that time, disturb the balanced generalities of social history' (p. 1). The introduction of the Welfare State after the war gave those girls different choices as it reified unspoken class lines. These stories, then, seek to differentiate the over-determination of class and gender, while they describe a rather fragmented episode of British life.

While the stories told here do indeed provide insights into that changing construction of British life, one wonders if this is indeed an articulated theoretical practice, or a sketch of social history. Of course, the distinction between social history and enunciative practice is a rather difficult one to define. However, we could say that social history is the documentation of the lived experiences of those who fall within the crevices of 'official' history: people's history as opposed to the stories of great men. Theoretical practice, then, is the overt political agenda behind this documentation; these voices are then used to problematize day-to-day relations: to render an historical present. At the same time, it has to be asked whether representations of the marginal, excluded, or silenced actually can lead to some form of empowerment. For instance, Gayatri Spivak maintains that 'the subaltern has no history and cannot speak . . . the subaltern as female is even more deeply in shadow' (Spivak 1988: 287). While I do not want to enter into a discussion of Spivak's important and complex project here, the stories in Heron's collection do provide us with snippets of unsanctioned history. The problem becomes what to do with them to make them more significant, not to universalize these childhood voices, but how to articulate them as a strategy. At the end of her own story Carolyn Steedman writes:

> I want a politics that will take all of this, all these secret and
> impossible stories, recognise what has been made on the
> margins, and then, recognising it, refuse to celebrate it; a

politics that will watching that past say: so what?; and abandon it to the dark.

(Steedman 1985: 126)

In her article 'Dreams from an ordinary childhood' Valerie Walkerdine also questions what to do with individual knowledge. Yet Walkerdine is more emphatic about the process of collecting these stories: 'It is as though those stories which are "nothing to write home about", in all their ordinary obviousness, were not themselves both constituted by, and constituted of, a history which has to be told' (Walkerdine 1985: 65). Here Walkerdine points to the ways in which ordinary lives are structured by discourses of which they are constitutive. The importance of this argument is that it raises history as made up of common lives and moments, and that it demands that another history be made up and told. Between Steedman's wish to capture her childhood only to then let it go and Walkerdine's insistence on the importance of this history, it would be difficult to identify one articulated politics, a unified feminist strategy. Furthermore, the recounting of one's growing up is not a panacea for all theoretical shortcomings. Indeed, it is normally only of interest to those near and dear, and the childhood memories of feminists do not guarantee their (political) interest. When Walkerdine states that 'there, caught in the threads of that ordinary life, is the basis for understanding what my subjectivity might be about' (p. 65), are we to cheer or yawn? In another article, Walkerdine (1986) attempts to integrate her own voice into an ethnographic and psychoanalytic analysis of a working-class family. While she clearly brings out the problematic power relations involved in the structure of the research situation, her wish to include herself, 'to examine my multiple positioning as both middle-class academic *and* working class child', operates on a different level. The dynamics of the relationship of researcher to researched, and the researcher's evident power in this situation, are obviously crucial. While one can see that Walkerdine's own experience of this situation would bring her to reflect on her positioning as both middle and working class, the two dynamics of her present and past are not immediately congruent. After all, she does represent authority and she is there, in the family living-room, watching *them*. It is also interesting that in several seminar situations, female students tend to react angrily to Walkerdine's story of her

117

childhood, and her imposed subjectivity as 'Tinkerbell'. While I mention this parenthetically, I think that this (at first, surprising) response may be due to the way in which her particular autobiographical voice re-centres the article around herself. The working-class family whom Walkerdine is nominally studying seems to recede. Nonetheless, Walkerdine ends the article with a key point: 'What is important is to understand the different conditions in which these pleasures – and their associated pains and hopes – are produced' (p. 197). While my reservations should not detract from what is an important analytic move, her article illustrates a potentially problematical aspect of autobiographical writing as a theoretical enunciative practice: is it possible for the autobiographical voice not to be self-centred, and does attention to one's self have to produce a hierarchy of selves?

These questions do not displace the importance within feminist theory of the work of Steedman, Walkerdine (along with Angela McRobbie [1984], Rosalind Coward [1985], and Meaghan Morris [1988]). They are not, of course, operating in a vacuum; the mode of theorizing from the ground has a solid history stretching from Raymond Williams, E. P. Thompson, and Stuart Hall to more recent ethnographic studies by Christine Griffin (1985) to Dick Hebdige's recent work (particularly, 'Some sons and their fathers' [1985]). What is striking about the feminist move to integrate an autobiographical voice with theoretical analysis is their balancing act between the self and politics, the specificity of their questioning of whether the personal is political. The tension here, as I suggested earlier, is between an ontological insistence on being and an epistemological analysis of how we come to know what we know (including who and what we are). Their work proposes, in different ways, that the conditions wherein the self or the personal come to be formulated must be paramount to any discussion of the present 'I am'. This obviously demands very specific histories and tales of the ways in which class, gender and race shoot through those histories. These are then not variable factors in various childhoods, but structuring discourses with evident and hidden effects. To do justice to the inequities of those discourses requires very talented and precise story-tellers. However, it is also here that things get sticky. As both Walkerdine and Steedman acknowledge, education was their ticket out of the local situations that they describe. Their story-telling techniques are evidently disingenuous and interwoven with acquired knowledge. They are, as Smith would tell us, products of being positioned in relation to knowledge with untold epistemological projects. Indeed, their relationship to their selves is a complex ideological one that can not be fully accounted for. Thus as we celebrate these voices, we have to remember that, in very real ways and for crude economic reasons, only some get to speak.

IN WORD AND DEED

When the Pankhursts were struggling with politicians who talked about women's franchise without doing anything, their motto was 'Deeds, not words'. What I have argued here is that the autobiographical or personal voice does not necessarily guarantee a feminist politics. On the whole though, it is a courageous voice; it is not particularly easy to set oneself out, to posit your beings on paper. Within academic discourses the autobiographical is still dismissed; in various subtle (and more blatant) ways it is written off for not being social scientific, as the domain of women's studies, or as just not serious. As I was writing my master's thesis on anorexia nervosa, I carefully omitted the fact that as a girl, I suffered from anorexia. Now, my being anorexic did not bear very heavily on my thesis except that my experience of being anorexic drew me to that subject. Nonetheless, I felt that if my advisors knew, it might somehow invalidate what I was doing, and 'drag it down to the personal'. And we all work with the personal, with texts and self-texts that interest us and compel our theoretical and effective attention. And these interests no more automatically ensure a politics than will the autobiographical voice. Simply put, the personal has to be worked upon and articulated with theoretical and political agendas.

This is also to say that the autobiographic does not belong to one theoretical camp. Looking at gynocritique we see the ways in which the ontology of women reading women writing is privileged within reading practices. In this way the autobiographical voice risks being taken as a transparent account of women's experience. If only read in this way, the very textual representation of a particular subjectivity is masked. Within Smith's account, on the other hand, the specificities of an autobiographical voice may get lost in an endless epistemological loop. It is important to remember the contributions of post-structuralism in building a more complex view of the subject, but also that the subject lives both in language *and* in day-to-day relations. Subjects do have individual lives and what they say of them intertwines with how they are discursively positioned as well as what they can do with them. Finally, a feminist cultural studies approach to the autobiographical reveals the voice as strategy. However, it is necessary to maintain a tension between the ontological pull inherent in writing one's being and the epistemological impulse to privilege the discourses that structure one's life. In conclusion then, the autobiographical can be seen as a way of writing, reading, and speaking. This is not to proclaim its politics as evident truths, but, if worked upon and worked over, these personal voices can be articulated as strategies, as ways of going on theorizing. And as such they (and we) need to be heard.

NOTES

1 The questions that I raise here result from a stimulating panel on ethnography (Re-appropriating Ethnography in Cultural Theory, International Communications Association conference, New Orleans, June 1988). I would like to thank the panellists, Gail Valaskakis and Janice Radway, and the respondents, Larry Grossberg and Ien Ang. I also thank Marty Allor for his comments and ideas on this draft.

2 My aim here is not to go into the intricacies of autobiography as a literary genre; rather I will only hope to raise some questions about what happens when we speak in a personal manner. For a more detailed and different argument about speaking our selves, see Probyn (forthcoming). For an interesting discussion of personal criticism in literary theory, see Nancy K. Miller (1991).

3 For detailed examinations by other black feminists about ways of reclaiming words and putting them to work in deconstructing racist patriarchal systems, see Wall (ed.) (1989).

4 While I cannot enter into all the intricacies of the concept of 'masquerade', it is important to note that in Joan Rivière's use of the term, the 'homosexual woman' masqueraded as feminine in order to avoid the retribution of male anger for having usurped the phallus. Also of interest is the fact that Rivière's case studies concerned women who spoke in public – lecturers in abstract intellectual matters (1929, reprinted 1986).

5 Marcus 1987: 77.

6 In a similar way, Michelene Wandor's (1990) collection of interviews, *Once a Feminist: Stories of a Generation*, also foregrounds the personal conditions of possibility that allowed for the re-emergence of

120

feminism in the 1970s and 1980s in Britain. Like Heron's collection it is a welcome change to have leading feminists portrayed as women with small and large individual conflicts and not, as in Showalter's generation, an amorphous up-rising.

REFERENCES

Berger, J. (1980) *About Looking*, New York: Pantheon Books.

Christian, B. (1988) 'The race for theory', *Feminist Studies* 14, 1, reprinted in Linda Kaufman (ed.) *Gender and Theory: Dialogues in Feminist Criticism* (1989) New York and Oxford: Basil Blackwell.

Coward, R. (1985) *Female Desires*, New York: Grove Press.

de Man, P. (1979) 'Autobiography as defacement', *Modern Language Notes* 94: 919–30.

Fox-Genovese, E. (1987) 'To write myself: the autobiographies of Afro-American women', in S. Benstock (ed.) *Feminist Issues in Literary Scholarship*, Bloomington and Indianapolis: Indiana University Press.

Frieden, B. (1963) *The Feminine Mystique*, New York: Dell Books.

Griffin, Christine (1985) *Typical Girls? Young Women from School to the Labour Market*, London: Routledge and Kegan Paul.

Hebdige, D. (1985) 'Some sons and their fathers', *Ten-8* 17: 30–9.

Henriques, J., Holloway, W., Urwin, C., Venn, C. and Walkerdine, V. (1984) *Changing the Subject: Psychology, Social Regulation and Subjectivity*, London: Virago.

Heron, L. (1985) 'Introduction', in L. Heron (ed.) *Truth, Dare or Promise: Girls Growing Up in the Fifties*, London: Virago.

Hoggart, R. (1963) 'A question of tone', *The Critical Quarterly* 5, 1: 73–91.

McRobbie, A. (1984) 'Dance and social fantasy', in A. McRobbie and M. Nava (eds.) *Gender and Generation*, London: Macmillan.

Marcus, L. (1987) ' "Enough about you, let's talk about me": recent autobiographical writing', *New Formations* 1: 77–94.

Miller, N. K. (1991) *Getting Personal: Feminist Occasions and Other Autobiographical Acts*, New York and London: Routledge.

Morris, M. (1988) *The Pirate's Fiancée: Feminism, Reading, Postmodernism*, London and New York: Verso.

Olney, J. (1980) 'Some versions of memory/some versions of "Bios": The ontology of autobiography', in James Olney (ed.) *Autobiography: Essays Theoretical and Critical*, Princeton: Princeton University Press.

Probyn, E. (forthcoming) *Sexing the Self: Gendered Positions in Cultural Studies*, New York and London: Routledge.

Rivière, J. (1986) [orig. 1929] 'Womanliness as a masquerade', in V. Burgin, J. Donald and C. Kaplan (eds) *Formations of Fantasy*, London: Methuen.

Rose, J. (1987) 'The state of the subject (II): the institution of feminism', *Critical Quarterly* 29, 4: 9–15.

Showalter, E. (1987) 'Women's time, women's space: writing the history of feminist criticism', in S. Benstock (ed.) *Feminist Issues in Literary Scholarship*, Bloomington and Indianapolis: Indiana University Press.

Smith, P. (1988) *Discerning the Subject*, Minneapolis: University of Minnesota Press.

Smith, S. (1987) *A Poetics of Women's Autobiography*, Bloomington and Indianapolis: Indiana University Press.

Spivak, G. (1988) 'Can the subaltern speak?', in C. Nelson and L. Grossberg (eds) *Marxism and the Interpretation of Culture*, Urbana: University of Illinois Press.

Stanton, D. (1984) 'Autogynography: is the subject different?', in D. Stanton (ed.) *The Female Autograph*, New York: New York Literary Forum.

Steedman, C. (1985) 'Landscape for a good woman', in L. Heron (ed.) *Truth, Dare or Promise: Girls Growing Up in the Fifties*, London: Virago.

Stimpson, C. (1987) 'Introduction', in S. Benstock (ed.) *Feminist Issues in Literary Criticism*, Bloomington and Indianapolis: Indiana University Press.

Suleiman, S. R. (1986) 'Malraux's women: A re-vision', in E. A. Flynn and P. P. Schweickart (eds) *Gender and Reading*, Baltimore: The Johns Hopkins University Press.

Walkerdine, V. (1985) 'Dreams from an ordinary childhood', in L. Heron (ed.) *Truth, Dare or Promise: Girls Growing Up in the Fifties*, London: Virago.

—— (1986) 'Video replay: families, films and fantasy', in V. Burgin, J. Donald and C. Kaplan (eds) *Formations of Fantasy*, London: Methuen.

Wall, C. A. (ed.) (1989) *Changing Our Own Words: Essays on Criticism, Theory, and Writing by Black Women*, New York and London: Routledge.

Wandor, M. (ed.) (1990) *Once a Feminist: Stories of a Generation*, London: Virago.

5

WHY ARE THERE NO GREAT WOMEN POSTMODERNISTS?

Geraldine Finn

This question, as far as I know, has not yet been asked.[1] I pose it now, not because I share its assumptions (that there are no great women postmodernists, for example) but to point to a process which is producing this question as one of its effects, under our very noses and even as we speak. The process I am referring to is an intellectual one: the process of production of *postmodernism* as a master discourse and discourse of mastery, whose mastery is accomplished through the active and systematic disappearance of women in general and feminism in particular from the framing of its terms and relevances and, correspondingly therefore, from contemporary descriptions and debates of and about culture inasmuch as it is constituted as postmodern.

At its simplest and most transparent the process consists in the pumping up of the familiar male canon into a new 'pantheon of proper names and authoritative texts' (Morris 1988: 12) – the old pantheon revised to include the new kids on the block: Barthes, Benjamin, Baudrillard, Deleuze, Derrida, Lacan, Lyotard . . . etc., names and texts which function not only as icons of intellect and intelligibility ('ritual objects of academic exegesis and commentary' [Morris 1988: 12]) but also, and more importantly, as the gatekeepers and guardians of the intellectual Holy Grail: legislators and legitimizers of what constitutes 'culture' in general and 'postmodern' critique in particular.

Identifying the mechanisms and effects of these processes of exclusion, of the containment and mastery of the terrain of the postmodern for men, for Man, is the subject of this paper. My comments fall into four parts: (1) a clarification of the term 'postmodern' and what I include in its category; (2) a description and exemplification of the processes whereby both the category and reality of the postmodern are hijacked to and for the old male canon (and thus to and for its continuing and relentless constitution of hegemony, inside and outside academe); (3) a discussion of what is wrong with this from an epistemological as well as political point of view, i.e. why it is bad social theory; and (4) a sketch of what good social theory should and could be doing in the light of the above.

POSTMODERNISM

I am using the term 'postmodernism' to refer to the after of modernism, i.e. to the world modernism has produced which modernist consciousness itself can no longer clarify, continue or control. The modernism of and after which postmodernists speak cannot be further defined because the *question* of modernity, of its precise content, configuration and effects, is in fact what constitutes and distinguishes the postmodern. 'Modernism' designates not so much a coherent or completed project, period or praxis, but rather a continuum of being and thought which calls itself 'modern' within which the problematic and possibility of a *post* modern has emerged as both a question and a demand. Since modernism (the appeal to and practices of the 'modern') has taken different forms at different times (in the different contexts of philosophy, science, economics, religion, politics, poetry, art, architecture, music and dance, for example) so too have the appeals to and practices of the postmodern. Nevertheless, all appeals to and practices of modernism, to one degree or another, espouse and promote the values and ends of the Enlightenment: of Humanism, History, Progress, Freedom, Reason, Transcendence and Man. And likewise all appeals to and practices of postmodernism *to one degree or another* (and this question of degree is central to the organizing question of this paper) put those values into question.

This process of questioning the values and ends of the Enlightenment, together with the perception of the inadequacy of the theories and practices of Enlightenment Reason – of modernism – to clarify, control, continue or change the world it has produced, has precipitated a series of crises amongst our intellectuals: a crisis of *authority*, for example, specifically the cultural authority vested in Western Europe, its history, culture and society; a crisis of *control*, specifically the control of nature and society vested in Science, Reason and Man (in the face of a modern technology which seems to destroy at least as much as it creates, and to control us as much as we control it); and a crisis of *faith*, specifically of the humanist faith in the ultimate wisdom, goodness and salvation of Man: in his technological and rational prowess, for example; in the dream of the global village which, in its reality, has not so much empowered or united its citizens as homogenized and passified us, fragmented and totalized us at one and the same time into both culture and the economy.

In the face of these crises of authority, control and faith, postmodernists sometimes describe our own era as an Apocalyptic one, as one marked by a series of ends: the end of Man, Reason, History and Transcendence, for example. Or, more precisely, as an era marked by the end of the master narratives of Man, Reason, History and Transcendence by which human experience and historical change have for so long in our culture been organized and understood according to a governing and benign teleology or logos (Reason) supposedly immanent within it (within Man, within History itself). In response to these crises and these 'ends' of and within modernity, postmodernist thinkers and activists have undertaken a series of radical revisions and initiatives, including the following:

1 A rethinking of the relationship between reality and representation in view of the demise of the self-evidence of the old solidities: of History, Reason, Freedom, Progress, Science and Man, for example.

2 A recognition that reality is socially constructed as are the organizing categories (of history, reason, self, subject, sex, sanity, etc.) by which it is known and reproduced. (This is how I interpret post-structuralist references to the arbitrariness of the sign, the instability of the referent, the disappearance of the real, the death of the author, the end of philosophy, and so forth.)

3 A revaluation of the old polarities which modernism has taken for granted as 'objective' categories of the real and in terms of which the real has been both organized and reproduced: the familiar, hierarchical oppositions of self/other, subject/object, reason/emotion, mind/body, transcendence/immanence, history/myth, knowledge/opinion, reality/illusion,

125

individual/society, man/woman, culture/nature, identity/
difference, order/chaos, sane/insane, etc.

4 A recognition that categories and the relationships between
them are always contingent, i.e. neither necessary nor essential, but socially constructed and imposed as well as
regulatory and productive of the realities they purport merely
to represent.

5 A revaluation or rejection of those Enlightenment values by
which modernism/modernity both animated and authorized
its practices: the values of freedom, individualism and autonomy, for example, taken to be the other side of alienation; of
truth as transparency; of knowledge as information; of
technology as control; of progress, change, rationality and
man as the indisputable and necessary ends of individual and
collective life.

THE HIJACK

How you respond to this crisis of the cultural authority of
Western Europe and this rethinking (or rejection) of its old
certainties – of its 'ancient compasses' as one canonized Canadian
scholar once expressed it[2] – depends very much, of course, on
your position in the Imperium over which it has ruled. And
herein lies the origin of the organizing question of this paper and
the exclusionary processes it is intended to address. Those heavily
invested in the terms and practices of the culture and institutions
of the Western European Cultural Imperium, who believe or
once believed in the various rhetorics and strategies of
modernism and in the values and ends of Enlightenment Reason,
may well find themselves in a panic, faced as they are with what
must indeed appear to them to be *the* Apocalypse: the end of the
known and signifying universe (of the universe as knowable and
'signifiant'), the second death of God. Faced with what they
proclaim to be (as they confuse rhetoric with reality and the
particular with the universal) the end of History *as such*: the
death of *the* Subject (as if there were only ever One), the loss of
the Social, the disappearance of *the* Real, the absence of *the*
Signified, the end of *all* Politics. In this version, which is
increasingly the Authorized Version of Postmodernism in some
intellectual locations, the collapse of the old certainties (of the
modernist myths of Reality, History, Freedom, Reason, and

126

Man) is translated into the collapse of *all* certainties and *all* possibilities of certainty and thence of *all judgement* (all possibility of discrimination, differentiation and interrogation of and *among* histories, realities, freedoms, and men) into the position of what I want to call 'lyrical nihilism' (Finn, forthcoming): a position which (I want to argue) *abdicates* ethics and politics and intellectual responsibility in the name of their contemporary impossibility. The following citation from a recent collection of essays *Sojourns in the New World* edited by Tom Darby exemplifies this position. Darby was a fellow speaker on the panel on Critical Theory and Canadian Culture at the conference *Cultural Studies and Communication Studies: Convergences and Divergences* held at Carleton University, Ottawa, in March and April of 1989, for which this paper was originally prepared. I thought I should read his book before delivering my paper to see to what extent his particular engagement with (post)modernism accorded with or departed from my argument(s). To my combined delight, disappointment and dismay, I found it demonstrated my case perfectly and it seemed appropriate to use it as a *local, particular and concrete working example* (a book written and edited by Canadian scholars and published by a Canadian university press) of the general processes of intellectual canonization, totalization, exclusion and mastery which are the focus of this paper. So although Tom Darby's book does not itself figure in the 'seminal' debates within and about (post)modernism, and is in fact a self-evidently 'modernist' text according to the criteria laid down above, it nevertheless illustrates *precisely* the kind of institutional and discursive hijacking of the contemporary critical intellectual terrain *for men/for Man* – the traditional would-be universal Man of the old world, with which I am concerned. Here is what Darby has to say about 'the post–modern man':

> Today, if a person is not a nihilist he can be one of only three things. First, he can simply be ignorant of the New World . . . Secondly, he can know of it yet . . . misunderstand it. Thirdly, he can know of it and deny it. The first is naive, the second foolish, the third cowardly.
>
> (Darby 1986a: 4)

From the standpoint of this subject, this masculine subject as the pronouns make clear, the collapse of the old modernist project leaves only one option: nihilism. Any other attitude or sentiment amounts to naivety, foolishness or cowardice. Note, however, how the speaker, while purporting to describe the exigencies of the *New* World, the *post* modern world, does so from the standpoint of the traditional subject of the old: from the standpoint of a universal pre-feminist, pre-post-colonial subject for whom all are One and One is always He.

Those of us not so heavily invested in nor so well served by the values and ends of modernism may well find much to celebrate and affirm in the collapse of its authority and control. For it would seem to open up spaces in culture and consciousness where we can speak, hear, and recognize other and heretofore subordinated histories, realities, reasons, subjectivities, knowledges, and values, which have been silenced and suppressed and certainly excluded from the formulations and determinations of the old modernist project. In Canada, for example, where I happen to be living, the postmodern condition (i.e. the breakdown of the authority of modernism) consists of among other things: the emergence of the particular voices and political presence of women, Quebec, aboriginal peoples, gays, lesbians, and blacks; of what English Canadians who live in Ontario call the 'regions'; of what white Anglo-Saxon Canadians refer to as 'ethnic' groups. That is, the postmodern condition in Canada consists in the emergence of what Linda Hutcheons (1988) has called the ex-centric voices of the borders and boundaries of Canada. Or as I have come to think of it, the voices of those who do not live in Toronto. Canada thus exemplifies one aspect of the postmodern scene: both constituting and constituted by the disappearance and fragmentation of the unitary Imperial Subject of Western Europe: that universal Man with his singular and monotonous History, Civilization, Reality, and Truth from which many of those who now call themselves Canadian (including myself) once fled.

It is of some concern to me, therefore, that the increasingly hegemonic voice of the Canadian postmodern, the voice which is claiming and controlling the category and thereby the rites of inclusion and exclusion into and from the theories, practices *and places* it organizes, is not the plural, varied, eccentric and changing voice(s) of Canada but the familiar voice of Imperium: of a Canada hitched to and thereby disappeared into the Western Imperium itself by way of an already familiar canon of Canadian spokesmen: George Grant, Harold Innis, Marshall McLuhan, Northrop Frye.[3] It is the unsituated (and therefore the decidedly un-postmodern) voice of what I recall Canadian author Margaret Atwood calling the 'free floating . . . citizen of the world'. It is a totalizing voice which presumes to speak on behalf of and in the name of (and here the examples are from *The Postmodern Scene: Excremental Culture and Hyper-Aesthetics*, by Arthur Kroker and David Cook [1986]): western civilization, modern culture, the European mind, the western mind, modern experience, western experience, modern self-consciousness, the citizen of this world, our culture. The same voice speaks less duplicitously perhaps in Tom Darby's *Sojourns in the New World* (1986) in the name of: the truly modern man, multinational man, the Last man, the masters of the earth, and most apt of all, in the name of the 'experience of being a man'. Let us listen as one of these voices describes the postmodern condition from *his* point of view, and it is clearly *his* not hers as we will see; a condition and a description which is subsequently situated and interpreted within the text in terms of the historic realization of Hegel's Universal and Homogeneous State.

> In the practical and everyday manifestation of the New World one can take a taxi down a Los Angeles freeway, catch a plane, and in less than ten hours be in Tokyo. One can stay at the Hilton, ring room service and have a meal of fresh sushi and chilled Rhine wine. When finished one can have a cognac along with Kenyan coffee, puff on a true Havana cigar, and while clad in a pair of genuine American Levis, throw a careless leg over the arm of a crafted piece of Danish furniture. The next day one can take the bullet train to Kyoto and have lunch at McDonald's next to an ancient Buddhist shrine. When this stay is over, one can fly to Toronto, take a taxi home to a California-style modern house between the English Tudor and the French Provincial homes of the neighbours, and relax in one's own hot tub that sits between a big stone and a Mugo pine in the glassed-in Japanese garden.
>
> (Darby 1986b: v)

Well, one can, can one? Who is this 'one', this subject of the postmodern, for whom these are the 'practical and everyday

129

manifestations of the New World' and who presumes as 'one' to speak for us all?

According to Fowler's *Dictionary of Modern English Usage* 'one' stands for: 'the average person, or the sort of person we happen to be concerned with, or anyone of the class that includes the speaker'. The sort of person we happen to be concerned with in this case, the class that includes this particular speaker, though never acknowledged is actually quite precisely specified in this text. It is people we may not have heard of before with names like Peter and Michael and Ian and Tom, and other people we are presumed to have heard of before with names like Strauss, Ellul, Kojève, Heidegger, Kant, Hegel, Plato, Rousseau, Nietzsche, Heraclitus, Deleuze, Guattari, and God. Need I say more?

Let us listen again to another speaker from the same collection of essays edited by Darby (1986). Notice this time the instability of the repeated use of 'one' in this passage. It does not always in this case stand for the class that includes the speaker, though it begins this way and the unacknowledged equivocation would have us believe it continues. In this case, the use of 'one' (and 'he') makes for not just bad (plain, old-fashioned modernist) theory, but also bad grammar.

> To be modern is to adopt a specific self-understanding or self-interpretation. One sees oneself as autonomous, independent of natural constraints, independent of God, and therefore free to create personal and social meaning. The absence of natural constraints is not, however, absolute. Human beings are not angels; they still have bodies. But for modern self-consciousness, one's body, one's gender, for example, does not constrain the meaning of one's sexuality: gay, straight or kinky, the options of an effectively androgynous existence may everywhere be displayed. Likewise the normal or natural consequences of gender differences have effectively been circumvented by the widespread use of contraception and abortion. And finally, what could be more trite than to observe that all this has been described and justified in terms of freedom? Why else would one leave the closet, take the pill, or submit to surgical therapy?
>
> (Cooper 1986: 35)

No prizes for guessing whether this particular writer is gay, straight, or kinky, has left the closet, taken the pill or submitted to surgical therapy. As Dorothy Smith might put it, the social relations which organized this particular text are manifest in the text if we have eyes to see it.[4]

Let me clarify what precisely it is that I am objecting to here besides sloppy English usage. I am not criticizing who or what this 'one' actually is or does, or who it stands for, or any particular 'lifestyle' it may represent (straight, straight or straight) – though there may well be good reasons for doing so, from an ecological perspective, for example, or from the perspective of political economy or studies in development. What I am objecting to is the presumption, the inscription, the deployment of this 'one' as *the* subject of (post)modern consciousness; as the sufficient foundation of a social theory which purports to speak for all of us: for 'our culture', 'modern self-consciousness', or even, and more specifically, 'the experience of being a man' in the New World. This is at one and the same time an epistemological, a logical and a political objection. I am objecting to the 'indifference' of this no one in particular, this everyone in general: a category you can step into and out of as it suits you and which thereby effectively delivers (post)modernism over to the worst excesses of intellectual opportunism. It is an 'indifference' which both marks and masks the specific (sexual, racial, and class) difference of the speaker and those with whom he is concerned as the traditional white male (subject) of the imperialist European civilization whose demise postmodernism purports to describe, but from whose position of continuing privilege he, the subject, continues to speak. I am objecting to this 'indifference' because it simply replicates (confirms and congeals) the rule of the (post)modernist techné it claims to critique, and the strategies of the 'global village', the new Imperium, it purports to deplore: in its totalizing and totalitarian erasure of the particular histories, experiences and realities of those over whom that Imperium continues to rule. (The particular histories of those whose labour provides the room service, the sushi, the chilled Rhine wine, the Havana cigar, the genuine American Levis, the crafted piece of Danish furniture, the lunch at McDonald's, etc. which Tom Darby exhibits as the 'practical and everyday manifestations of the New World'; the particular experiences of those who leave the closet, take the pill or submit to surgical therapy, exhibited by Barry Cooper as evidence of his claim that 'for modern self-consciousness, one's body, one's gender, for example, does not constrain the meaning of one's sexuality'.)

Instead of resisting or disrupting the 'desiring machine', the homogenizing regime of modern technological culture, this version of (post)modernism, its increasingly Authorized Version, merely exploits it and reproduces it in its own tendency to become global. You can take this brand of postmodernism anywhere in the world market of ideas (as Tom Darby obviously does) and it will continue to work for you, the 'free floating citizen of the world'. (It is in this respect that John Rajchman once referred to postmodernism as the 'Toyota' of thought: 'produced and assembled in several different places and then sold everywhere' [Rajchman 1987: 52].) This totalizing tendency of postmodernism replicates the processes and effects of television by disappearing people in particular into the seductive appearances, the simulacra, of every one in general (the one who takes the taxi home to his California style modern house between the English Tudor and the French Provincial). It constitutes bad social theory (from a logical, epistemological, aesthetic, political and moral point of view) inasmuch as it continues the modernist practice of *universalizing the particular* – over and over and over again, reinstating under the guise of a 'post' the old modernist illusion of the bourgeoisie that takes itself for a universal class. In this sense it is a social theory that has forgotten Marx and therefore scarcely qualifies as *post* modern.

BAD SOCIAL THEORY

More precisely then, I am criticizing a certain tendency in postmodernism because it is not critical enough, if it is critical at all. In its tendency to go global, to universalize the contingencies of its own unexamined particularity and thereby disappear the experiences and realities of the many into the unified consciousness of the one of western civilization (modern culture, truly modern man), this increasingly authorized and authorizing version of postmodernism fails as *critical* social theory and as *post* modern theory on the following counts:

1 It does not acknowledge the politics of knowledge: its location within a social context organized by and for systematic inequalities of power – of race, class, region, nation, culture,

age, sexuality, etc. It does not, for example, acknowledge or examine the politics of its own knowledge-claims and interests; nor the politics of the knowledge it chooses to draw upon as the context of its own thought and self-consciousness; nor the politics of that very selectivity itself: of why Hegel, Heidegger, Kojève and Nietzsche are *in*, for example, and Marx, Marcuse, Freud, and Sartre are *out*. It is particularly disturbing that so much of what passes for *post*modernism maintains a characteristically modernist silence on its own relationship to the violence and violations of the Western Imperium whose demise it purports to describe; its relationship to the practices and effects of colonization, for example, which are so clearly one of the conditions of its own possibility.

2 More particularly, for the purposes of this paper, the totalizing tendency of postmodernism does not take gender into account, i.e. sexual difference *and the difference it makes*, either in its use of language or in its conceptualization of its problematic: the History, Culture, Man, Consciousness, and Civilization which it presumes to be constitutive of the (post)modern world. Where gender is acknowledged, as in Barry Cooper's piece cited above, the difference sexual difference makes is disavowed by way of the typically modernist strategy of division and denial: reduced to more of the Same ('gay, straight or kinky, the options of an effectively androgynous existence may everywhere be displayed. Likewise the normal or natural consequences of gender differences have effectively been circumvented by the widespread use of contraception and abortion'), or more of the Other (gay, straight or kinky, leaving the closet, taking the pill, submitting to surgical therapy). By the exclusivity of its inclusiveness this globalizing tendency in postmodernism reproduces and reconstructs *women's absence* from history, culture, consciousness and thought and thereby *women's silence* in its own would-be *post* modern discourse. A discourse which has been precipitated, at least in part, by the emergence of women's voices into history, culture and consciousness as a political and theoretical force to be reckoned with – as a difference which does, indeed, make a difference.

3 This tendency to go global in postmodern thought thus fails to take into account its own contingency: its own specificity as

both a theory and a practice, a description and a way of being, an ideology and a reality which is not always and everywhere the same, nor always and everywhere the necessary and inevitable consequence of modernism. It does not, that is, acknowledge the specificity and limits of what it claims to know and know as real, or the location of its knowledge-claims in particular persons, places, uses and times: in a specific relationship to power and desire, for example, which is constitutive of the presumptive subject of modernity.

4 The political effect of this kind of generalizing postmodernist discourse is not the promotion of difference and change or the disturbance of a 'culturally suspicious trouble-making reader' (Bennett 1989) but rather the reproduction and reification of the Same: the same structures of atomization, fragmentation, alienation, homogenization, totalization, and technological imperialism which constitute its own condition of possibility as well as the content and form of its own praxis. It is, therefore, neither critical nor transformative in its effects but complicit with and reproductive of the political status quo ante. Like all master discourses/discourses of mastery it stirs up a smoke-screen of *achieved universality* behind which lies a very particular (modernist) subjectivity with very particular interests and investments at stake. Speaking for modern experience, our culture and the truly modern man, this tendency of postmodernism is both reassuring to the established order (of power and privilege, control, and influence, prestige, and penetration) and easily recuperated by and within it, precisely because it speaks the universal. Hence its hegemonic spread across, between and within the various academic disciplines, the arts and culture.

5 Postmodernism of this kind does not open up speaking positions for previously subordinated/silenced subjectivities and knowledges – for women, for example – in either discourse or institutions but ignores them (as in Darby above) or speaks for them (as in Cooper above), incorporating them into its own seamless and would-be anonymous voice. It thereby forgets Foucault for whom speaking for others was the greatest indignity[5] and once again disqualifies itself from the *post* of modernism. On the contrary, it continues modernism's sclerosis of privileged ideas into religions of meaning and its

corresponding organization of political and discursive closure.

6 It is an unreflexive discourse which accepts no responsibility for the position from which it is spoken nor, therefore, for that which is spoken from it. It is in this respect a typically modernist discourse. In Sartre's terms it assumes the perspective of the *false* intellectual because it universalizes the particular, the particular sensibilities and realities of the petit bourgeois academic, the salaried intellectual (his boredom, frenzy, and panic, for example), without confronting the specific contradictions (the suffering and violence) of his very particular situated existence.[6]

7 From my perspective, this tendency in postmodern discourse is profoundly ideological: it mystifies reality by presenting particular local and partial truths as if they were the Whole Truth, and reifies it by presenting those local and particular truths as if they were the ineluctable, necessary conclusions of History itself. Or, as Althusser might say, the globalizing tendency in postmodernism alludes to reality – the reality of the lives of those who speak it – in an illusory way: representing the imaginary relationships of individuals ('one sees oneself as autonomous, independent of natural constraints, independent of God and therefore free to create personal and social meaning') to their real conditions of existence (petit bourgeois academics, salaried *male* intellectuals) (see Althusser 1971).

8 Inasmuch as it is ideological, postmodernist discourse is not just bad social theory. It is also, I suggest, bad for your mental health in that it actually accomplishes the death of the social it claims to merely diagnose or describe. Like television and pornography it is a discourse in which no body speaks. Like television and pornography it is a discourse which privileges performance over presence: its medium is the message. Its very form (the generality and anonymity of its address, for example) contains, organizes and constructs its content and its constituency: a collectivity (or series, in Sartre's terms) of anonymous no/bodies (disembodied subjects of the gaze) organized by and around the spectacle of some body else made object: some body else who takes the pill, leaves the closet, submits to surgical therapy, throws a careless leg over the arm of a crafted piece of Danish furniture, and so forth. Like

television and pornography, the globalizing tendency of postmodernism seduces us by its anonymous and sophisticated appeal away from human presence and the discipline and demands of a reciprocating reality, into the simulacra, the appearances, the imaginary surfaces of its own performance. As such it disarms the already disarmed, passifies the passified, and pre-empts the production of the culturally suspicious troublemaking reader, which would be the minimum requirement of *critical, dissident* social theory.

Two recent Canadian enquiries into the agency and effects of television give substance to this claim that postmodernism, pornography and television collude in the production of the death of the social, though this collaboration is not the explicit concern of the two texts in question. In *Cambodia: A Book for People Who Find Television Too Slow* (1986), Brian Fawcett demonstrates how the implicit telos of North American television and the explicit logos of the Khmer Rouge in Cambodia converge in the politics of what he calls *genocide*: i.e. in the obliteration of local memory and imagination (our only resources for struggle, difference and change); in the extermination of consciousness and the liquidation of particularity (as Sartre would say) upon which contemporary Imperium depends. Joyce Nelson in *The Perfect Machine: Television in the Nuclear Age* (1987) develops a similar and supporting argument from a different set of premises. She traces the concrete and specific personal, political and economic links between the historical production and dissemination of television and the production and dissemination of nuclear weapons, to demonstrate how television and nuclear weapons perform, project and produce the same *intentional* political ends: social death, the disappearance of the body, what she calls the 'flesh-free' environment upon which the contemporary North American Imperium of patriarchal capitalism depends.

Obviously, I cannot do justice to the arguments of these two texts here, nor substantiate my own suggestion of a collusion between television, pornography and postmodernism (some versions of) in the active production of the death of the social (but see Finn 1985 and 1989 for further details). I cite them here as counter-examples to the master discourses of postmodernism referred to above which are the specific focus of this paper. For, in spite of the fact that both of these writers are systematically and self-consciously engaged in a fundamental and radical critique of and disaffection from the authority, control, and faith of modernism, neither of them invokes the category of postmodernism in their work and neither of them, correspond-ingly, is included within its canon, in the footnotes and biblio-graphies of its scholars. And this, I believe, is precisely because they *put the universal into question* from the standpoint and on behalf of the particular. That is, they insist on *embodying* and exploring the globalizing tendency of 'Western' discourse (taken for granted and reproduced by the Authorized Version of postmodernism, by Cooper and Darby for example) to disclose its specific, concrete and historical roots in particular persons, places, interests, uses and times and its specific and concrete political logos in Imperium: in the continuing organization of power and privilege in the hands of the few who speak as 'one'. As such, both texts exemplify what in my opinion good social theory which is both radical and responsible (in the very literal meaning of those terms) should be doing and is doing, behind the scenes of the mystifying master discourses of the postmodern.

GOOD SOCIAL THEORY

In the light of the above I would like then to conclude with some positive indications of what good social critique could and should be doing in the face of the collapse of the modernist project:

1 Producing counter-cultural theory and practice focused on events (ideology made concrete and practical) rather than texts (ideology made abstract and ideal). That is, critical social theory develops theory from and for the sake of the political and practical urgencies of the moment: specific, concrete, local and particular theory; and correspondingly struggles to resist the traditional intellectual trajectory of theory for theory's sake: theory for the sake of theoretical mastery, for the sake of the mastery of discourse and the discourse of mastery.

2 Critical social theory is committed to *interrogating the appearances* of the (post)modern world and *not* submitting to or being seduced by them: to interrogating the 'practical and everyday manifestation of the new world' as they reveal

themselves to the likes of Tom Darby in the Tokyo Hilton Hotel in the shape of chilled Rhine wine, Kenyan coffee, Havana cigars, Danish furniture, genuine American Levis, or 'the options of an effectively androgynous existence . . . everywhere . . . displayed' to Barry Cooper. It means *contesting* dominant ideologies and demystifying ruling representations (of the 'everyday' and the 'everywhere'), not throwing up our hands in despair ('if a person is not a nihilist . . .') or complacency in the face of its (false and falsifying) universalizing rhetoric. Fascination with the object, with the objectivity of the object (with chilled Rhine wine, Kenyan Coffee, Havana cigars or 'one's own hot tub that sits between a big stone and a Mugo pine in the glassed-in Japanese garden') is not critical social theory (neither critical nor social nor theory) and is certainly no substitute for the concrete and specific *deconstruction* of it: of the object, of the objectivity of the object; and likewise no substitute for the investigation of its social and political conditions of possibility, its social and political (re)productivity, and our own implication in what it is and does. (How precisely, for example, is Tom Darby implicated in his chilled Rhine wine, his genuine American Levis, his Mugo pine, California-style modern house in Toronto? How precisely is Barry Cooper implicated in the widespread use of contraception and abortion, coming out of the closet, taking the pill, submitting to surgical therapy?)

3 Deriving social theory from events rather than texts and from the systematic deconstruction of the objectivity of their appearances means revealing the *human presence/praxis* in the making of reality and in the making of its meaning and/ or meaninglessness, in the making of the illusion of its universality and/or its end, for example, instead of obscuring the local and historical (racial, sexual, and class) specificities of that presence/praxis beneath the mystifying categories of no one in particular and everyone in general. In the case in question, for example, it would mean revealing the identities of those whose unacknowledged, unspoken and *invisible labour and lives* provide our would-be anonymous intellectuals, our free-floating citizens of the world, with their Havana cigars, their room service, their Kenyan coffee and their taxi rides to and from the Tokyo Hilton Hotel, and with their flattering visions of themselves as having circumvented

the 'normal or natural consequences of gender differences', to be 'autonomous, independent of natural constraints, independent of God and therefore free to create personal and social meaning'.

4 Revealing the specific and local human presence/praxis in the making of a reality and in the making of its meanings necessarily entails a perpetual reversal of perspectives – of the world through self and the self through world. It entails an *interrogation of self* as well as of the world of meaning and sense. In the case in question it means calling oneself into question as, for example, a jet-setting salaried intellectual of the (post)modern world. Critically contesting contemporary thought and culture means critically contesting ourselves, our tastes and our knowledge, inasmuch as we have been made both by and for it. It entails, as Sartre once put it, a traversal of the research through the singularity of the researcher, of the universal through the particular (Sartre 1974). Deconstructing the object, demystifying the objectivity of the object, requires a corresponding deconstruction of the subject: in this case, for example, a demystification of his presumption of universality, knowledge and truth ('Today, if a person is not a nihilist he can be only three things . . .'; 'To be modern is to adopt a specific self-understanding or self-interpretation . . .'). Producing critical counter-cultural theory, interrogating appearance to reveal the specific and local human presence/praxis beneath the veil of achieved universality, requires the researcher ceaselessly to combat the (class, gender, and racially specific) petit-bourgeois ideology embedded in his own social formation, therefore, and his own sentiments and thoughts as these are made manifest in his everyday life: in his taste for fresh sushi, chilled Rhine wine, Havana cigars and genuine American Levis, for example; in his assumption that his body, his gender does not constrain the meaning of his sexuality: that 'gay, straight, or kinky, the options of an effectively androgynous existence may everywhere be displayed', that 'the normal or natural consequences of gender differences have effectively been circumvented by the widespread use of contraception and abortion'. (*Whose* widespread use of contraception and abortion? The natural consequences of *whose* gender differences?) Interrogating oneself as part of the process of critical interrogation of the reality and appearances of one's

culture means being prepared to give something up in the interest of social and political change. It means modifying one's own sensibilities and thoughts as well as those of 'culture' and 'society': one's taste for sushi, Havana cigars and taxi rides, as well as one's cheerful embrace of nihilism and the unthinking presuppositions of the sensibilities of a white, urban petit-bourgeois heterosexual male intellectual who thinks his experience entitles him to speak for all.

5 Producing counter-cultural critical theory also means resisting in our practice as intellectuals what Naomi Goldenberg (1990) has called the Apocalypse in Everyday Life, referring to the progressive and systematic disappearance of people from each other in the routine practices of daily life in the (post)modern world. Particular persons, histories and lives are disappeared into texts, screens, and machines, for example, into bureaucratic forms and functions, and then again into the hermetic patois of abstract universals of those who would make sense of it all. Producing theory that resists this disappearing tendency of the (post)modern world means *revealing ourselves* in our work: owning the knowledge and experience we attribute to the (post)modern condition and *taking responsibility* for it; for our part in our investment in its production and reproduction. It means saying 'I' and renouncing the use of the anonymous 'he', 'one', or 'man' which only and always obfuscates the reality in question by concealing the local, concrete and specific determinations of local, concrete and specific thought beneath a blanket of impersonal generalization. Being a concrete, specific and particular and thereby response-able intellectual means not simply reading the appearances and ideas (the simulacra) of (post)modernity against the appearances and ideas of earlier times immortalized in texts, but investigating the origins and effects of those appearances in and on particular persons and populations. In the case in question, the case of the Authorized Versions of postmodernism as exemplified here by Darby and Cooper, this would entail some reflection upon the relationship of white male privilege and domination to the postmodern condition under review, together with some acknowledgement of the specific contradictions, violences and pain particular to this particular privilege; contradictions, violences and pain which must surely underlie that tendency

140

to nihilism which characterizes so much of this kind of global theorizing.

Revealing oneself in one's intellectual work means acknowledging the politics of the work itself and taking a side, a position, in that politics. It means passing judgements and taking risks, both personal and intellectual. While assuming the (false) position of the universal global intellectual, the free-floating citizen of the world, allows you to avoid that and thereby to support the ruling order (if only implicitly) by reproducing its *ex cathedra* discourse of singular Truth(s).

6 Finally, critical social theory which aims to trouble the status quo and resist its reification of reality and politics should strive to create space within theoretical discourse for the voices, knowledges and realities of previously subordinated and silenced subjects, instead of continuing to speak for them as Barry Cooper does in the passage cited earlier where he hijacks (appropriates) the experiences of Man's Others, of women and gays for example (those who come out of the closet, take the pill or submit to surgical therapy), for his own particular version of what it means to be (post)modern. Critical social theory would, on the contrary, systematically avoid closure to maintain *the openness* of the world and its possible truths by speaking always from the contingencies, borders and boundaries of its master discourses, its discourses of mastery, instead of from the necessities of its dead (fixed, still, enclosed) centre.

CONCLUSION

Why, then, are there no great women postmodernists? What I have tried to show here is the process which produces the conditions for posing questions like this: the active process of *disappearing people* from the collective consciousness which interprets and shapes our culture and what counts as knowledge of it or even resistance to it. It is a process which disappears not only women, of course, though that has been the focus of this particular essay. It also disappears Canada as you may have noticed,[7] and the particularity of a Canadian experience of the (post)modern. And as indicated earlier it disappears the labour and lives of those who produce the reality of the postmodern condition for its spokesmen and their illusion of its universality and/or end.

Dorothy Smith addresses these discursive processes of exclusion and their relationship to the ruling apparatus in her work which she calls 'institutional ethnography'. Ten years ago she described these processes as they operate in sociology. I would like to end therefore with a quotation from that essay, modified very slightly to highlight its relevance to the contemporary discourse(s) of postmodernism. Notice as you read how you can replace 'men' here with a reference to any ruling elite, and 'women' with any subordinated group and the description will work for the discursive organization of every and any hierarchy, hegemony or institutionalized order of dominance.

> Women do not appear to men as men do to one another, as persons who might share in the common construction of a social reality where that is essentially an ideological construction. There is, we discovered a circle effect – men attend to and treat as significant what men say and have said. The circle of men whose writing and talk has been significant to one another extends back in time as far as our records reach. What men were doing has been relevant to men, was written by men about men for men. Men listened and listen to what one another say. A tradition is formed, traditions form, in a discourse with the past within the present. The themes, problematics, assumptions, metaphors, and images form as the circle of those present draws upon the work of those speaking from the past and builds it up to project it into the future. From the circle women have been almost entirely excluded. When admitted, it has been only by special licence, and as individuals, never as representatives of their sex. They could share in this circle only by receiving its terms and relevances. These have been and still are to a large extent the terms and relevances of a discourse among men.
>
> (Smith 1979: 137)

And for those of you who are still wondering whether there are any (great) women postmodernists I have attached a bibliography (Appendix I) to help you decide.[8] It consists entirely of women's names and women's writing and is a partial (and now rather dated) list of what is available, the likes of which has provided the context (not the canon) of my own reflections over the last twenty years. I suggest you read *all* of these titles and only books by women until you are through. In the meantime do all your research and writing entirely in the terms and relevancies of this discourse among women (not all of whom are dead or European). I predict that before long you will see more to being human, or even to being a man, than the options currently on offer from the Orthodox Versions of Postmodernism: the lyrical nihilism of those who bespeak the end of modernity (History, Freedom, and Man), exemplified here, perhaps, by Tom Darby; or the nostalgic rationalism of those who would revive its dead and dying social body, exemplified perhaps by Barry Cooper. Well, why not? You have obviously nothing to lose. Or do you? That is the question I would like you to think about as you consider this discourse of (post)modernism among women.

APPENDIX I: BIBLIOGRAPHY FROM *THE PIRATE'S FIANCÉE* BY MEAGHAN MORRIS

For the reasons discussed in the Introduction [to *The Pirate's Fiancée*], I have included in this bibliography only works signed or cosigned as written by women. Since it combines entries about feminism, theories of reading, and postmodernism, it is for practical reasons mostly limited to works I have drawn on in some way for the essays in this book. Essays published in anthologies are not listed separately under their authors' names.

Abel, Elizabeth, ed., *Writing and Sexual Difference*, Brighton 1982.
Allen, Judith and Grosz, Elizabeth, eds, *Feminism and the Body, Australian Feminist Studies*, no. 5, 1987.
Allen, Judith and Patton, Paul, eds, *Beyond Marxism? Interventions After Marx*, Sydney 1983.
Atkinson, Ti-Grace, *Amazon Odyssey*, New York 1974.
Bell, Diane, *Daughters of the Dreaming*, Melbourne 1983.
Bergstrom, Janet, 'Enunciation and Sexual Difference (Part 1)', *Camera Obscura*, nos. 3–4, 1979.
Bergstrom, Janet, 'Violence and Enunciation', *Camera Obscura*, nos. 8/9/10, 1982.
Bergstrom, Janet, 'Androids and Androgyny', *Camera Obscura*, no. 15, 1986.
Bernstein, Cheryl, 'Performance as News: Notes on an Intermedia Guerilla Art Group', in Michel Benamou and Charles Caramello, eds, *Performance in Postmodern Culture*, Milwaukee 1977.
Braidotti, Rosi, *Féminisme et philosophie: La philosophie contempor-*

aine comme critique du pouvoir par rapport à la pensée féministe,
Université de Paris-1, 1981.

Brooke-Rose, Christine, *A Rhetoric of the Unreal,* Cambridge 1981.

Brown, Denise Scott, Izenour, Steven and Venturi, Robert, *Learning from Las Vegas: The Forgotten Symbolism of Architectural Form,* Cambridge, Mass. and London 1977.

Bruno, Giuliana, 'Postmodernism and *Blade Runner*', *October,* no. 41, 1987.

Bruss, Elizabeth W., *Beautiful Theories: The Spectacle of Discourse in Contemporary Criticism,* Baltimore and London, 1982.

Burchill, Louise, 'Either/Or: Peripeteia of an Alternative in Jean Baudrillard's *De la séduction*' in André Frankovits, ed., *Seduced and Abandoned: The Baudrillard Scene,* Sydney 1984.

Cameron, Deborah, *Feminism and Linguistic Theory,* London 1985.

Chow, Rey, 'Rereading Mandarin Ducks and Butterflies: A Response to the "Postmodern" Condition', *Cultural Critique,* no. 5, 1986-7.

Cixous, Héléne *et al.,* *La Venue à l'écriture,* Paris 1977.

Clément, Catherine, and Cixous, Hélène, *La Jeune Née,* Paris 1975.

Clément, Catherine, *Miroirs du sujet,* Paris 1975.

Clément, Catherine, *Les Fils de Freud sont fatigués,* Paris 1978; *The Weary Sons of Freud,* London 1987.

Clément, Catherine, *Vies et légendes de Jacques Lacan,* Paris 1981; *The Lives and Legends of Jacques Lacan,* New York 1983.

Collins, Felicity, 'A (Sad) Song of the Body', *Screen,* vol. 28, no. 1, 1987.

Cornillon, Susan Koppelman, *Images of Women in Fiction: Feminist Perspectives,* Ohio 1972.

Coventry, Virginia, *The Critical Distance: Work With Photography/ Politics/Writing,* Sydney 1986.

Coward, Rosalind, *Female Desire,* London 1984.

Coward, Rosalind and Ellis, John *Language and Materialism: Developments in Semiology and the Theory of the Subject,* London 1977.

Creed, Barbara, 'From Here to Modernity – Feminism and Postmodernism', *Screen,* vol. 28, no. 2, 1987.

Daly, Mary, *Beyond God the Father; Towards a Philosophy of Women's Liberation,* Boston 1973.

Daly, Mary, *Gyn/Ecology: The Metaethics of Radical Feminism,* Boston 1978.

Davidson, Robyn, *Tracks,* London 1980.

Delphy, Christine, *The Main Enemy: A Materialist Analysis of Women's Oppression,* London 1977.

Doane, Mary Ann, 'Woman's Stake: Filming the Female Body', *October,* no. 17, 1981.

Doane, Mary Ann, 'Film and the Masquerade: Theorizing the Female Spectator', *Screen,* vol. 23, no. 24, 1982.

Doane, Mary Ann, 'When the Direction of the Force Acting on the Body is Changed: The Moving Image', *Wide Angle,* vol. 7, nos. 1-2, 1985.

Doane, Mary Anne, *The Desire to Desire: The Woman's Film of the 1940s,* Indiana 1987.

Dubreuil-Blondin, Nicole, 'Feminism and Modernism: Paradoxes' in

Benjamin Buchloh *et al.*, eds, *Modernism and Modernity*, Nova Scotia 1983.

Duras, Marguerite and Gauthier, Xavière, *Les Parleuses*, Paris 1974.

Ecker, Gisela, ed., *Feminist Aesthetics*, London 1985.

Eisenstein, Hester and Jardined, Alice, eds. *The Future of Difference*, Boston 1980.

Ellmann, Mary, *Thinking About Women*, London 1969.

Ewen, Elizabeth and Ewen, Stuart, *Channels of Desire: Mass Images and the Shaping of American Consciousness*, New York 1972.

Felman, Shoshana, *La Folie et la chose littéraire*, Paris 1978; *Writing and Madness*, Ithaca 1986.

Felman, Shoshana, ed., *Literature and Psychoanalysis, the Question of Reading: Otherwise, Yale French Studies*, nos. 55–6, 1977.

Felman, Shoshana, *Le Scandale du corps parlant: Don Juan avec Austin ou la séduction en deux langues*, Paris 1980.

Ferguson, Frances, 'The Nuclear Sublime', *Diacritics*, vol. 14, no. 2, 1984.

Fraser, Nancy, 'The French Derrideans: Politicizing Deconstruction or Deconstructing Politics', *New German Critique*, no. 33, 1984.

Fraser, Nancy, 'What's Critical About Critical Theory? The Case of Habermas and Gender', *New German Critique*, no. 35, 1985.

Freadman, Anne, 'On Being Here and Still Doing It', in P. Botsman, C. Burns and P. Hutchings, eds. *The Foreign Bodies Papers*, Sydney 1981.

Freadman, Anne, 'Sandpaper', *Southern Review*, vol. 16, no. 1, 1983.

Freadman, Anne, 'Riffaterrra Cognita: A Late Contribution to the "Formalism" Debate', *SubStance*, no. 42, 1984.

Freadman, Anne, 'Reading the Visual', *Framework*, nos. 30–31, 1986.

Gaines, Jane, 'White Privilege and Looking Relations: Race and Gender in Feminist Film Theory', *Cultural Critique*, no. 4, 1986.

Gallop, Jane, *Intersections: A Reading of Sade with Bataille, Blanchot, and Klossowski*, Nebraska 1981.

Gallop, Jane, *Feminism and Psychoanalysis: the Daughter's Seduction*, London 1982.

Gallop, Jane, *Reading Lacan*, Ithaca and London 1985.

Gaudin, Colette, *et al.*, *Feminist Readings: French Texts/American Contexts, Yale French Studies*, no. 62, 1981.

Gould, Carol, C. and Wartofsky, Marx W., eds, *Women and Philosophy: Toward a Theory of Liberation*, New York 1976.

Gross, Elizabeth, 'Derrida, Irigaray and Deconstruction', *Leftwright, Intervention*, no. 20, 1986.

Gross, Elizabeth, 'Irigaray and the Divine', Local Consumption Occasional Paper 9, Sydney 1986.

Grosz, Elizabeth, 'Every Picture Tells a Story: Art and Theory Reexamined', in Gary Sangster, ed., *Sighting References*, Sydney 1987.

Grosz, Elizabeth, 'The "People of the Book": Representation and Alterity in Emmanuel Levinas', *Art & Text*, no. 26, 1987.

Grosz, Elizabeth, *et al.*, eds, *Futur*fall: Excursions into Post-Modernity*, Sydney 1986.

Gunew, Sneja, 'Feminist Criticism: Positions and Questions', *Southern Review*, vol. 16, no. 1, 1983.

Gunew, Sneja, and Reid, Ian, *Not the Whole Story*, Sydney 1984.

Gusevich, Miriam, 'Purity and Transgression: Reflections on the Architectural Avantgarde's Rejection of Kitsch', Working Paper, Center for Twentieth Century Studies, University of Wisconsin-Milwaukee, 1986.

Haraway, Donna, 'A Manifesto for Cyborgs: Science, Technology and Socialist Feminism in the 1980s', *Socialist Review*, no. 80, 1985.

Hartsock, Nancy C. M., *Money, Sex, and Power: Toward a Feminist Historical Materialism*, Boston 1985.

Hermann, Claudine, *Les Voleuses de langue*, Paris 1976.

Hill, Ernestine, *The Great Australian Loneliness*, Melbourne 1940.

Hutcheon, Linda, *Narcissistic Narrative: the Metafictional Paradox*, Ontario 1980.

Hutcheon, Linda, 'A Poetics of Postmodernism', *Diacritics*, vol. 13, no. 4, 1983.

Hutcheon, Linda, *A Theory of Parody: The Teachings of Twentieth Century Art Forms*, New York and London 1985.

Hutcheon, Linda, 'Beginning to Theorize Postmodernism', *Textual Practice*, vol. 1, no. 1, 1987.

Irigaray, Luce, *Speculum de l'autre femme*, Paris 1974; *Speculum of the Other Woman*, Ithaca 1985.

Irigaray, Luce, *Ce sexe qui n'en est pas un*, Paris 1977; *This Sex Which is Not One*, Ithaca 1985.

Jacobus, Mary, ed., *Women Writing and Writing About Women*, London 1979.

Jardine, Alice, *Gynesis: Configurations of Woman and Modernity*, Ithaca and London 1985.

Jardine, Alice, and Smith, Paul, *Men in Feminism*, New York and London 1987.

Jayamanne, Laleen and Rodrigo, Anna, 'To Render the Body Ecstatic', *Fade to Black*, Sydney College of the Arts Occasional Publication, 1985.

Jayamanne, Laleen, Kapur, Geeta and Rainer, Yvonne, 'Discussing Modernity, "Third World", and *The Man Who Envied Women*', *Art & Text*, nos. 23/4, 1987.

Jennings, Kate, *Come To Me My Melancholy Baby*, Melbourne 1975.

Johnson, Barbara, *The Critical Difference: Essays in the Contemporary Rhetoric of Reading*, Baltimore and London 1980.

Johnson, Barbara, 'Thresholds of Difference: Structures of Address in Zora Neale Hurston', in Henry Louis L. Gates, ed., *'Race', Writing, and Difference, Critical Inquiry*, vol. 12, no. 1, 1985.

Johnston, Jill, *Gullibles Travels*, New York and London 1974.

Jones Lyndal, 'Prediction Piece # 9', *Art & Text*, no. 9, 1983.

Kaplan, Cora, *Sea Changes: Culture and Feminism*, London 1986.

Kelly, Mary, 'Re-viewing Modernist Criticism', *Screen*, vol. 22, no. 3, 1981.

Kofman, Sarah, *Nietzsche et la métaphore*, Paris 1972.

Kofman, Sarah, *Comment s'en sortir?*, Paris 1983.

Kofman, Sarah, *Un métier impossible*, Paris 1983.

Kofman, Sarah, *L'Enigme de la femme*, Paris 1980; *The Enigma of Woman*, Ithaca 1985.

Kramarae, Cheris and Treichler, Paula A., *A Feminist Dictionary*, Boston, London and Henley 1985.

Krauss, Rosalind E., *The Originality of the Avant-Garde and Other Modernist Myths*, Cambridge, Mass. and London 1985.

Kristeva, Julia, *Desire in Language: A Semiotic Approach to Literature and Art*, Oxford 1980.

Kristeva, Julia, *The Kristeva Reader*, ed., Toril Moi, Oxford 1986.

de Lauretis, Teresa, *Alice Doesn't: Feminism, Semiotics, Cinema*, Indiana 1984.

de Lauretis, Teresa ed., *Feminist Studies/Critical Studies*, Indiana, 1986.

de Lauretis, Teresa, *Technologies of Gender: Essays on Theory, Film and Fiction*, Indiana 1987.

Lawson, Sylvia, *The Archibald Paradox: A Strange Case of Authorship*, London and Sydney 1983.

Le Doeuff, Michèle, 'Women and Philosophy', *Radical Philosophy*, no. 17, 1977.

Le Doeuff, Michèle, 'Operative Philosophy: Simone de Beauvoir and Existentialism', *Governing the Present, I&C*, no. 6, 1979.

Le Doeuff, Michèle, *L'Imaginaire philosophique*, Paris 1980.

Le Doeuff, Michèle, 'Pierre Roussel's Chiasmas', *Life, Labour and Insecurity, I&C*, no. 9, 1981/2.

Lewitt, Vivienne Shark, 'Why Egyptian Mods Didn't Bother to Bleach Their Hair or More Notes about Parkas and Combs', *Art & Text*, no. 3, 1981.

Lewitt, Vivienne Shark, 'The End of Civilisation Part 2: Love Among The Ruins', *Art & Text*, no. 10, 1983.

Lippard, Lucy, *Changing: Essays in Art Criticism*, New York 1971.

Lloyd, Genevieve, *The Man of Reason: 'Male' and 'Female' in Western Philosophy*, London 1984.

Long, Elizabeth, 'Reading Groups and The Postmodern Crisis of Cultural Authority', *Cultural Studies*, vol. 1, no. 3, 1987.

McRobbie, Angela, 'Settling Accounts with Subcultures', *Screen Education*, no. 34, 1980.

McRobbie, Angela, 'The Politics of Feminist Research: Between Talk, Text and Action', *Feminist Review*, no. 12, 1982.

McRobbie, Angela, 'Strategies of Vigilance, an Interview with Gayatri Chakravorty Spivak', *Block*, no. 10, 1985.

McRobbie, Angela, 'Postmodernism and Popular Culture', *Postmodernism*, ICA Documents 4, London 1986.

McRobbie, Angela and Nava, Mica, eds, *Gender and Generation*, London 1984.

Marini, Marcelle, *Territoires du féminin avec Marguerite Duras*, Paris 1977.

Marks, Elaine and de Courtivron, eds, *New French Feminisms*, Amherst 1980.

Mellencamp, Patricia, 'Film History and Sexual Economics', *Enclitic*, vol. 7, no. 2, 1983.

Mellencamp, Patricia, 'Postmodern TV: Wegman and Smith', *Afterimage*, vol. 13, no. 5, 1985.

Mellencamp, Patricia, 'Situation and Simulation', *Screen*, vol. 26, no. 2, 1985.

Mellencamp, Patricia, 'Uncanny Feminism: The Exquisite Corpses of Cecilia Condit', *Framework*, nos. 32/3, 1986.

Mellencamp, Patricia, 'Images of Language and Indiscreet Dialogue – 'The Man Who Envied Women'' ', *Screen*, vol. 28, no. 2, 1987.

Mellencamp, Patricia, 'Last Seen in the Streets of Modernism', Hawaiian Film Festival, publication forthcoming.

Miller, Nancy K., ed., *The Poetics of Gender*, New York 1986.

Millett, Kate, *Sexual Politics*, London 1970.

Minh-ha, Trinh T., 'The Plural Void: Barthes and Asia', *SubStance*, no. 36, 1982.

Minh-ha, Trinh T., ed., *The Inappropriate/d Other*, *Discourse*, no. 8, 1986/7.

Mitchell, Juliet, *Woman's Estate*, London 1971.

Mitchell, Juliet, *Psychoanalysis and Feminism*, London 1974.

Mitchell, Juliet, and Oakley, Anne, eds, *The Rights and Wrongs of Women*, Harmondsworth 1976.

Modleski, Tania, *Loving with a Vengeance: Mass-Produced Fantasies for Women*, New York and London 1982.

Modleski, Tania, 'Femininity as Mas(s)querade: A Feminist Approach to Mass Culture' in Colin MacCabe, ed., *High Theory/Low Culture*, Manchester 1986.

Modleski, Tania, ed., *Studies in Entertainment: Critical Approaches to Mass Culture*, Indiana 1986.

Moi, Toril, *Sexual/Textual Politics: Feminist Literary Theory*, London and New York 1985.

Montrelay, Michèle, *L'Ombre et le nom, sur la fémininité*, Paris 1977.

Moore, Catriona and Muecke, Stephen, 'Racism and the Representation of Aborigines in Film', *Australian Cultural Studies*, vol. 2, no. 1, 1984.

Morgan, Robin, ed., *Sisterhood Is Powerful*, New York 1970.

Morgan, Robin, *Monster*, private printing, 1972.

Mouffe, Chantal, 'Radical Democracy: Modern or Postmodern' in Andrew Ross, ed., *Universal Abandon? The Politics of Postmodernism*, Minnesota 1988.

Mouffe, Chantal and Laclau, Ernesto, *Hegemony and Socialist Strategy: Towards a Radical Democratic Politics*, London 1985.

Mulvey, Laura, 'Visual Pleasure and Narrative Cinema', *Screen*, vol. 16, no. 3, 1975.

Pateman, Carole, *The Problem of Political Obligation*, Cambridge 1985.

Pateman, Carole and Gross, Elizabeth, eds, *Feminist Challenges: Social and Political Theory*, Sydney, London and Boston 1986.

Penley, Constance, 'The Avant-Garde and Its Imaginary', *Camera Obscura*, no. 2, 1977.

Penley, Constance, 'Time Travel, Primal Scene, and the Critical Dystopia', *Camera Obscura*, no. 15, 1986.

Petro, Patrice, 'Mass Culture and the Feminine: The "Place" of Television in Film Studies', *Cinema Journal*, vol. 25, no. 3, 1986.

Petro, Patrice, 'Modernity and Mass Culture in Weimar: Contours of a Discourse on Sexuality in Early Theories of Perception and Representation', *New German Critique*, no. 40, 1987.

Petro, Patrice, *Joyless Streets: Women and Melodramatic Representation in Weimar Germany*, Princeton 1988.

Pratt, Mary Louise, 'Interpretive Strategies/Strategic Interpretations: On Anglo-American Reader-Response Criticism', in Jonathan Arac, ed., *Postmodernism and Politics*, Manchester 1986.

Probyn, Elizabeth, 'Bodies and Anti-Bodies: Feminism and the Postmodern', *Cultural Studies*, vol. 1, no. 3, 1987.

Rich, Adrienne, *Of Woman Born: Motherhood as Experience and Institution*, London 1977.

Rich, Adrienne, *On Lies, Secrets and Silence, Selected Prose 1966–1978*, London 1980.

Richard, Nelly, 'Body Without Soul: On the Mechanism of Quotation in the Pictorial Materialism of Juan Davila', *Art & Text*, nos. 12–13, 1984.

Richard, Nelly, 'Notes Towards a (Critical) Re-evaluation of the Critique of the Avant-Garde', *Art & Text*, no. 16, 1984.

Richard, Nelly, 'Love in Quotes: On the Painting of Juan Davila', in Paul Taylor, ed., *Hysterical Tears: Juan Davila*, Melbourne 1985.

Richard, Nelly, 'Margins and Institutions: Art in Chile Since 1973'. *Art & Text*, no. 21, 1986.

Rose, Jacqueline, *Sexuality in the Field of Vision*, London 1986.

van Rossum-Guyon, Françoise, ed., *Ecriture, fémininité, féminisme*, *Revue des sciences humaines*, no. 168, 1977-4.

Rowbotham, Sheila, *Hidden from History*, London 1974.

Russ, Joanna, *How to Suppress Women's Writing*, Austin 1983.

Schor, Naomi, *Breaking the Chain: Women, Theory and French Realist Fiction*, Columbia 1985.

Schor, Naomi, *Reading in Detail: Aesthetics and the Feminine*, New York and London 1987.

Schor, Naomi and Majewski, Henry F., eds, *Flaubert and Postmodernism*, Nebraska 1984.

Showalter, Elaine, *A Literature of Their Own; British Women Novelists from Bronte to Lessing*, Princeton 1977.

Showalter, Elaine, ed., *The New Feminist Criticism: Essays on Women, Literature, Theory*, New York 1985.

Silverman, Kaja, *The Subject of Semiotics*, New York and Oxford, 1983.

Smock, Anne, 'Learn to Read, She Said', *October*, no. 41, 1987.

Solanas, Valerie, *The Scum Manifesto*, London 1983.

Sontag, Susan, *Against Interpretation*, New York 1966.

Sontag, Susan, *On Photography*, London 1977.

Sontag, Susan, *I, etcetera*, London 1979.

Sontag, Susan, *Under the Sign of Saturn*, New York 1981.

Spivak, Gayatri Chakravorty, 'Displacement and the Discourse of Woman', in Mark Krupnick, ed., *Displacement: Derrida and After*, Indiana 1983.
Spivak, Gayatri Chakravorty, *In Other Worlds: Essays in Cultural Politics*, New York and London 1987.
Stanton, Domna C., ed., *The Female Autograph*, New York, 1984.
Stein, Gertrude, *How Writing is Written*, Los Angeles 1974.
Stein, Gertrude, *How to Write*, Toronto and London 1975.
Stern, Lesley, 'The Body as Evidence', *Screen*, vol. 23, no. 5, 1982.
Suleiman, Susan Rubin, *Authoritarian Fictions: The Ideological Novel As a Literary Genre*, New York 1983.
Suleiman, Susan Rubin, ed., *The Female Body in Western Culture*, Cambridge, Mass. and London 1986.
Whiteside, Anna and Issacharoff, Michael, eds, *On Referring in Literature*, Indiana 1987.
Williamson, Judith, *Consuming Passions: The Dynamics of Popular Culture*, London and New York 1986.
Wilson, Elizabeth, *Adorned in Dreams: Fashion and Modernity*, London 1985.
Wolff, Janet, 'The Invisible Flaneuse: Women and the Literature of Modernity', *The Fate of Modernity, Theory Culture & Society*, vol. 2, no. 3, 1985.

The above bibliography has been reprinted by kind permission of Verso publishers.

NOTES

1 The question is anticipated, however, by Meaghan Morris in her discussion of the absence of women's names and women's voices from postmodern texts written and referenced by contemporary male critics who, as is customary, continue to cite each other and not the work of women even as they lament our absence. See especially the Introduction to Morris (1988).

2 'Our present is like being lost in the wilderness, where every pine and rock and bay appears to us as both known and unknown, and therefore as uncertain pointers on the way back to human habitation. The sun is hidden by the clouds and the usefulness of our ancient compasses has been put into question. Even what is beautiful – has been made equivocal for us both in detail and in definition' (Grant 1969: 52).

3 See for example *The Canadian Journal of Political and Social Thought*, and the series of collections edited by Arthur Kroker *et al.* and published by New World Perspectives, Montreal.

4 For example, see Smith (1987).

5 For example, see Foucault (1980).

6 For example, see Sartre (1974).

7 This paper was originally presented at a Conference on Cultural Studies and Communication Studies: Convergences and Diver-

gences, Carleton University, Ottawa, in March/April 1989. It was prepared for a session on Critical Theory and Canadian Culture. The speakers were myself originally from England, Tom Darby originally from the United States, and Bela Egyed originally from Hungary, all of us speaking with the appropriate accents.

8 Appendix 1. Taken from Meaghan Morris (1988: 17-23).

REFERENCES

Althusser, L. (1971) 'Ideology and ideological state apparatuses', *Lenin and Philosophy*, London: New Left Books.

Bennett, T. (1989) Presentation at Carleton University, March/April.

Cooper, B. (1986) 'Hegelian imperialism', in T. Darby (ed.) *Sojourns in The New World*, Ottawa: Carleton Library Series, Carleton University Press.

Darby, T. (1986a) 'Preface' in T. Darby (ed.) *Sojourns in The New World*, Ottawa: Carleton Library Series, Carleton University Press.

Darby, T. (1986b) 'Reflections on technology: an excursus as introduction' in T. Darby (ed.) *Sojourns in The New World*, Ottawa: Carleton Library Series, Carleton University Press.

Darby, T. (ed.) (1986) *Sojourns in The New World*, Ottawa: Carleton Library Series, Carleton University Press.

Fawcett, B. (1986) *Cambodia: A Book for People Who Find Television Too Slow*, Vancouver: Talon Books.

Finn, G. (1985) 'Patriarchy and pleasure: the pornographic eye/I', *Canadian Journal of Political and Social Theory* ix, 1-2: 81-95.

—— (1989) 'Nobodies speaking: subjectivity, sex and the pornography effect', *Philosophy Today*, Summer: 174-82.

Foucault, M. (1980) *Power/Knowlege*, C. Gordon (ed.), New York, Pantheon Books.

Goldenberg, N. (1990) *Returning Words to Flesh: Feminism, Psychoanalysis, and the Resurrection of the Body*, Boston: Beacon Press.

Grant, G. (1969) *Time as History*, Toronto: Canadian Broadcasting Corporation.

Hutcheons, L. (1988) *The Canadian Postmodern: A Study of Contemporary English-Canadian Fiction*, Oxford, Oxford University Press.

Kroker, A. and Cook, D. (1986) *The Postmodern Scene: Excremental Culture and Hyper Aesthetics*, Montreal: New World Perspectives.

Morris, M. (1988) *The Pirate's Fiancée: Feminism, Reading, Postmodernism*, London and New York: Verso.

Nelson, J. (1987) *The Perfect Machine: Television in the Nuclear Age*, Toronto: Between the Lines.

Rajchman, J. (1987) 'Postmodernism in a nominalist frame', *Flash Art* 137, November/December: 49-51.

Sartre, J. P. (1974) *Between Existentialism and Marxism*. Trans. J. Matthews, London, New Left Books.

Smith, D. (1979) 'A sociology for women' in J. Sherman and E. T. Beck (eds) *Prism of Sex: Essays in the Sociology of Knowledge*, Madison: University of Wisconsin Press.

—— (1987) *The Everyday World as Problematic: A Feminist Sociology*, Toronto: University of Toronto Press.

Part III

CULTURAL STUDIES AND THE LOCAL

6

POSTCARDS OF MY PAST
The Indian as artefact
Gail Guthrie Valaskakis

Postcards of Indians have always attracted me. As a child
growing up on the Lac du Flambeau reservation in Wisconsin, I
remember watching cultural tourists search postcard racks for
images of Indians, familiar faces overpowered by buckskin and
beadwork, horses and headdresses, evidence to supplement the
memories mirrored in their photographs:

> And here's one of an Indian
> selling Ralph a trinket –
> I suppose he'll use the money
> to buy some wine and drink it.
>
> (Bacon 1988: 346)

Even then I knew that Indian postcards had little to do with
Indians. I was drawn to postcards not because they touched some
chord of displaced history or identity, but because they did not.
N. Scott Momaday (1976: 22) writes about the experience of being
a Kiowa Indian: 'Some of my mother's memories have become
my own. That is the real burden of the blood'. These silent,
decorated images masking our struggles for empowerment
remain so removed from memory and daily life in Flambeau.
Postcard Indians have to express another heritage. These are the
representations of others, aboriginals transformed in the non-
native social imaginary and frozen in fragments: Indians as
academic artefacts. Yet I claim them as my own.

Postcard Indians have long been appropriated in Canadian
cultural products and processes, where they stand in silent
contradiction to the memories and lived experiences of Indians.
From the romantic representations of Canadian Pacific Railway
ads on the beauty of Banff and vulgar stereotypes of plastic,

CULTURAL STUDIES AND THE LOCAL

pot-bellied Indian banks and cross-eyed, wind-up toys, to the marginalized Indians of historical and political process, Canadian images of Indians have worked to construct a discourse of subordination.

In the summer of 1990, this discourse expanded to absorb images of Oka: sovereignty filtered through the lenses of Mohawks and police; army and politicians, townspeople, and reporters; negotiating, stone-throwing, scuffling; guns and gambling.[1] Today, representations of warriors stand as postcards of Indians asserting self-determination. And as Indians themselves struggle over claiming and disclaiming the warriors, over the threats and promises of appropriated images and their polarized assertions of identity, Indians and others are locked in broader confrontations of identity and power voiced in issues of aboriginal rights and resources, cultural tourism and cultural trespassing. Logging in British Columbia and northern Ontario; hydro development in Alberta and northern Quebec; low-level flights in Labrador; hunting in New Brunswick; fishing on the West Coast; art and artefacts and 'grave goods'; Indian stories and films – all contested territories with struggles over cultural identity, sovereignty and self-determination related to what Michael Ames (1987: 14) calls the 'ethnological fate' of Indians. And across Canada, Indians stood behind Elijah Harper, the only native in the Manitoba legislature, as he acted to block the nation's tenuous constitutional accord, a merger pasted together without assuring the participation or rights of women or multicultural and aboriginal Canadians.[2]

The pan-Indian support for Elijah Harper's action was reminiscent of 1988, when Indians across the country joined the land claims struggle of the Lubicon Nation in Alberta by protesting the Glenbow Museum exhibit of the Olympic Arts Festival in Calgary. The protest of 'The Spirit Sings: Artistic Traditions of Canada's First People' revealed the political relationship between museums and aboriginal rights, and the extent to which the ethnographic constructions fundamental to both are reflected in historical, literary, and artistic practice. Bruce Trigger, an anthropologist who joined the protest, writes:

> The Spirit Sings has shown that at least one major Canadian museum is still prepared to mount an exhibition in the face of protests from associations representing almost

all native groups across Canada who in this instance were outraged that a show glorifying the creativity of native peoples at the time of European discovery should be sponsored by an oil company that is currently engaged in destroying the traditional economy and way of life of the Lubicon Lake Cree.

(Trigger 1988a: 15)

Tom Hill, who is the Director of the Woodland Cultural Centre Museum of the Six Nations Reserve in Ontario, has remarked that this exhibit might more accurately have been named, 'The Tourist Sings' in celebration of the souvenirs collected from 'real red Indians' by the earliest European tourists in America (Hill 1988). And Indian artist Joane Cardinal-Shubert (1989: 23) writes: 'The exhibition was called "The Spirit Sings" but it pushed the notion that native culture was dead, wrapped up, over and collected'. These are new voices arising from Indians and anthropologists. Like People of First Nations and artists, they are tenuous allies whose current practice and concerns threaten to freeze them in opposition to each other.

Reflexive writing in anthropology continues to propel an increasingly tired and incestuous ethnographic turn. Fabian (1983), Marcus and Fischer (1986), Clifford (1987, 1988), Geertz (1988) and others discuss the extent to which ethnography is caught by the definition of the task, in the conflicting social realities of experiencing and researching and writing. It is a perspective which, in the process of turning in upon itself, confronts the distance reflecting time and culture and technique which forms a symbiotic knot between the aboriginal and the academic other. Grounded in the axis of encountering and textualizing otherness, this anthropological discourse struggles with 'the reign of worn codes' (Minh-ha 1989: 47), concepts that constrain Indian practice to the past of an 'ethnographic present' and the stasis of empirical analysis. But the problem revealed in the politics of difference is even more basic than as Geertz (1988: 84) suggests 'to represent the research process in the research product'. To the studied, the critique of ethnography is significant because it probes the framework of the subaltern experience and provokes a discursive opening to expose and to understand the subordinated voice. As Lawrence Grossberg writes: 'A reconception of ethnography must begin by recognizing precisely

157

that there is a "reality", an otherness which is not merely its mark of difference within our signifying systems' (Grossberg 1988: 381-2). Without devaluing the conditions of subordination which produce silence (Spivak 1988), Grossberg challenges ethnography to recognize that 'it does matter who is acting and from where; it does matter that the subject is both an articulated site and a site of ongoing articulation within its own history' (Grossberg 1988: 384).

It is this 'reality' embedded in the intertwined, articulating positions of history and heritage that is played out in the memories and lived experience of Indians, both among themselves and with outsiders in the contemporary sites of Canadian Indian cultural struggle: the representational practice of ethnography and art, museums and literature; and the political process of land claims, treaty rights and more recently, constitutional change. In these arenas, Indians and others are engaged in pitched battles over issues of appropriation: territorial, cultural, personal. This struggle to assert control over images, and identities and localities is, at another level, a dispute about representation, power, and identity, and the social reality in which these are expressed and lived in political process and popular culture.

Native reality is grounded in the kaleidoscopic experience of being inscribed as subaltern in the history of others and as subjects in one's own heritage. For Indians, these are placements built upon contradictory social imaginaries, representations of otherness prescribed by the missionary, the merchant, the military which, as Virginia Domingues writes, 'are inherently appropriative and hierarchical' (Domingues 1987: 131-2). These images, entrenched in the relationship between aboriginal peoples and outsiders are widely acknowledged in literary criticism as manifestations of 'American double-mindedness about the Indian' (Pearce 1967: 76). The way in which this 'double-mindedness' works to construct what Homi Bhabha (1984) calls 'the ambivalence of colonial discourse' has been less important to anthropology than reconstructing historical Indian practice and, more recently, the practice of ethnography itself. How the contradictions embedded in discourse are enacted among insiders, and are acted upon by outsiders, is of interest to writers from Memmi (1965) and Fanon (1967) to Said (1979), Spivak (1988) and Stuart Hall (1981). Their enquiries reveal a bond between academic construction and the domination of discourse, a position which prods ethnography to move beyond the description and meaning of texts (Clifford 1988: 23) to voice the reality of the other, and lays bare the web connecting academic and artistic representations of Indians, personal experience, collective memory, and political process.

In the resurgent Indianness of the mid-1970s, I remember being among a group of Indians who protested an auction of native artefacts at the Ritz Carlton Hotel in Montreal. We circled the entrance, then stood silently in the ballroom. Someone carried a sign saying 'How many beaver pelts for the Mona Lisa?' We watched as people bid: a pair of Blackfoot burial moccasins, a child's doll, a ceremonial dress, and a piece of parflesh. Just before the police ushered us out, a Cree from Mistassini named Morley Loon slipped off one of his workboots, held it high and said, 'How much will you pay for this Indian boot, worn by a real Indian?'

Indians have always known that collecting is at the heart of ethnographic practice. This reality is expressed by Tom Hill (1988) who, in the ambiguity of humour, speaks of Indians experiencing the earliest tourists in America through their propensity to collect souvenirs – and those who made the souvenir – all for European markets. It is collecting as conceptualized in James Clifford's 'salvage anthropology' with its 'desire to rescue "authenticity" out of destructive historical change' (Clifford 1987: 121) which is the basis of what a Mohawk artist calls 'the politics of primitivism' (Jacobs 1986: 3), a discourse which constructs what outsiders – and Indians – know about native peoples in representations of Indianness: tribal and traditional, other and unequal. In the words of Deborah Doxtator 'People growing up in the 1950's and 60's were conditioned to believe that "Real Indianness" had something to do with not talking very much, never smiling, wearing fringed clothing, being mystical, being poor, riding horses' (Doxtator 1988: 26).

As we worked to renew Indian identity through education in the 1970s, I remember the wars of heritage we waged at Manitou College.[3] One long night we sat, Mohawk and Ojibway, Chippewa, and non-Indian, pressed together in words over a soul-searing question of the times: Is it Indian to watch Rudolf Nureyev dance?

Collecting – customs and clothes; images and memories and idioms; spoons and songs and spirits – removes or redefines the lived significations of identity and power. The significance and the extent of this cultural appropriation is suggested in a conversation between the anthropologist Irving Hallowell and an Ojibway elder: 'Since stones are grammatically animate, I once asked an old man: "Are all stones we see about us here alive?" He reflected a long while and then replied, "No! But some are" ' (Hallowell 1960: 24).

For Indians, objects and subjects are collected by someone else, then absorbed or transformed to disappear or reappear as something else. But because meaning is never confined to the text in these negotiations, it is misleading to assume that 'From cigar store Indian, to cowboy and Indian movies, to the "noble savage", native people live in a prison of images not of their own making' (Alexander 1986: 45). Indians may claim these images as their own; and they also internalize the experience suggested by artist Norval Morriseau who has said: 'Whenever you are looking at my pictures, you are looking at my visions' (quoted in the *Globe and Mail*, 4 March 1989: C13). In the words of Paula Gunn Allen: 'A contemporary American Indian is always faced with a dual perception of the world: that which is particular to American Indian life, and that which exists ignorant of that life' (Allen 1986: 161).

Indians live in a *prism* of images, experienced in 'contradictory symbols of Indianness' (Doxtator 1988) related to history and experience, consumerism and popular culture which a recent exhibition at the Woodland Cultural Centre in Ontario called 'Fluffs and Feathers':

> What is Fluff? Fluff is artificial, highly coloured decorative soft stuff ornamenting Indian tourist products. What is Feather? Feather is from a creature that soars between earth and the heavens, symbolizing the spiritual, social, political reality of Indian culture.
>
> (Bedard 1989: 2)

There is, of course, no border between feather and fluff. The two are interwoven in Indian heritage: transformed, enacted, and contested. The struggle to inscribe the reality of Indian experience in the memories of others is a disquieting task. For historians who recognize that 'native people have been a determining factor in Canadian history' (Fisher and Coates 1988: 2), Indian heritage is valued to mark the difference within dominant signifying systems rather than for its historical substance. Bruce Trigger writes about the silence of Indian history:

> Even less has been done to integrate what native people write about their past with academic studies of native history. It is, however, clearly wrong to dismiss such work as only polemical or of ethnological interest. On the contrary, what native people currently believe about their history may provide valuable insights into the significance of that history.
>
> (Trigger 1988b: 35)

This distinction between native heritage and 'real' history is linked to representations which in Canada reinforce the dominant culture's understanding of the Indian as, in the words of Margaret Atwood, 'both tormentor and sufferer; the villain and the victim' (Atwood 1972: 102). Drawn from the image of the savage as noble or evil, neither representation allows newcomers to identify native peoples as equal, to recognize them as 'real inhabitants of a land' (p. 105). Like the companion myths of the frontier or the pioneer, these representations conceal the structured subordination of Indians in a country carved out by companies and charters, proclamations and promises. Like so many other countries, Canada illustrates that 'the nation has played a critical historical role in defining what a modern conception of history should be' (Dirks 1990: 25). As '[h]istory came to mean the deployment of reason in the real world' (p. 25), postcard images of Indians glossed over the reality of aboriginal peoples and their respective political structures. Louis Hall writes of the Iroquois Confederacy:

> The European immigrants call us tribes. A tribe is primitive man's first attempt at social order . . . It's an insulting term . . . When the Europeans came to America they made treaties with the Indians and in doing so, recognized them as nations . . . Only nations can make treaties.
>
> (L. K. Hall n.d.: 32)

From the Indian perspective, even Canada's Royal Proclamation of 1763, which speaks of 'the several Nations or Tribes of Indians with whom we are connected' (Asch 1984: 57–8), is grounded in contradictory representations of Indians. And these diverging representations form the framework for continuing, conflicting perceptions of native rights on ceded and reserved land, and of the treaties themselves.

> Indian people view treaties as reaffirmations of their sovereignty and rights and as agreements to allow settlement in certain areas, non-Indians regard treaties as an extinguishment of rights, an acceptance of the supremacy of the Crown, and a generous gift of land to the Indians so they might have land of their own.
>
> (House of Commons 1983: 12)

In the spreading pan-Indianism of the 1970s, I remember being among a group of Indians who travelled to Ottawa for the memorial of Nelson Small Legs, Jr.[4] We were absorbed in ambivalence as we listened to the rhetoric of raised fists echoing from Alcatraz, Wounded Knee, and Rosebud.[5] But there among the appropriated red berets and armbands, we recognized something of ourselves in the death masks of the tenuous Canadian connection to the American Indian Movement: Anna Mae Aqwash, Richard Oakes and his daughter, and Nelson Small Legs, Jr. In the sullen darkness of the journey home, someone spoke of the 1969 White Paper, the 'Statement of the Government of Canada on Indian Policy' proposing to remove the status of Indian people entrenched in Canada's Indian Act, recalling that '[u]nderscoring every contemporary struggle by indigenous peoples – be it against specific damage, or for cultural and political self-determination – is the demand for land rights' (Moody 1988, vol. I: 355). In the silence, we could almost hear the drumbeats begin, signalling the Mohawk occupations of Racket Point, Ganyiegeh and Akwesasne.[6]

To the non-native, treaties are the historical products of benevolent conquest, artefacts of reasonable (if not equitable) surrender. To aboriginal peoples, treaties are a process, exercises of ritualized land acquisition and resource exploitation. For Indians, there is no surrender, only mutual sovereignty, nations abstracted from nation-states, recognized through agreements in which self-determination is the common ground. This is not the self-government of Indian councils grafted onto Canadian municipalities; but self-determination 'bound up with sovereignty in all its ramifications – social, cultural, political, econ-

omic'; that which in the Mohawk language, translates as 'carry-
ing ourselves' (*Tribune Juive* 1989: 5).

The political distance between native reality and others in
Canada is represented in the four Constitutional Conferences
held between 1983 and 1987 to define aboriginal rights, each of
which became mired in the discursive questioning of identity and
power. Who is aboriginal? Whose values? Whose self-government? Whose land? Whose God? This framework was established
at the outset when the first conference opened with Chief Many
Bears beginning an Indian prayer and Prime Minister Pierre
Trudeau interrupting: 'Are you going to pray every morning, in
public?' To the answer, 'Yes, Sir', Trudeau replied, 'Then
everybody should pray to his own God, and we'll have a moment
of meditation' (Bulbulian 1987). Everyone did, and the subsequent isolation, ambiguity and confusion of political prayers in
English and French, Indian languages and Inuktitut echoed the
cultural distance between the reality of aboriginal land and life
and the treaty table. The provincial premiers left the last meeting
with no sense of common ground, unaware of the irony in
announcing: 'We will go home and solve the real problems of
aboriginal peoples' (Bulbulian 1987).

In the resurgent Indianness of today, Jim Thunder, a Plains
Cree from Alberta, remembers a dream about the 150-year-old
medicine bundle from the American Museum of Natural History
in New York, and he says, 'I wouldn't run from Alberta for an
historical artefact. This is alive. It has power' ('Newswatch', CBC
TV, 21 Feb 1989).[7]

> The bundle, a sack containing sweetgrass, a bear's paw and
> tobacco was turned over to an anthropologist from the
> museum in 1934 by Big Bear's son, Jim Pimi . . . [who]
> asked the museum to 'keep it well, keep it there . . . Is the
> museum to violate the trust placed in it by persons who
> deliver things to the museum?'
>
> (*The Gazette*, 23 March 1989: B5)

In the non-native cultural construction of the museum, so far
removed from the treaty table and the experience of sweat lodges
and story-telling elders, beaded history belts, and mnemonic
birch bark scrolls, Indians remember their heritage. This is not
an exercise in remembered identity stripped off, then pasted back
on to become the anthropologist's 'revitalization' (Minh-ha 1989:

59). It is the collective memory about which Homi Bhabha writes: 'Re-membering is never a quiet act of introspection. It is a painful remembering, a putting together of the dismembered past to make sense of the trauma of the present' (Bhabha 1987: 123). But Indian heritage which is framed in historical reconstruction of the past draws equally upon the contemporary social memory of lived experience: real and imagined, ambivalent and prescribed, tentative and transforming. As Paul Connerton (1989) suggests, societies remember through historical reconstruction and the celebration of collective events. And in the cultural formation of everyday life – individual and collective – Indians entrench the social memory and identity of heritage. It is the intertwined experiences and collapsed time of cultural formation which make the academic tasks of unravelling and interpreting the meaning in 'traces' of cultural evidence so problematic. And as the conceptual approach of historians and anthropologists positions them as 'their own authority' (Connerton 1989: 13) through the collection of cultural evidence and the interpretation of its meaning, the recognition and understanding of native social reality remains elusive and rare.

For Indians, museums like art and literature are sites of re-membering, re-collecting; living locations of the contradictory articulations Indians experience in history and heritage and everyday life. Here, amid the feathers and fluffs of Indian cultural and political process – the condolence cane and the bear claw necklace, the silver cross and the raven mask and Hudson Bay blanket coat – and the skeletal remains, 'grave goods' and medicine bags of tribal ancestors (Preston 1989: 66) – Indians and anthropologists confront each other over issues which are aptly expressed in Bruce Trigger's question: 'Who owns the past?' (1988a: 13). Along with land and treaty rights, Indians are laying claim to native objects and images, to museums and to history; in short, to aboriginal heritage, reconstructed, lived and imagined. In Canada, this move to transform the present by recovering the past has contributed to a new debate reclaiming memory, experience and imagination.

As I worked to reconstruct my own identity as an academic and an Indian in the 1970s, I remember reading *Mountain Wolf-Woman, Sister of Crashing Thunder: the Autobiography of a Winnebago Indian*, a text tape-recorded in Winnebago and English, transcribed, then written and annotated by Nancy Lurie

(1966), Curator of Indian Ethnography at the Milwaukee Public Museum. I recognized glimpses of my Chippewa great-grand-mother in Mountain Wolf Woman's story. My great-grand-mother lived across the road and I remember being there as vividly as I remember being home until I was eighteen years old, when I went away to school and she died. I listened in that book to the whispers of my great-grandmother's history and her heritage. But it was years later, reading N. Scott Momaday's *The Way to Rainy Mountain* (1969) and *The Names* (1976) when I realized that, beyond all the contradictions which I myself represent, some of her memories have become my own:

> The journey herein recalled continues to be made anew each time the miracle comes to mind . . . It is a whole journey, intricate with motion and meaning; and it is made with the whole memory, that experience of the mind that is legendary as well as historical, personal as well as cultural.
>
> (Momaday 1976: 4)

In Lac du Flambeau, where postcards were once the reflection of our otherness, Indians today associate cultural tourism with cultural trespassing. This perspective is equally evident in the Canadian literary community, where the 'Women's Press Debate' 'began with whether white writers should be allowed to publish work in which they adopted the voices of persons of colour' (Begamudre 1989: 11–12). For Indian writers and artists, this debate has revealed the power of appropriated identity.

As we worked to build urban Indian services in the 1970s and 1980s, I remember someone at the Native Friendship Centre passing me a book written by W. P. Kinsella, a non-Indian who has published six collections of Indian stories about the Ermine-skin family of Hobbema Reserve in Alberta, all a mixture of fact and fiction drawn from his real experience as a taxi driver in Edmonton, Alberta, and his construction of Indian social imaginaries: Frank Fence-post, Silas One-wound, Mad Etta. I remember being among a group of Indians who travelled the western powwow circuit in the summers of those years. We moved from the elder's speeches and buffalo feasts in the lush foothills of Morley through the dusty back roads to celebrate the struggle of Hobbema and the Métis spirit of 'Back to Batoche'. And I remember George Brown, Sr, the first Tribal chairman of my own reservation in Lac du Flambeau. George Brown seemed to hold that position for all the years of my childhood, a dignified full-blood living out at the old village who spoke in a ponderous voice, trying his best to manoeuvre us through the forced appropriation of foreign political process. No one had ever doubted that he was a real Indian. Yet W. P. Kinsella writes of his namesake at Hobbema:

> The family name was originally Two-brown-bears, and both of Lester Brown's brothers still carry that name. For as long as I can remember Lester and his family just called themselves the Browns. Then four or five years ago Lester hired himself a lawyer and get his name, and his wife and kids' names, changed from Two-brown-bears to Brown. I remember seeing the change-of-name notice on the back page of the *Wetaskiwin Times* newspaper. 'Why carry around a ten pound name when a two pound one will do?' Lester joke with everybody. But it be kind of a sad joke, and us *real* Indians look down our noses at the Browns, take that name change as just another way Lester Brown have of turning himself into a white man. Lester is a friend of our chief, Tom Crow-eye, who, though he ain't changed his name yet, is whiter than most people born with pink skin.
>
> (Kinsella 1983: 45)

Today, Indians and others struggle over the stereotyping, appropriation and the politics of primitivism expressed in Aislin's cartoon of the mafia-warrior (*The Gazette*, 30 April 1990);[8] or the question put by Ven Begamudre: 'Do we really need another rediscovery of Saskatchewan's native peoples by a white photographer born in Britain?' (Begamudre 1989: 12); or the shamanistic adaptations of new age Indian philosophy with its White Warrior Society. This dispute over ownership and authenticity is expressed in the spontaneous, pained, often vulgarized voices of Indians asserting control over the instrumentality of indigenous cultural forms. Their concerns focus on the discourse of conflicting representations basic to academic argument, political discourse and commodity culture: public access and profit. Joane Cardinal-Shubert writes from the Indian perspective: 'Money, that is what appropriating is all about. Whether the issue is land or art or iconography or ceremonial reliquae, the focus of the deprivation is money. Something to be gained by imitation, copying, stealing' (Cardinal-Shubert 1989: 20).

In Quebec's so-called 'Indian Summer of 1990', I remember images of barricades and bulldozers, gunshots in the woods and sudden death. I remember helmets pitted against bandanna masks, interceding women, soldiers struggling, and crying children. And in the silence of all the negotiators' calls for peaceful resolution, I remember two non-natives from Oka who rushed to the patent office to copyright every marketable aspect of the Oka crisis, more than 100 copyrights for games, toys, dolls and bicycles; more than 400 for names such as 'Lasagna' and 'Spudwrench' (CBC News, 19 Oct 1990). This is an open-ended list of ambiguous images for profit – the tormentor and the sufferer, the villain and the victim transformed in the current discourse of identity and power – all used to sell the memories of Kanesatake and Oka.

In the aftermath of Oka, the recollection and expression of our personal and collective memories – ethnographic, artistic, literary and Indian – take on new significance. We stand apart, living together in an increasingly hostile and distrustful social reality in which land, sovereignty and self-determination are ever more urgent in the lived experience of native people. We stand opposed, unaware that we are all rooted to each other in the construction and the appropriation of the contradictory Indian social imaginaries which make native sovereignty and self-determination so important to understand and so difficult to achieve.

NOTES

1 The events that have come to be called 'Oka' are explained in the Introduction to this volume. Prior to the events of 'Oka' which occurred during the summer of 1990, there had also been confrontations between non-aboriginal authorities and Mohawk Indians over bingo games on reserves in Quebec and (adjacent) New York state.

2 Along with 'Meech Lake' and 'Oka', references to Elijah Harper have become common in Canada's political discourses on relationships between First Nations Peoples and the Canadian state. Harper gained national attention when there was an eleventh hour effort to extend the deadline for ratifying the Meech Lake accord. The Manitoba legislature had to agree to an extension, but their rules required unanimity, and Harper withheld his consent.

3 Manitou College was a native junior college initiated and operated by First Nations in Quebec from 1973 to 1976, when it was closed by the Canadian government.

4 Nelson Small Legs, Jr committed suicide in the early 1970s to protest Canadian inattention to the conditions on Indian reserves.

5 Alcatraz, Wounded Knee and Rosebud were critical sites of Indian struggle in the United States during the late 1960s and early 1970s. In 1973, a confrontation between police and the American Indian Movement lasted over two months and involved the deaths of both FBI agents and Indians.

6 Racket Point, Ganyiegeh and Akwesasne were sites of Canadian Indian protest over land rights in the late 1960s and early 1970s.

7 Jim Thunder ran from Alberta to New York City in 1989 in an attempt to recover the sacred Medicine bundle from the Museum of Natural History.

8 This cartoon, like many others in the summer of 1990, criminalized Indian warriors through association with illegal activities.

REFERENCES

Alexander, D. (1986) 'Prison of images: seizing the means of representation', *Fuse* February/March: 45–6.

Allen, P. G. (1986) *The Sacred Hoop: Recovering the Feminine in American Indian Traditions*, Boston: Beacon.

Ames, M. (1987) 'Free Indians from their ethnological fate', *Muse* Summer, V, 2: 14–19.

Asch, M. (1984) *Home and Native Land: Aboriginal Rights and the Canadian Constitution*, Toronto: Methuen.

Atwood, M. (1972) *Survival: A Thematic Guide to Canadian Literature*, Toronto: Anansi.

Bacon, B. (1988) 'Tourist/home movies', in R. Moody (ed.) *The Indigenous Voice: Visions and Realities*, I, London and New Jersey: Zed Books.

Bedard, J. (1989) 'Fluffs and feathers: a conference on stereotyping', *Wadrihva* January, 3, 1. Brantford, Ontario: Woodland Cultural Centre.

Begamudre, V. (1989) 'On cultural justice and cultural revenges', *Blackflash*, Fall.

Bhabha, Homi (1984) 'Of mimicry and man: the ambivalence of colonial discourse', *October* 28, Spring: 125–33.

—— (1987) 'What does the black man want?', *New Formations* 1, Spring.

Bulbulian, M. (1987) Director, *Dancing Around the Table* (1 & 11) National Film Board of Canada.

Cardinal-Shubert, J. (1989) 'In the red', *Fuse* Fall.

Clifford, J. (1987) 'Of other peoples: beyond the salvage paradigm', in H. Foster (ed.) *Discussions in Contemporary Culture*, 1, DIA Art Foundation Seattle: Bay Press.

—— (1988) 'On ethnographic authority', in J. Clifford (ed.) *The Predicament of Culture: Twentieth Century Ethnography, Literature and Art*, Cambridge and London: Harvard University Press.

Connerton, P. (1989) *How Societies Remember*, Cambridge: Cambridge University Press.

Dirks, N. B. (1990) 'History as a sign of the modern', *Public Culture* 2, Spring: 25–32.

Domingues, V. (1987) 'Of other peoples: beyond the salvage paradigm', in H. Foster (ed.) *Discussions in Contemporary Culture*, 1, DIA Art Foundation, Seattle: Bay Press.

Doxtator, D. (1988) 'The home of the Indian culture and other stories in the museum', *Muse* Autumn, VI, 3: 26–8.

Fabian, J. (1983) *Time and the Other: How Anthropology Makes Its Object*, New York: Columbia University Press.

Fanon, F. (1967) *Black Skin, White Masks*, New York: Grove Press.

Fisher, R. and Coates, K. (1988) *Out of the Background: Readings in Canadian Native History*, Toronto: Copp Clark Pittman.

The Gazette, Montreal, Quebec. 17 March 1990, A3; 23 March 1989, B5; 30 April 1990, B2.

The Globe and Mail, Toronto, 4 March 1989, C13.

Geertz, C. (1988) *Works and Lives: The Anthropologist as Author*, California: Stanford University Press.

Grossberg, L. (1988) 'Wandering audiences, nomadic critics', *Cultural Studies* 2, 3, October: 377–91.

Hall, L. K. (n.d.) 'Rebuilding the Iroquois Confederacy', monograph.

Hall, S. (1981), 'Notes on deconstructing "the popular" ', in R. Samuel (ed.) *People's History and Socialist Theory*, London: Routledge and Kegan Paul.

Hallowell, A. I. (1960) 'Ojibway ontology, behavior and world view', in S. Diamond (ed.) *Cultural in History: Essays in Honor of Paul Radin*, New York: Columbia University Press.

Hill, T. (1988) Paper delivered on 'The pressures of tourism' Panel, Interpretation and Tourism, Ottawa: National Conference on Heritage Interpretation.

House of Commons (1983) Issue no. 40 *Minutes of Proceedings of the Special Committee on Indian Self-Government*, K. Penner, Chair, 12 October and 20 October.

Jacobs, A. A. K. (1986) 'The politics of primitivism: concerns and attitudes in Indian art', *Akwekon* 2/3: 1–3.

Kinsella, W. P. (1983) *The Moccasin Telegraph and Other Stories*, Harmondsworth: Penguin Books.

Lurie, N. O. (ed.) (1966) *Mountain Wolf Woman, Sister of Crashing Thunder: The Autobiography of a Winnebago Indian*, Michigan: Ann Arbor Paperbacks.

Marcus, G. E. and Fisher, M. M. J. (1986) *Anthropology as Cultural Critique*, Illinois: University of Chicago Press.

Memmi, A. (1965) *The Colonizer and the Colonized*, Boston: Beacon.

Minh-ha, T. T. (1989) *Woman Native Other*, Bloomington and Indianapolis: University of Indiana Press.

Momaday, N. S. (1969) *The Way to Rainy Mountain*, Albuquerque: University of New Mexico Press.

—— (1976) *The Names*, New York: Harper and Row.

Moody, R. (ed.) (1988) *The Indigenous Voice: Visions and Realities*, vols. I and II. London and New Jersey: Zed Books.

'Newswatch', Montreal: CBC TV, 21 February 1989.

Pearce, R. H. (1967) *Savagism and Civilization*, Baltimore: Johns Hopkins Press.

Preston, D. J. (1989) 'Skeletons in our museums' closets', *Harpers Magazine*, February: 66–75.

Said, E. W. (1979) *Orientalism*, New York: Vintage Books.

Spivak, G. C. (1988) 'Can the subaltern speak?', in C. Nelson and L. Grossberg (eds) *Marxism and the Interpretation of Culture*, Urbana and Chicago: University of Illinois Press.

The Toronto Star, 22 October 1988, D5.

Tribune Juive (1989) 'Kahnawake'.

Trigger, B. (1988a) 'Who owns the past?', *Muse* Fall, VI, 3: 13–15.

—— (1988b) 'The historian's Indian: Native Americans in Canadian historical writing from Charlevoix to the present', in R. Fisher and K. Coates (eds) *Out of the Background: Readings on Canadian Native History*, Toronto: Copp Clark Pittman.

7

VALUE AND POWER IN MUSIC
An English Canadian perspective[1]
John Shepherd

This chapter is concerned with questions of value and power in music, and, in particular, with the role of value and power in the processes through which cultural identities arise. Despite the considerable attention cultural studies has given recently to issues of nationhood and national and cultural identities, it nonetheless remains customary in everyday common sense to think of national and cultural identities as having an existence or 'substance' over and above that produced by the specific social processes through which they are constructed and reproduced. Nowhere has this notion of substance or 'essence' been more influential than through the terms in which questions of national or cultural identity *in music* have been couched.

Music is frequently thought of as having a culture-specific sound. Sounds are identified in geocultural terms: the Liverpool sound, the Chicago sound, the sounds of reggae, juju and so on. The 'essence' of a geocultural identity is thought, somehow, to be manifest from within music's sounds. Cultural theorists, however, are quick to point out that music's sounds and music's identities are but cultural constructs. In the final analysis, this is undoubtedly the case. However, there is rather more at stake. In being concerned with the everyday, with lived awareness, cultural studies has had a considerable amount to say on the topic of music. However, unlike the study of literature, language, film and television, the study of music has contributed little if anything to the development of cultural studies itself. Reasons for this are discussed below. The point, however, is that the traffic between cultural studies and the analysis of music has been remarkably one-way. Faced with the intensity with which people invest in personal, cultural and national identities through music, and faced with the considerable time and effort expended by musicologists and ethnomusicologists in attempting to pin down this phenomenon in its cultural and sonic dimensions, it will not do simply to fall back on the truism that music's identities and music's sounds are but cultural constructs.

If it is accepted that music's articulation of identity is powerful, and that this power relates intimately and intensely to music's co-ordinates of value (music tends to be loved and hated more than most other cultural forms – acceptance or rejection are the norms, not reasoned response or indifference), then there is something to be explored. The relationship of power to identity has long been a theme of importance in various trajectories of cultural studies. Yet theorizing power's effectivities and theorizing its sources have proved difficult. There remains a tension in cultural studies between those who think of power as being concentrated in the last instance in material processes, and those who conceptualize its sources as being closer to the sites of its effectivities. The difference is a subtle but important one. Those who remain closer to the spirit of Marx do not deny the pervasiveness of processes of power throughout the social formation. However, they tend to think of the operations of power as being characterized and shaped by the social formation (including its cultural aspects) being (to use Althusser's words) 'a structure in dominance'. Those influenced by Foucault tend to conceptualize power as being in a more intrinsic and less extrinsic relation to the specific moments of social and cultural process wherein it is manifest. Power is 'dispersed'.

The particular case of music can be helpful in theorizing relations of power and identity. Music, as we shall see, points up a particular kind of relationship between material processes (in this case – specifically – structure, relations and textures of sound) and the cultural realm, one not traditionally embraced by cultural studies in theorizing processes of signification. The material figures little in traditional theories of signification, except in providing pathways or grounds for the conventional mapping of significance. Yet, outside the realms of the 'textual' or the 'aesthetic' (realms where processes of signification are taken to figure most importantly), material processes (in this case – more generally – material productive forces and material as opposed to social relations of production) can be argued to have more efficacy. In contrast, questions of aesthetics and textuality on the one hand and political economy on the other have receded as concerns oriented towards a more integral conceptualization of institutions and policy become more prominent.

To point out that music's sounds and music's identities are but cultural constructs is to assign them effectively to the realms of the textual and the aesthetic, realms which seem to provide few answers to questions of power and identity. If, as Bennett suggests in his contribution to this volume, it is beneficial to dispense with the time-worn and troubling dichotomy of context and text – to do away with the seeming opposition between the governmental, the institutional and policy fields on the one hand, and postmodernism, textuality and aesthetics on the other, then a reconsideration of music is, indeed, helpful. This is because music's 'textuality', its 'aesthetics', function in a governmental and institutional manner. Music's materiality functions as a medium of placement and as an instrument of power at the same time as it encapsulates and articulates established patterns of social relations. The materiality of music positions and structures, but not in a determining fashion. People position and structure sounds as much as they are positioned and structured by them. Contestedly so. There is perhaps no more a concrete manifestation of Williams' 'structure of feeling' than these materials as they are implicated in processes of identity, both individual and collective.

But is not to claim that music articulates structures of feeling in a concrete fashion from within its material processes once again to essentialize *music*'s processes and to essentialize identities in relation to them? A careful distinction needs to be drawn not only between the sounds of music and music as cultural process, but also between cultural identities as they arise in specific social and historical circumstances, and cultural identities as they take on a life in everyday common-sense consciousness independent of the specificities of the social and historical processes which produced them. The reality of the former, imbricated with music's concrete yet symbolic power, can frequently become the essence of the latter.

If this paper is concerned with questions of value and power in music from the particular perspective of music's involvement with processes of identity, then it is important that this perspective be grounded in a set of cultural processes where a transfer from reality to essence is difficult. Such a grounding is provided

173

through a consideration of processes of cultural identity in English Canada. While it would be wrong to imply that English Canadian identity is 'unformed' or 'lacking in substance' (which in this context is to say 'reality'), it is clear that this identity is not *easily* or *transparently* recognizable. It is curiously a reality of absences and silences. If music acts powerfully and with persuasion in English Canada (and there is no reason to think that it does not), then processes of identity through music become that much more transparent.

AUTHENTICITY, COMMERCIALISM AND MEANING IN MUSIC

There are two reasons why the development of cultural studies has been little affected by cultural theoretical analyses of music. Firstly, little cultural theoretical work in music is concerned with music's sounds. Although, as Grenier correctly observes, the term 'music' displays a 'highly polysemic nature' and 'encompasses distinct notions' (Grenier 1990: 28), its various discursive constitutions have one thing in common: music is in one way or another taken to be involved with sounds through processes that go beyond sound's involvement in language. Music's involvement with sounds has meant that cultural theoretical treatments of sounds in music have come overwhelmingly from musicologists with a background in cultural theory (for example, McClary 1990; Middleton 1990; Shepherd 1991a). Only recently have there been signs that a concern with sounds might characterize work on music which is more symptomatic of the mainstream of cultural studies (Grossberg 1991). If the study of music is to make a distinctive contribution to the further development of cultural studies, then 'the emergence of a set of problematics . . . which subsume[s] the concerns both of critically minded musicologists and ethnomusicologists, and . . . musically interested cultural theorists' (Shepherd 1991b: 260) is crucial. In this dialogue, the contribution of ethnomusicologists *is* important. While, in considering the social and cultural nature of music, the tension between questions of text and context has been 'more inescapably and sharply focussed [in popular music studies] than it has been in musicology or ethnomusicology' (Shepherd 1991c: 102), it is nonetheless the case that 'some of the most interesting work on the subject of music as a signifying practice within human communities has come from ethno-musicologists' (Shepherd 1991c: 111).

Second, a majority of cultural theoretical writings on popular music have been stamped indelibly with the hallmark of British subcultural theory and the concept of the structural homology (for a critique of this concept, see Middleton 1990: 127–69 – note, however, Middleton's statement that 'I would like to hang on to the notion of homology in a qualified sense. For it seems likely that some signifying structures are more *easily* articulated to the interests of one group than are some others; similarly, that they are more easily articulated to the interests of one group than to those of another' [p. 10]). Within this tradition there was a feeling, as Frith has put it, that 'good music is the authentic expression of something – a person, an idea, a feeling, a shared experience, a *Zeitgeist*'. Bad music, on the other hand, 'is inauthentic – it expresses nothing' (Frith 1987a: 136). Conse-quently, 'different groups possess different sorts of cultural capital, share different cultural expectations and so make music differently – pop tastes are shown to correlate with class cultures and subcultures; musical styles are linked to specific age groups; we take for granted the connections of ethnicity and sound'. This, concludes Frith, 'is the sociological common sense of rock criticism' (Frith 1987a: 134–5). Although, unlike high culture accounts of music, this 'sociological common sense of rock criticism' allows for the social grounding of musical meaning, it nonetheless buys into important aspects of high culture dis-courses. Good music is authentic and exists independently of the forces of commercialism. In encountering the forces of commer-cialism, good music is drained of its meanings and becomes inauthentic and bad. The villain of the piece is the transnational 'music industry'. Discourses constructed around the opposed notions of authenticity and commercialism have posed a con-siderable problem in understanding musical signification. Since modern times, the production of virtually all music has been mediated in one way or another by the forces of commercialism. In this connection, Frith's comment on the autobiography of John Culshaw, for many years head of the classical division at Decca Records, is instructive. Culshaw, writes Frith, 'takes for granted that classical music records are produced commercially. The tension between judgements of commercial value and judge-ments of musical value are ever present in his decisions' (Frith

1990: 92). Music, then, is not something that exists initially outside commercial forces – it is not something on which commercial forces operate. It is, as Frith argues, something which in recent history has itself been inalienably commercial in nature. 'The industrialization of music', observes Frith, 'cannot be understood as something that happens to music, but describes a process in which music is made – the process, that is, which fuses (and confuses) capital, technical and musical arguments' (Frith 1987b: 54).

If critical musicology (and ethnomusicology) is to maintain a dialogue with the cultural theory that informs it (and thus be more than just the recipient of a monologue), it needs to make two advances. Firstly, it needs to theorize more fully than it has done the relations between the sounds of music and the forms of awareness that are in some way constructed in relation to those sounds. However, in order to do this, it needs to be critical of and hold at a distance the contradictory discourses of the classical, the folk and the popular that have circumscribed so much cultural theoretical work on music. In analysing the substance and workings of these discourses Frith has observed that a 'comparative sociology would reveal far less clear distinction between these worlds than their discursive values imply' (Frith 1990: 101). Although contradictory (both internally and in their mutual relations), all these discourses have nonetheless understood meanings in music to be in some way immanent, fixed in music's sounds. Discourses of the classical understand music's meanings to be autonomous, explicable by reference to nothing other than music's sounds (see Leppert and McClary 1987 and Wolff 1987). The culturalist implications of folk and popular discourses (see Middleton 1990: 127–69) can lead to the conclusion that the sounds of music are in a fixed relation to the external meanings they homologously articulate from within themselves. If the sounds change then so must the meanings. That is how music becomes inauthentic.

The problem is this. On the one hand, if the meanings of music are assumed not to be immanent in the materials of music, then the traditional semiological model of how sound in language signifies becomes very attractive (because of the arbitrary connection of the signified to the signifier). On the other hand, to apply this model to an understanding of how sound in music signifies inevitably renders music as a special, but,

176

unfortunately, inferior case of language. The nature of this choice is hinted at strongly by Frith in his discussion of musical discourses. 'What I have been trying to suggest', says Frith:

> is that arguments about the value of particular pieces of music can only be understood by reference to the discourses which give the value terms concerning their meaning. Arguments about music are less about the qualities of the music itself than about how to place it, about what it is in the music that is actually to be assessed. After all, we can only hear music as having value, whether aesthetic or any other sort of value, when we know what to listen to and how to listen for it. Our reception of music, our expectations from it, are not inherent in the music itself – which is one reason why so much musicological analysis of popular music misses the point: its object of study, the discursive text it constructs, is not the text to which anyone listens.

(Frith 1990: 96–7)

'Ordinary' listeners are not concerned about the question of the supposedly immanent meanings of music, in other words. They are concerned about what music means to them. What Frith *seems* to be suggesting is that if the meaning and value of music are not located in the materials of music themselves, then the only alternative is to locate them within the contradictory discourses through which people make sense of and assign value to music. If the nature of this assigning is so contradictory, he concludes, 'if the meaning of "good music" is so unstable how can we possibly assign it to the notes alone?' (Frith 1990: 101).

According to the traditional semiological model of how sound in language signifies, sound in music would be taken to signify in fundamentally the same way as sound in language, but with one notable difference. Sounds in music are understood to work differently from sounds in language in the sense that they do not invoke or call forth signifieds coterminous with the world of objects, events and linguistically encodable ideas as that world is understood to be structured and called forth by language: there is little disagreement, in other words, on the question of music's non-denotative effectivities. According to this traditional semiological model, sounds in music have to be understood as occasioning a ground of physiological and affective stimulation which is subsequently interpellated into the symbolic order of language. It is at this point that the sounds of music are taken to enter the social world and take on significance. Meanings in music are in this way taken to be discursively constituted, *and exclusively so.* Sounds in music are thus taken to be equally as arbitrary in their relationship to processes of signification as is sound in language, except that, to the extent that sounds in music depend upon the arbitrary signifying processes of language in order to take on meaning, they are more distanced from and not as immediately implicated in processes of meaning construction as is sound in language. Sounds in music could thus be said to float even more free in their relationship to processes of signification than does sound in language because they are not as directly burdened by the conventions of traditional associations between signifiers and signifieds. There is more of a sense, according to this understanding of signifying processes in music, in which sounds in music can take on meanings assigned to them arbitrarily than can sound in language.

The objection can at this point be raised that although sound in music can be argued in theory to be completely polysemic in its signifying potentials – capable of having all meanings because it has none – it never appears to be completely polysemic in practice. That is, people situated in specific conjunctures of social and historical forces appear to be affected only by certain ranges of structures, processes and textures in the sounds of music. Sounds, in other words, do seem to be implicated in processes of meaning construction through music. The scholars whose work has faced this conundrum most squarely are Nattiez (1975 and 1990) and Wicke (1989 and 1990). Nattiez has in one sense unpacked the notion of immanent meaning in music by applying to the analysis of music the tripartite semiological model of Jean Molino (1975 and 1978). In another, however, he has retained a *certain* notion of immanence in quite rightly refusing to allow that just any meaning can be passed through or assigned to musical materials themselves. In retaining a certain notion of immanence, Nattiez's work unfortunately retains strong resonances of traditional high culture positions on questions of meaning and value in music. A careful reading of Nattiez reveals that the notion of the *niveau neutre* is handled ambiguously – it is constructed discursively according to the context of its use. As a consequence Nattiez frequently experiences trouble in not assuming that meaning and value reside, immanently, in music's 'neutral level'. This problem occurs precisely because Nattiez is unclear on the question of the relations of music's sounds as physical phenomena to music as a cultural process. Because Wicke's work *does* make a clear distinction between sound and music in arguing that music's sounds are implicated intrinsically in the construction of music's meanings, the problem of immanence does not arise. Yet, as we shall see, Wicke is able to argue that the attachment of people to the sounds of music is grounded in something other than the purely conventional.

The particular intimacy of music's sounds and music's meanings has been noted by Frith himself in relation to the passion with which fans embrace some musics and vehemently reject others. 'The intensity of this relationship between taste and self-definition', he writes, 'seems peculiar to popular music – it is "possessable" in ways that other cultural forms . . . are not' (Frith 1987a: 144). 'Other cultural forms – painting, literature, design – can articulate and show off shared values and pride', he observes, 'but only music can make you *feel* them' (p. 140). 'We are not free', he concludes, 'to read anything we want into a song' (p. 139).

I have quoted Frith extensively, not to suggest that he is contradicting himself (I hope to show why he is not in this paper), but to establish that a leading popular music scholar who is not a musicologist has identified a problem that critical musicology needs to address. This problem revolves around the related issues of authenticity, commercialism and meaning in music. The bankrupt nature of discourses founded on the opposed notions of authenticity and commercialism can, paradoxically, be exposed graphically by examining the role of rock music in the collapse of the German Democratic Republic (Wicke and Shepherd 1993, forthcoming). In order to address the bankrupt nature of these concepts in relation to the issue of music's meanings, however, I wish to ground my discussion in the cultural and musical dynamics of English Canada, the cultural 'identity' about which I know most. English Canada is assumed not to have much of a cultural or musical identity, apart, perhaps, from the music produced during the period 1968 to 1972 (this phenomenon will be discussed later in the paper). However, English Canadians consume popular music just as voraciously and intensively as any other population whether the music is that of Canadians or other nationals. A good part of this music (whether written or performed by Canadians or other nationals) is typical of the transnational mainstream. Is it as a consequence to be assumed that the relationship between English Canadians and their preferred musics is somehow less 'authentic', less 'real' than in other geocultural locations? Is it the case that because English Canada appears to have little 'music of its own' (because it was in a subordinate relation to the United States and transnational industries from the outset) it stands as a particularly stark example of what happens to the world's musics when they are 'appropriated' by the transnational industries? Or is it that musical practices in English Canada, arguably as 'real' and 'authentic' as in any other part of the world, point to the need to think about the relation of music's sounds to music's meanings in ways which get round the seemingly inescapable notion that music's meanings somehow travel inevitably with music's sounds?

This paper considers the possibility that the 'music industry' is not, in fact, monolithic, determining the trajectories of musical practices and tastes in a unitary and one-dimensional fashion. It suggests instead that there are music *industries* which are always partially fractured and contradictory, opening up new spaces in their constantly shifting and conflicting formations for the practice of music at more local levels. It considers also the way in which the creation of affect and meaning through music provides opportunities – at the local level, and within the spaces opened up by the contradictory functioning of the music industries – for the construction of affects and meanings, not only in relation to local music *but also* in relation to transnational musics as disseminated and received at the local level. Finally, it points to the way in which affect and meaning in music are not simply aesthetic, textual phenomena, but are rather of an institutional order, articulating established social relations and positioning social and individual bodies within them in ways which are instrumental yet contested.

In order to argue for the greater control of affect and meaning through musical processes at the local level, it is necessary to take issue with the dominant but not exclusive museological orientation of academic music, an orientation which is indeed based on the opposed notions of the authentic and the commercial. It is

180

argued that this orientation is based on two assumptions (the authenticity of good music and the immanence in good music of meaning) which belie and hide from view the realities of musical politics. The politics of museology, of resistance as opposed to articulation, is only made possible by the existence in most societies of musics and musical traditions which speak, however complexly, and however mediated externally, to affective states and structures of meaning retaining a demonstrable specificity in relation to those societies. Despite the specificity of its political and cultural dynamics, English Canada has little such musics or musical traditions. A politics of resistance is thus difficult to construct in the case of English Canada. The case of English Canada thus helps to lay bare some of the basic dynamics of musical politics. Before moving on to this discussion, however, it is necessary to consider some major dynamics of the transnational music industries in relation to local markets, and the framework this provides for understanding the English Canadian situation in particular.

THE TRANSNATIONAL AND THE LOCAL

Recent years have witnessed a number of important changes and changing trends within the transnational music industries. First, in line with the growing globalization of capital, there has been a reduction in the number of major phonogram corporations. Second, with the advent of the video, music industry corporations have been absorbed into the corporations of the entertainment industry. Videos not only made possible the advertising and marketing of popular music through audiovisual means. They provided the principle in terms of which popular music could be inserted into the very structure of television programmes (for example, *Miami Vice*) and films (for example, *9½ Weeks* [1986] and *Ghost* [1991]), and the principle in terms of which television advertisements could in the future be structured. Many television advertisements now either copy or make explicit reference to well-known videos (the famous, or infamous, Madonna *Pepsi* advertisement provides as good an example as any of this particular trend).

Third, the increasing scope of the music and entertainment industries, while not detracting from their power and influence, has resulted in them becoming more distanced from local music

181

scenes. Their increasingly comprehensive spread over the surface of the planet has paradoxically opened up spaces for local, regional and national popular music activities. Perhaps this was what John Preston, the head of British BMG, was referring to recently when he said that the music industries guarantee cultural diversity. They guarantee it, that is, to the extent that more localized music scenes can constitute markets capable of supporting local music industries and to the extent that these industries from time to time produce music that can cross over into transnational marketplaces. Yet, despite this inevitable articulation to the practices of the transnational industries, many musicians now earn a reasonable living within these local markets and have no aspirations to a transnational career.

Fourth, and linked to this, the increasing miniaturization of recording technologies and their increasing financial accessibility has resulted in the possibility of making high quality recordings independently of recording company studios. This has given many musicians an increasing degree of control over the immediate circumstances in which music is created and recorded. And this, in turn, has resulted in the music industries becoming less concerned with controlling the actual circumstances of musical creativity, and more concerned with the management of complex copyright structures, as well as processes of promotion, marketing and distribution. The overall structure of the industries thus resembles less that of a pyramid with an apex, and more that of a centre with margins.

Fifth and finally (and within all this), while the contents and formats of the United States' cultural industries remain as pervasive and as influential as ever (witness the attempts of the USA to enter the de-regulated European radio market), the ability of the USA to remain economically superior in the transnational entertainment business is in question. It seems not unlikely that the domination of world markets by Anglo-American music will in the future decrease (Frith 1991). The recent appointment of a Frenchman (Alain Levy) as the international head of Polygram (80 per cent owned by Phillips, a corporation which originated in the Netherlands and whose headquarters are there), is perhaps symptomatic of these changes. So also is the statement made less than a year ago by the vice-president of the BMG music group, who was quick to point out that there are now 150,000,000 people living in central Europe who speak, read and write German and now have access to the global free market. European economic union in 1992 is likely to result in some significant shifts within the structures of the global entertainment industries.

What all this points to is that the 'music industry' is not a monolith with uncontested centralized control over the music consumption of the world's peoples. While undoubtedly of very great power and significance, it is at best an uneasy alliance of different institutions and sectors which are in relation to each other both vertically and horizontally, and which are frequently owned by entertainment corporations who have major interests other than that of music. These institutions and sectors frequently have interests in common, but just as frequently they also have different interests which cause them to be in tension, if not competition, with one another. The 'music industry' is therefore made up of complex and contradictory structures which are constantly shifting, not only as a result of their own internal dynamics, but also as a result of major changes in the corporate, economic and political climates around them.

Local music practices are inevitably in some kind of relation to the transnational industries. While some local music scenes (those whose markets can viably sustain a local industry) are relatively autonomous in their relations to the transnational industries, others (those most notably of the 'Third World') are not. The question of whether or not a local scene can sustain a local industry has in a significant number of cases been influenced by the prior actions of the transnational industries. In their desire constantly to create and exploit new markets in the 'First World', the transnational industries have drawn increasingly on the musics of the 'Third World' and small nations. These nations in themselves have frequently provided marginal markets in which music already profitable in the 'First World' can be 'dumped' for additional profits (Wallis and Malm 1984). Such actions militate against the possibility of the growth and maintenance of a financial and technological infrastructure sufficient to sustain a local industry whose relation to the transnational industries is relatively autonomous.

Yet, despite the overall logic of relations between the transnational industries and local scenes, it is important to remember that the internal complexities and contradictions of the industries, together with the specificities of each local scene, do render each set of relations unique at any particular point in history. Paul Rutten, for example, has constructed a typology (Rutten 1991) in which the positions of countries in relation to processes of transnational production and consumption are located in one of four categories: firstly, those of countries with a big phonogram market, a big share of local music in the turnover of that market, and a relatively important role for local sounds in transnational markets; secondly, those of countries with a big phonogram market, a big share of local music in the turnover of that market, and a relatively unimportant role for local sounds in transnational markets; thirdly, those of countries with a small phonogram market, a big share of local music in the turnover of that local market, and a relatively unimportant role for local sounds in transnational markets; and, finally, those of countries with a small phonogram market, a small share of local music in the turnover of that local market, and a relatively unimportant role for local sounds in transnational markets. Countries in the first category are the USA and the UK. Of particular interest is the fact that Brazil is to be found in the third category, while the Netherlands (the country of the author of this typology) and Canada (the country of the author of this paper) are to be found in the fourth. In the realm of the cultural industries, distinctions between 'First' and 'Third World' countries are not as easy to make as is sometimes supposed.

Typologies such as the one developed by Rutten are helpful in thinking through the logic of relationships between the transnational and the local. But as Rutten notes, they can only function as a starting point for research into 'the position of a country and its local music within the force field outlined here' in this typology (1991: 301). 'Having determined the specific situation of each country that interests us,' concludes Rutten, 'we must grasp those structural factors which shape the context within which the music industry operates' (1991: 303).

My intention in this paper is to undertake this exercise in relation to English Canada. This exercise requires first an analysis of English Canadian political culture, and then the relations of various musical practices to this culture. English Canada as opposed to French Canada differs from most 'Third World' countries in two important respects in its relationship to the transnational industries. First, it has a highly sophisticated communications and media network which might allow for a strong national cultural identity. Second, and paradoxically, its cultural and musical identity is relatively 'unformed'. In one sense, it is tenuous, fragmented and unspoken, folded within a double articulation of silence and absence (Shepherd and Giles 1989). In another, it can be spoken about as being in a complex relation to the identities of United States musical cultures (Wright 1988). Generally speaking, English Canada – itself fragmented as a market – provides a sector of the global market towards which the industries target their products. It does not, notably, provide the industries with *identifiably* Canadian 'marketable sources'. It is this absence of musical capital deriving from a 'formed' and recognizable cultural identity that helps to lay bare some of the dynamics operating between the industries and their sources and markets.

ENGLISH CANADIAN POLITICAL CULTURE

The ambivalences and paradoxes which surround the English Canadian identity (which is to say, more precisely, the hegemonic anglophone identity of Central Canada) have to be understood historically as well as structurally. The settlement of the United States in the eighteenth and nineteenth centuries involved a substantial migration westwards of diverse English-speaking and a large variety of other ethnic groups. In this move, the identity of these groups, and particularly those of the white English-language groups, became less discernible and distinct as an inevitable intermingling took place. Central and Western Canada have, by contrast, tended to be populated from the south, largely by English-speaking settlers moving further north, either in search of more land or to escape the republican and independent environment of the United States. Isolated settlements involving different ethnic groups were established and linked subsequently by the Trans-Canada railroad, a railroad funded by interests in anglophone Central Canada. This form of development established the logic of the relationship between the local and the national in much of Canada. The 'national' has tended to be a veneer – a veneer of Central Canadian anglophone economic and cultural interests – visited on the rest of the country (and particularly the west) initially as a consequence of Western Canada's claims to sovereignty *vis-à-vis* the United

States. The Canadian experience in this regard has been very different from that of the United States.

There is another way in which the development of Canada has differed significantly from that of both the United States and Britain. At no point has more than 25 per cent of Canada's population been employed in manufacturing and related industries. In a country of vast geographical proportions and a relatively small population this has meant that no identifiable set of working-class institutions and cultural activities has emerged *at the national level*. This renders the Canadian experience very different from the British, for example, which has been marked and formed at least over the last 200 years by significant class tension and opposition. The working out of these tensions and oppositions in a densely populated small island has resulted in cultural identities easily, although variously, recognized by British and non-British alike.

In Canada, on the other hand, the lack of a national working-class identity resulted in the absence, until the 1930s, of a political party with alternative, anti-bourgeois intentions. A consequence of the absence of a class-driven politics in English Canada has been that Canadian political culture has not been social democratic in nature, characterized by a corporatism through which the labour movement is customarily involved in state-level economic planning. Canadian political culture has been characterized by its unmitigatingly bourgeois character, in which the state governs the country in a distanced fashion with less reference to the lived experiences and legitimate interests of its citizens than is customary in Western Europe.

There is a sense, therefore, in which the bourgeoisie has always maintained an uncontested control in English Canada. English Canada has not experienced a challenge to the extensive bourgeois conception of authority which Habermas identified as central to the reproduction of capitalist economic relations in the nineteenth century. A traditional historical and geographic disengagement of the national interests of the state from the more local interests of its citizens has thus been reinforced by the character of the political development of English Canada. This does much to explain the well-known English Canadian respect for authority, and it is on this notion of respect for the established social and moral order that any understanding of English Canadian political culture must centre. It constitutes the ground, the substance of 'the specifically bourgeois form of hegemony that exists at the political level in English Canada' (Taylor 1987: 211). While 'Liberalism has succeeded, until recently, in persuading the mass of Canadians of an alternative agenda more conducive to the dynamic advances of a capitalist economy' (Taylor 1987: 212), it has not, in its openness towards the international capitalist order, succeeded in supplanting conservative beliefs as the actuality of an English Canadian identity. Multicultural pluralism as 'bonded' by advanced technology has, if anything, given rise to an identity founded on silence and absence.

The particular dynamics of Canadian political culture take on added significance against the shift to the right in politics which took place in Britain and the United States during the 1980s. In Britain in particular, the move to dismember the social democratic contract came as a result of the manifest failure of 'authoritarian statism' to reverse the widely felt decline of the British economy. 'Authoritarian statism' was replaced by 'authoritarian populism' as Thatcherism took unerring aim at the welfare state and state planning. Corporatism was replaced by a stress on the free market, on the responsibility of the individual, and on the need for moral and legal discipline. In both Britain and the USA, through Thatcherism and Reaganism, popular support was mobilized for the effective disenfranchising of significant sections of the population in terms of real political influence. Cultural formations increasingly became privatized as an outward gaze towards the political was replaced by an inward, narcissistic gaze towards the fulfilment of individual pleasures and desires.

English Canadian culture is likewise characterized by a postmodern quality of narcissism and consumerism. Yet, as Taylor has argued, it is largely inappropriate to conceive of this English Canadian form of privatism in hegemonic terms. Although traditional conservative beliefs have supplied the only easily recognizable substance of hegemonic processess in English Canada, they have not convincingly constituted the overarching framework within which a recognizable national identity forged of intense political debate could emerge. That overarching framework has been provided by, if anything, the open and insubstantial approaches of liberalism.

If there is an attempt to understand the traditional disaffection of Canadians with public political discourse in hegemonic terms (Chorney and Hansen 1980), then it must be through a conception which views that disaffection *not* as a forced dropping away of significant segments of the population from meaningful political intervention at the national level to concerns which are more local and private, but as a pulling away of people's gaze from the civil and family-vocational privatism of traditional nineteenth-century capitalism to a national political discourse that is lacking in easily recognizable substance. This conception, a re-working of traditional hegemonic analysis to fit the particular circumstances of a 'liberal democracy within a bourgeois social order with a longstanding conservative political culture' (Taylor 1987: 212), then comes to constitute a specifically English Canadian gloss on the dynamics of the Habermassian crisis of motivation (Habermas 1979). The Habermassian analysis is particularly apposite to Canada because there never was, at the national level, the forging of encompassing and powerful processes that crossed class lines. The dynamics of a lack of class dialectics lends paradoxical specificity to this application of Habermas' concepts: a specificity, a substance born of absence and silence.

Any application of Habermas' thought to other situations must take account of the contextualization of welfarism and de-skilling within the forging and continued articulation of the social democratic order. If Habermas' analysis has become more pertinent with the falling away of political cultures once participated in, then the privatization that ensues must be understood to carry with it residues and traces of battles won and lost, of familiar cultural terrains renegotiated so as to become increasingly indifferent to purposeful political engagement. In Canada, on the other hand, cultural life has never been able to subsume within itself the world of politics. This led Taylor to a depressing prognosis:

> . . . assumptions about 'Canada' derive . . . from the sense that this is a national culture that has not developed and may not develop its own . . . autonomous rhetoric which would be capable of holding Confederation together in changing economic and political circumstances. Many astute observers have interpreted the caution and conservatism of Canadians as a fear of the ever-present possibility of

defeat of the culturally pluralistic, politically consensual, and essentially bourgeois concept of 'Canada'. There is widespread anxiety that the building is built on sand.

(Taylor 1987: 217)

Whether or not the reading of Taylor and his 'astute observers' is well taken is open to question. Nonetheless, Taylor's words take on a prophetic quality in the context of a post-Free Trade, post-Meech and post-Oka Canada. The culturally familiar, disengaged from the politically unfamiliar and the politically absent, has come to constitute the only matrix through which the political can be structured in apprehension and hence in projection. Such a matrix has been problematic in facing the very real political issues that have confronted Canada since 1989 and 1990. As Taylor concludes: 'politics in Canada has become almost indistinguishable from consumer marketing . . . political issues . . . are almost invisible and the only important question is the appearance and technical competence of leaders and candidates' (Taylor 1987: 217). The feeling of the people is, however, another matter.

ENGLISH CANADIAN MUSICAL CULTURE

It is against this background of political culture that the dynamics of English Canadian musical culture have to be understood. Only once has a seemingly distinctive English Canadian musical culture emerged, and this during the period 1968 to 1972, when a number of folk music singer-songwriters (for example, Gordon Lightfoot, Leonard Cohen, Bruce Cockburn, Neil Young and Joni Mitchell) gained international reputations without 'losing' their national identities as Canadians.

The background to the emergence of these singer-songwriters was the clear disparity (clear, at least, to most Canadians) between the calm and orderliness of the north – the 'secure and peaceable Kingdom' – and the strife of the south. Riots in Newark and Detroit were followed in 1968 by the assassination of Robert F. Kennedy and Martin Luther King Jr. Canadians would have to wait some fourteen years before economic difficulties and a series of high profile murders, deaths and hostage takings would significantly unsettle their own sense of security (Taylor

1983). During the late 1960s and early 1970s there was therefore every reason for Canadians to celebrate smugly their sense of nationalism (officially sanctioned as a result of the centennial celebrations of 1967) by looking with distaste at the civil strife south of the border. Gordon Lightfoot's 'Black Day in July' (a song about the race riots in Detroit) was, as it were, the flip side of 'Canadian Railroad Trilogy' (a song about one of the major events in the formation of 'Canada').

Yet the relationship of the singer-songwriters to the political and cultural life of the United States was more complex than that of many fans and media commentators, and would ultimately have to be interpreted as a projection of United States' musical culture. The Canadian sense of moral and social order, of moral and social justice, became a bedrock of recognizably Canadian musical expression, not because it betrayed anything 'originally' or 'distinctively' Canadian, but because it provided, from a safe and secure distance, a critical reprise of key aspects of United States cultures that, perhaps, had been temporarily lost to view. As Robert Wright has concluded:

> For all that [these performers] disliked and feared in the United States of the turbulent 1960s, they recognised that there were many Americans who shared their estrangement. They also knew that Canada was no Utopia, that it was naive to look to life in Canada, or to any rural myth, as a panacea for the ills of the United States. These conflicting impulses produced a remarkable ambivalence in the protest music Canadians wrote: they were able to judge life in America from the vantage point of the outsider and insider simultaneously, blending toughness and sympathy in a new way that was unique to the American musical scene.
>
> (Wright 1988: 37)

'In the end', concludes Wright, 'it was the natural affinity of Canadians for the American folk tradition and their uniquely ambivalent perception of American society, not anti-Americanism, that accounted for their remarkable ascendance as heroes of the Sixties generation' (Wright 1988: 39).

The political commitment evidenced in much of the music of the 1960s and early 1970s has long since evaporated in line with the shift to the right of Thatcherite and Reaganite politics. 'Resistance' is now much more subtly articulated within the mainstream in terms of the private and individual relevance of style, not in terms of unambiguous public, political or cultural discourse. Yet to read the conformity of contemporary English Canadian consumption patterns simply as a reflection of wider trends, simply as a passive acceptance of the incursions of the transnational music industries, might be a mistake. Folded within the layers of self-referring desire and pleasure there may lurk a silence that is specifically English Canadian, a silence whose substance of frustration and repression remains largely unspoken because of the situation of created dependency responsible for the silence in the first place.

If English Canadian culture did not occupy its national space with a hegemonic order forged of the articulation and mediation of issues specifically grounded in its geographical space, then this was because that space had been otherwise occupied by outside interests. There is a certain sense in which English Canadian culture, as it has looked up from its local, conservative, nineteenth-century roots, has not easily been able to avert its gaze from the seductive glare of the United States mass media. Yet the condition of created dependency, of invaded space and transgressed boundaries, is *not* identical, even in the lived experience of the 'popular mind', with a condition manifesting an identifiable sense of cultural self-sufficiency and self-confidence. The logic of the English Canadian experience can bear a different set of relationships to mass-mediated transnational musics, even when produced by Canadians, than the experiences of those born and raised in the United States can. 'American' and Canadian experiences of the 'same' cultural symbol can, in other words, be markedly different.

It is against this possibility that Grant's (1986) arguments for the 'generic subversion' of United States rock music by Canadian rock music must be read. Although Grant does not theorize the source of this supposed subversion, and although the examples he gives are insufficiently interrogated, there are resonances that provide food for thought. Is it completely coincidental that the world's most financially successful impersonator, Rich Little, is Canadian, and if not, is this instructive for understanding the musical development of his fellow Ottawan Paul Anka away from an adoption of an imitative role to the role of an established United States Tin Pan Alley figure? Should the ironic self-presentations of Carol Pope (of Rough Trade) be read simply as another, individual instance of related presentations widely perceptible within the transnational music industry, or should they be read as revealing something specifically Canadian to those able to crack the code?

Within this possibility of a double articulation of silence, these questions are not easy to answer. Indeed, it is the central thesis of this paper that they should not be. The history of popular and mass culture yields many examples of social groups attempting to protect their cultural space by throwing up barriers around them – barriers which are not recognized for what they are by the dominant culture. When blacks, after Emancipation, engaged in minstrelsy, a double layer of protection was involved. The black behaviour, imitated and savagely commented on by the whites who blacked up their faces and performed for white audiences, was itself a parody of what the blacks saw as the pretentious and 'high falutin' manners of their white masters. The whites seldom recognized this. When blacks imitated whites to make money out of them, cultural and existential survival was again guaranteed by a level of parody unrecognized by whites. The vacuous stylistic renegotiations of working-class British punk culture of the late 1970s were not recognized for what they were by the dominant culture – a portrayal of the emptiness of a culture without hope of employment – 'no future'. The culture was written off in the media either as unnatural, completely 'beyond the pale', or as natural, simply the kids next door going through yet another 'stage'. The English Canadian situation is, however, more difficult to identify, theorize and understand. With both blacks and punks there was a previously recognizable culture to draw on, respectively of Africa and of British bourgeois life. If there was a sense of betrayal, then there was the spectacle of a culture against which, in different ways, it was possible to take stock of that betrayal. In English Canada, there is little such history. The yardstick has never existed against which betrayal and invasion can be identified and measured.

Canada does have a music industry. It is a branch plant. As of 1989, 87 per cent of recordings manufactured in Canada were from imported master tapes. Canadian independents received only 11 per cent of the national revenues from record sales. Seventy per cent of their production has what is referred to as 'Canadian content'. Yet the concept of 'Canadian content', not being publicly recognizable in any musical or affective terms, has to rest on criteria such as citizenship and the location of performance. Since most Canadian musicians, writers and producers do not view the 49th parallel as an insurmountable barrier to musical creativity, the concept becomes problematic, questionable and even, in some cases, amusing. And since there is little recognizable musical and affective identity to draw on, protectionist measures such as the CanCon regulations and the Sound Recording Development Program effectively replace an absence of cultural capital with financial capital and orient Canadian musicians even further towards mainstream sounds (Berland 1986, 1991; Laroche 1988; Laroche and Straw 1989; Robinson *et al.* 1991; Wright 1991). More recently, free trade legislation has resulted in a number of Canadian independents folding. Protectionist measures, paradoxical and contradictory in the first place, have become 'increasingly fragile both economically and politically' (Berland 1991: 323). This contradiction and fragility has created an environment in which 'Canadian agents, producers, musicians and owners of independent labels have been angry and disturbed at the difficulty of working within their own national market' (Berland 1991: 324).

CAPITAL, POWER AND AFFECT

The English Canadian situation is instructive for an understanding of the exercise of cultural power through music because there is little recognizably indigenous musical culture around which discourses of resistance can be constructed. It is a particular cultural dynamic which is specific to the English Canadian situation, not a particular musical culture. It is for this reason, as Berland has observed, that 'in a time when controversies about local, national, and international cultural identities, movements and economies have moved to the forefront of academic discussion, Canada's situation is . . . both exemplary and anomalous'. In Canada, continues Berland, 'the cultural and economic problems accompanying nationalization–denationalization–internationalization of the media have been very visible where they are elsewhere more latent . . . and invisible where elsewhere they are more overt' (Berland 1991: 317). In this sense, English Canadian musical culture tends to be translucent in the invisibility of its identity, thus revealing more clearly the dynamics of musical power.

193

The only form of critical engagement with the processes of the transnational music industries that is possible from the situation of English Canada is one based on a politics of articulation, that is, a politics that engages in ironic subversion through the production of music or in the investment of different, altered and rewritten meanings in received musical symbols through processes of consumption. This ability – indeed, the necessity – of being able to invest established symbols and symbolic codes with ironic and subversive meanings as a basis for engaging more powerful cultural forces brings into question the two assumptions on which a politics of resistance has hitherto been founded. These assumptions were identified at the beginning of the paper.

The first assumption has to do with the distinction between 'authentic' music, which means something and is of value and 'inauthentic' music, which means nothing and is of no value. As it has been constituted and influenced through the discourses of academic music, the insistence on a culture of resistance has rested on exactly this distinction as it has been taken to exist between 'folk' or 'traditional' music on the one hand, and 'popular' music on the other. There has been a tendency to assume that before the incursions of the industrialized world the musics of 'traditional' societies existed in a state of purity and grace. Music created 'mutually' and 'organically' was taken to reflect a world of egalitarian and just social relations. Many ethnomusicologists and folklorists have seen it as their responsibility to collect and preserve these musics before they were lost to the forces of commerce. The problem with this museological approach to the politics of music is that it fails to recognize the realities of such politics. The discursive constitution of the 'folk' has, in fact, resulted in certain musical practices being removed from the context of these realities and reconstituted in an objectified and reified form, as Middleton has indicated in his succinct and biting criticism of this particular discursive formation:

> The politics of the folk centre, through all interpretative nuance, on the 'authenticity' of the music. Its value – particularly when set against other, less favoured kinds of music – is guaranteed by its provenance in a certain sort of culture with certain characteristic processes of cultural production. Thus the supposed 'purity' of folk society (or

194

in liberal accounts, of the essential processes of folk creation) goes hand in hand with the 'authenticity' of the music
. . . both are myths. Culturally they originate in the romantic critique of industrial society; politically they derive from
the bourgeoisie's attempts to make such critique comfortable, providing an ideologically functioning fantasy which
can be used to counter the threat of real workers' culture. The
judgement of 'authenticity' is always directed at the practice
of someone else. Either it removes this practice from its own
mode of existence and annexes it to the system of an
imperialist cultural morality, or it scapegoats undesirable
('inauthentic') practices and casts them beyond the pale.

(Middleton 1990: 139)

While it would certainly be wrong to reduce music to the social
and political circumstances of its creation and use, it would
equally be wrong to ignore music's politically contingent characteristics. Music is not a sanctified icon which is then affected by
social, political and economic forces. To think of music in this
way is as misleading in relation to the politics of its creation and
use in 'traditional' societies as it is in relation to its creation and
use in the modern, industrialized world. The flaw in this
argument as it relates to music's situation in the modern world,
argues Simon Frith: '. . . is the suggestion that music is the
starting point of the industrial process – the raw material over
which everyone fights – when it is, in fact, the final product'
(Frith 1987b: 54).

The presence within many societies of music which seems to
speak, however complexly, and however mediated by external
forces, to the affective identities constructed through the cultural
processes of such societies can thus serve to hide from view the
political contingencies of their music. Politically contingent
affective presence is rendered essential, objectified, taken to exist
only within the musical materials themselves, thereby constituting a *musical* essence that can only be distorted, diluted and
devalued through contact with the political contingencies
evidenced through the commercial forces of the modern world.
Within the English Canadian situation such essentialization is
difficult to achieve. Processes of political contingency are laid
bare, made visible for all to see.

The politically contingent nature of music's creation and use is characterized, therefore, by the negotiability of its meaning and significance, by the embeddedness of meaning construction through music in those kinds of process which, as Frith observes, 'fuse (and confuse) capital, technical and musical arguments' (1987b: 54). As the English Canadian situation demonstrates, music – no matter how powerful its sources, no matter how consequential the conditions of its production and dissemination – is always in play politically. Its meanings can always be renegotiated. This leads to an examination of the second assumption underpinning a politics of resistance, which is that the meaning of music is somehow immanent and therefore fixed in its technical characteristics. This assumption underwrites essentialized views of music in the sense that if music's meaning is specific to technical characteristics, fixed and immutable, then it cannot be changed, but only distorted, diluted and devalued in being subject to mass commercial processes. Meaning in music is not, however, fixed. As Wicke has argued (see Wicke 1989 and 1990), music is a social medium in sound. While music's sounds can provide a medium or matrix through which people can construct meanings, and in which they can invest them, the sounds of music do not 'contain' or 'possess' the meanings thus constructed and invested. The sounds of music are material phenomena – no more. Music – as distinct from its sounds – arises only in specific situations through the interactions of people and those sounds. However, unlike the sounds of language, the sounds of music are in themselves structured and structuring in relation to the range of meanings that can be constructed through them and invested in them. The sounds of music will admit the investment of certain ranges of meaning and resist others. In this sense, while they do not 'contain' or 'possess' meanings, the sounds of music are nonetheless implicated from the outset in their construction and investment: no sounds, no music!

As Middleton indicates, despite the problems that have been associated with it, the notion of the structural homology is worth retaining in a qualified sense. This is because there must to some degree exist a 'fit' between the structures, processes and textures of music's sounds and the range of meanings that the sounds can 'accept'. This notion of 'fit' becomes more comprehensible when it is understood that the primary appeal of music's sounds is to the body. The sounds of music empathetically and sympathetically call forth the physiologically grounded and socially mediated affective states implicated in their production (Shepherd 1991c). It is in this sense that music's sounds both structure and position bodies (social as well as individual) at the same time as they are structured and positioned by the actions of human bodies as collectively and socially mediated. While sounds and bodies do not mutually determine structures and positions, it nonetheless remains the case that there must exist a certain 'fit' or 'docking' between the two. As Middleton argues, 'actors' and 'texts' act as mutual limitations on one another within history:

> it seems likely that there are, inscribed in the musical form and in its cultural history, *limits* to the transmutation of meaning and hence to the re-construction of homologies; 'culturalist' social actors are not free to express themselves by inventing or interpreting *ab novo*, and 'structuralist' texts are not free to wander infinitely away from the cultural contexts within which their meanings have been defined. It seems likely, too, that in the relationship of form and what can provisionally be called 'experience' . . . the two must 'dock' – rather than the one completely producing the other or the conjunction being purely one of juxtaposition. The docking may be relatively loose; but the parties must meet within certain *limits of tolerance*.
>
> (Middleton 1990: 154)

While music seems to work in a significantly iconic fashion and while, therefore, the structures, textures and processes of music's technical characteristics are heavily implicated in processes of meaning construction, they do not determine them. The technical characteristics of music limit the range of meanings and affective states that can be 'passed' through them. They do not, however, originate meanings from within themselves. Music, then, is not the source of its own meaning. People acting in their collectivities are. People recognize in the structures, textures and processes of music's sonic medium a potential to invest therein their own affective states and meanings. Music as a social medium in sound is affective to the extent that it can successfully invite engagement and conversation.

These two assumptions (the 'authenticity' of good music and the 'immanence' in good music of meaning) have between them underwritten a politics of resistance. The idea that certain musics

197

are authentic to certain sets of shared experiences has been present in nearly all discursive contructions of value and power in music. The removal of 'good' music from the circumstances of its presumed authenticity has been taken to demean it, to distort and dilute its essential meanings. Therein lies the supposed power of the music industries. However, a re-theorization of music's affective power and an understanding that music's meanings are always politically contingent leads to the realization that while the sounds of music may travel quite easily, the affective states and meanings which resulted in the creation of those sounds and were the first to be invested in them do not travel quite so easily. Music does not actually 'communicate' anything. It does not 'carry' its meaning and 'give it' to participants and listeners. Affect and meaning have to be created anew in the specific social and historical circumstances of each instance of music's creation and use. This does not mean, of course, that the sounds of music can be successfully recontextualized within just any set of political contingencies. The sounds of music restrict significantly the range of affective states and meanings that can be invested in them. For that reason, the sounds of a particular musical event will always be likely to encourage the investment of certain traces and resonances. That is why it is frequently difficult for the people of one culture to 'get into' the music emanating from another, and why, in the context of the transnational industries, the sounds of music taken from other times and places are frequently 'adjusted' or changed.

Notwithstanding this invitation to invest certain traces and resonances, the sounds of music do not, however, have any privileged or authentic meanings. If the sounds of music from the 'Third World' have on many occasions become raw materials for the music industries, then this does not detract from the point made by Frith. The interpellation into industrial processes of musics taken from the 'Third World', together with the subsequent changes and recontextualizations that occur, can result only in the creation or re-creation 'anew' of music from within those processes. This music is as endemically contingent on those processes as is music 'actually' created anew. Its sounds offer up the possibility for the investment of certain states and meanings, and do not offer up the possibility for the investment of others. Since the sounds have no intrinsic meanings, music itself can have no original or authentic meanings in the sense of these meanings displaying a certain ontological priority over all others possible. The starting and finishing point for meaning and affect in music is people acting together in specific social and historical circumstances.

In a recent article, Will Straw drew an important distinction between the older notion of a musical community – which 'may be imagined as a particular population group whose composition is relatively stable . . . and whose involvement in music takes the form of an ongoing exploration of a particular musical idiom said to be rooted organically in that community' – and that of a musical scene ('the most appropriate term for designating centres of musical activity today') – which is 'that cultural space within which a range of musical practices co-exist, interacting with each other within a variety of processes of differentiation and according to widely varying trajectories of change and cross-fertilization' (Straw 1991: 373). It is probably the case that the concept of a musical scene as described by Straw has always been appropriate for 'designating centres of musical activity' in the sense that there have always been migrations of peoples and the constant mixing and cross-fertilizations of the world's sounds. There is a hint of this line of thinking in Straw's observation that cultural theorists like himself 'encountering ethnomusicological studies for the first time after an apprenticeship in the hermeneutics of suspicion may be struck by the prominence within them of notions of cultural totality or claims concerning an expressive unity of musical practices' (1991: 369).

It can, of course, be argued that notions of cultural totality and expressive unity derive from the politics of the folk. A symptomatic reading of such notions against these politics does allow, however, for a critical assessment of the notions' appropriateness in terms of the realities of migration, musical cross-fertilization and the politics involved. Such an assessment would reveal that travel and communication in previous times have been dramatically more slow and circumscribed than they now are in the global cultures of late capitalism. Processes of sedimentation had longer to concretize and establish a firm grip on the structures and margins of realities. Dislodging the consequences of this sedimentation could require considerable commitment and energy. A critical assessment would reveal also that cultures of other times and other places have placed great stress on the iconic potential of symbols, on the potential of symbols to be at one with what modern and postmodern people might take them to represent (see, for example, Shepherd 1991a: 19–35).

Processes of signification in music are instructive for gaining an insight into the indissoluble tightness of relationship between a symbol and its 'referent' that operates within this principle of this iconicity. Words in such cultures can only exist if their 'referents' exist and a 'referent' can only exist if its word exists. Equally, words are powerful over and above the 'meaning' that modern and postmodern people might invest in them or distill from them. They are powerful in their very materiality and can affect people's lives in a direct and concrete manner. In such cultures the manipulation of symbols is thus of very great consequence because the manipulation of a symbol's materiality represents a direct and concrete manipulation of the world. To remove a symbol from the circumstances of its creation and continued use can therefore be to remove a part of the culture. Thus, although a 'hermeneutics of suspicion' is necessary and welcome in revealing and unseating the politics of the folk, certain elements characteristic of the notion of a musical community may nonetheless remain of use in theorizing processes of sedimentation and iconicity within the more pliable and multidimensional notion of the scene, allowing as it does for the more sophisticated theorization of the circulation of people and music.

Notions of sedimentation and iconicity square nicely – perhaps too nicely – with a politics of resistance. However, the global terrain on which the politics of music is currently played out is both modern and postmodern. Modernity not only permitted but was, indeed, built on the conscious dichotomy of form and meaning (and later, 'signifier' and 'signified'). That is why the modern world has had such difficulty in grasping conceptually the power of music (Shepherd 1991a: 9–74), and has been so careful in music's discursive management. Postmodernity, if we are to believe many of its analysts, has 'drained' symbols of their meaning. Depending on the line of analysis, such draining is either empowering, allowing consumers almost complete latitude in the assignation of meaning, or nihilistic, creating panic and hysteria in the overheated search for meaning in a sea of momentary fragmentations. The reality, however, is that it is more difficult to invest heavily, even

200

iconically, in cultural symbols when they are circulated with the contemporary speed and effectiveness that they are, and when their exposure can only be momentary and fragmentary in the context of the competing clamour of numerous other symbols. In addition, symbols which compete successfully in transnational marketplaces have to be both inviting of investment but also open in the considerable range of investments that they can accommodate. This means neither that they approach 'meaninglessness', nor that they invoke only the lowest common denominator in homogenizing processes of taste formation within the markets in which they operate. It means that they must be complexly and sophisticatedly structured to a degree that allows investment from a wide range of subject positions symptomatic of complex permutations and combinations of numerous social variables. Meaning has to be invited, not 'prescribed'. This, essentially, was the achievement of the Michael Jackson *Thriller* album, which sold approximately 40,000,000 copies worldwide. This achievement means, however, that 'meaning' may not be as evident as it seems to be in some other musical traditions, where sounds may be structured in a less open fashion.

Since local music scenes are inevitably in some kind of relation to the transnational industries, they must to a degree operate in a world of fast circulating cultural commodities whose manner of production and distribution emphasizes, if not exaggerates, the way in which all symbols (including music) ultimately signify: through the investment in them of meanings and affective states arrived at subjectively through the social interaction of individual people. This is not to say that principles of iconicity should not continue to obtain and operate in those cultures for which they have meaning. However, cultures such as these exist fully within the modern and postmodern worlds, on occasion with considerable measures of political and economic success. These cultures also know fully about the modern split between symbol and meaning and about postmodern 'meaninglessness', if through no other route than their dealings with white politicians.

Every local music scene can therefore realize that the presence of their sounds in the matrices of transnational production and consumption does not mean that their characteristic meanings and affective states are likewise there, although certain traces and resonances may, indeed, be in the process of being renegotiated. It is necessary to evade the politics of resistance and the way in which these politics may have gained support and strength, first, from the presence in certain cultures of musics and musical traditions which speak to affective states and structures of meaning retaining a demonstrable specificity in relation to those cultures, and second, from musics and musical traditions displaying significant degrees of sedimentation and iconicity. Such evasion is guaranteed through the examination of analysis of musical practices in situations such as that of English Canada.

Meaning and affect cannot help but always remain negotiable, even under circumstances as stark as of those of English Canada. Whatever their political and economic circumstances, it is in principle possible for people to retain control over the affects and meanings they invest in music. This is the case whether music is produced and consumed within a local scene or whether it is produced transnationally and distributed and received within a local scene. The capacity to exercise this control rests in no small measure on the realization that the ability to invest affect and meaning is, indeed, an inalienable attribute of human and social existence. *The capacity is diminished only to the extent that people are persuaded to misrecognize in music an ability to originate and determine its own meanings.* In this sense, discourses of resistance and authenticity have hardly been helpful.

The crucial questions that remain, of course, are those of political economy. No matter how much control is exercised over the investment of meanings and affective states in music of whatever origin, the hard fact remains that building up a local scene, a local market and a local industry can be extremely difficult, if not impossible, in the face of the enormous power of the transnational industries to promote, market and distribute their music. Nonetheless, it is wrong to reduce questions of affect in music to those of political ecnonomy. Musicians who leave a local scene and make their music available transnationally do not necessarily serve their music in terms of the mass dissemination of the culturally mediated affective states it articulated within that scene. For reasons already argued, things are likely to change, not only in terms of structures, textures and processes of sound, not only in terms of the affective states and meanings invested in those sounds, but also in the subjective constitution of the individuals who make this particular move. That is why it is always so difficult to go back. It is not only a question of money. It is frequently also a question of cultural and subjective identity. There is something to be learnt, perhaps, from musicians who restrict their careers and recording activities to a local scene.

If local musicians wish to have their music recorded in order to disseminate it further – and there is no local industry – then the benefits of going elsewhere may be severely circumscribed from the point of view of making the music 'more extensively available', particularly if there are no significant copyright agreements capable of being enforced which would create the possibility of capital returning to a local scene. It seems more likely that local industries are built successfully by keeping the recording local and then negotiating in a legally enforceable manner with transnational companies. While it has to be admitted that this is not always a possible or realistic strategy, it has also to be accepted that markets are ultimately underwritten, not by economic capital, but by cultural and affective capital. No one can be made to buy a record if they do not want to, which is why the history of the transnational industries is littered with examples of music heavily promoted that essentially failed, and music slightly promoted that succeeded spectacularly. Thankfully, cultural capital is more inalienable than economic capital. That is the basis of value and power in music, and, whatever difficulties may in practice exist, it has to be recognized that it is also the basis of value and power in local music scenes. As the English Canadian situation demonstrates, the starting point for the exercise of this power cannot be a politics of resistance. It has to be a politics of articulation and rearticulation. As Straw notes, 'basing a politics of local or Canadian music on the search for musical forms whose relationship to musical communities is that of a long-term and evolving expressivity will lead us to overlook ways in which the making and remaking of alliances between communities are the crucial processes within popular music' (Straw 1991: 370). Music will always change – whatever the political economic circumstances of its production and consumption – and no music, in and of itself, is ever more privileged or authentic than any other.

NOTE

1 Certain parts of this paper have previously appeared in Shepherd
(1991b) and Shepherd and Giles (1989). I am grateful to Routledge, the
editors of *Australian–Canadian Studies*, and Jennifer Giles for permission to use this material here.

REFERENCES

Berland, J. (1986) 'Regulating diversity: radio music, audiences, and the
regulatory double bind', *IASPM-Canada Working Papers*, Ottawa:
IASPM-Canada.
—— (1991) 'Free Trade and Canadian music: level playing field or
scorched earth', in W. Straw and J. Shepherd (eds) *The Music Industry
in a Changing World*, special issue of *Cultural Studies* 5, 3: 317–25.
Chorney, H. and Hansen, P. (1980) 'The falling rate of legitimation: the
problem of the capitalist state in Canada', *Studies in Political
Economy* 4: 65–98.
Frith, S. (1987a) 'Towards an aesthetic of popular music', in R. Leppert
and S. McClary (eds) *Music and Society: The Politics of Composition,
Performance and Reception*, Cambridge: Cambridge University Press.
—— (1987b) 'The industrialization of music', in J. Lull (ed.) *Popular
Music and Communication*, Newbury Park: Sage.
—— (1990) 'What is good music', in J. Shepherd (ed.) *Alternative
Musicologies/Les Musicologies Alternatives*, special issue of the
Canadian University Music Review 10, 2: 92–102.
—— (1991) 'Anglo-America and its discontents', in W. Straw and J.
Shepherd (eds) *The Music Industry in a Changing World*, special
issue of *Cultural Studies* 5, 3: 263–9.
Grant, B. (1986) ' "Across the great divide": imitation and inflection in
Canadian rock music', *Journal of Canadian Studies* 21, 1: 116–27.
Grenier, L. (1990) 'The construction of music as a social phenomenon:
implications for deconstruction', in John Shepherd (ed.) *Alternative
Musicologies/Les Musicologies Alternatives*, special issue of the
Canadian University Music Review 10, 2: 27–47.
Grossberg, L. (1991) 'Rock, territorialization and power', in W. Straw
and J. Shepherd (eds) *The Music Industry in a Changing World*,
special issue of *Cultural Studies* 5, 3: 358–67.
Habermas, Jürgen (1979) *Communication and the Evolution of Society*,
Boston: Beacon Press.
Laroche, K. (1988) 'The sound recording development program: making
music to maintain hegemony', MA Thesis, Institute of Canadian
Studies, Carleton University, Ottawa, Canada.
Laroche, K. and Straw, W. (1989) 'Radio and sound recording policy in
Canada', *Australian–Canadian Studies* 7, 1–2: 163–6.
Leppert, R. and McClary, S. (1987) 'Introduction', in R. Leppert and S.
McClary (eds) *Music and Society: The Politics of Composition,
Performance and Reception*, Cambridge: Cambridge University Press.

McClary, S. (1990) 'Towards a feminist critique of music', in J. Shepherd (ed.) *Alternative Musicologies/Les Musicologies Alternatives*, special issue of the *Canadian University Music Review* 10, 2: 9-18.

Middleton, R. (1990) *Studying Popular Music*, Milton Keynes: Open University Press.

Molino, J. (1975) 'Faits musical et sémiologie de la musique', *Musique en jeu* 17: 37-62.

—— (1978) 'Sur la situation du symbolique', *L'Arc* 72: 20-5; 31.

Nattiez, Jean-Jacques (1975) *Fondements d'une sémiologie de la musique* Paris: Union générale d'éditions.

Nattiez, Jean-Jacques (1990) *Music and Discourse: Towards a Semiology of Music*, trans. C. Abbate, Princeton: Princeton University Press.

Robinson, D., Buck, E., Cuthbert, M. and the International Communication and Youth Consortium (1991) *Music at the Margins: Popular Music and Global Cultural Diversity*, Newbury Park: Sage.

Rutten, P. (1991) 'Local popular music on the national and international markets', in W. Straw and J. Shepherd (eds) *The Music Industry in a Changing World*, special issue of *Cultural Studies* 5, 3: 294-305.

Shepherd, J. (1991a) *Music as Social Text*, Cambridge: Polity Press.

—— (1991b) 'Introduction', in W. Straw and J. Shepherd (eds) *The Music Industry in a Changing World*, special issue of *Cultural Studies* 5, 3: 251-61.

—— (1991c) 'Music and the last intellectuals', *Journal of Aesthetic Education* 25, 3: 95-114.

Shepherd, J. and Giles, J. (1989) 'The politics of silence: problematics for the analysis of English Canadian musical culture', *Australian-Canadian Studies* 7, 1-2: 113-25.

Straw, W. (1991) 'Systems of articulation, logics of change: communities and scenes in popular music', in W. Straw and J. Shepherd (eds) *The Music Industry in a Changing World*, special issue of *Cultural Studies* 5, 3: 368-88.

Taylor, I. (1983) *Crime, Capitalism and Community*, Toronto: Butterworths.

—— (1987) 'Theorizing the crisis in Canada', in R. S. Ratner and J. L. McMullan (eds) *State Control: Criminal Justice Politics in Canada*, Vancouver: University of British Columbia Press: 198-224.

Wallis, R. and Malm K. (1984) *Big Sounds from Small Peoples*, New York: Pendragon.

Wicke, P. (1989) 'Rockmusik-Dimensionen Eines Massenmediums' *Weimar Beträge* 35, 6: 885-906.

—— (1990) 'Rock Music: Dimensions of a Mass Medium – Meaning Production through Popular Music', in John Shepherd (ed.), *Alternative Musicologies/Les Musicologies Alternatives*, special issue of the *Canadian University Music Review* 10, 2: 137-56.

Wicke, P. and Shepherd, J. (1993, forthcoming) ' "The cabaret is dead": rock culture as state enterprise – the political organization of rock in East Germany', in T. Bennett, S. Frith, L. Grossberg, J. Shepherd and G. Turner (eds) *Rock 'n' Roll: Politics, Policies, Institutions*, London: Routledge.

Wolff, J. (1987) 'The ideology of autonomous art', in R. Leppert and S. McClary (eds) *Music and Society: The Politics of Composition, Performance and Reception*, Cambridge: Cambridge University Press.

Wright, R. (1988) ' "Dream, comfort, memory, despair": Canadian popular musicians and the dilemma of nationalism, 1968-1972', *Journal of Canadian Studies* 22, 4: 27-43.

—— (1991) ' "Gimme Shelter": observations on cultural protectionism and the recording industry in Canada', in W. Straw and John Shepherd (eds) *The Music Industry in a Changing World*, special issue of *Cultural Studies* 5, 3: 306-16.

8

WEATHERING THE NORTH

Climate, colonialism, and the mediated body[1]

Jody Berland

A farmer one cold morning in winter went to his back door
to holler for his pigs. It was so cold out that as he yelled his
words froze in the air. His pigs didn't come home until his
words thawed out in spring – then the pigs heard it.

(Halpert 1976: 183)

A body becomes a useful force only if it is both a productive
body and a subjected body.

(Horne 1986: 82)

WEATHER AND IMPERIALISM: THE NORTHERN DILEMMA

From a Canadian perspective, one can hardly say that the
weather is getting worse. A worsening of weather would be
constituted by a more intense polarization of seasonal extremes,
the summers growing hotter, and the winters colder, which
would very quickly become unbearable. But the greenhouse effect
should provide us Canadians with singular relief, at least in
winter, and at an experiential level, if not in terms of responsible
political cognition. Scientists predict that the average annual
temperature will rise nearly five degrees in the coming decades,
which is almost as much as our present global average temperature has increased since the last Ice Age. The increase will be
greater in the north, where our winters will grow shorter, and
growing seasons longer. It is pleasant to think about warmer
weather, but unpleasant to think about droughts: dry earth,
dying animals, dwarfish plants, and other agricultural disasters.

This imminent development obviously carries important implications for the collective experience of national culture north of the 49th Parallel.

Weather is the condition that mediates between ourselves, which is to say our bodies, and the vast landscape that (as it is so often claimed) enfolds and defines us as a distinctive Canadian culture. In some weird and fundamental way, we *are* our weather. If we have nothing else very tangible in common, our reciprocal recognition as citizens 'North of the 49th' is naturalized annually by our shared encounter with our weather. The prospect of radical change in the weather thus challenges the very foundation of our collective material histories: in farming, politics, culture, trade, temperament, and the continental balance of power, it is our geography and weather, or in other words 'nature', which have been most often proffered as explanation for our plight. Of course this climatic mediation between us and nature is itself mediated; it is shaped by the everyday practices of our culture, by ritual, economy, technology, and systems of representation; and by the ways that these have been the subject of colonizing transformations by the economic and representational practices of European and American machineries of power. The consequently complex relationship which we have with the weather in turn modifies our daily interactions, our senses, our physiologies, as well as our meteorological conditions, and its cumulative history has produced a colonized morality of the body as well as a polluted sky.

Perhaps it goes without saying that this historical culturation, this shaping of uses and representations of the cold that is our indigenous condition, contains subtle but profound political consequences. Now that weather has been made the subject of overtly political international controversy, perhaps it is more evident that the inverted and repressed significance of Canada's weather presents a key to our past and future. Has weather not been transformed from privileged vehicle to privileged victim by 'postindustrial' and 'postnational' global imperialism? (In the southern hemisphere, where tropical heat invites more explicit connotation from the point of view of climatically moderate nations of middle Europe and middle America, the active term for this relationship has been 'civilization'.) Are we not, in Canada, in a privileged position (perhaps increasingly so, however ironic this may seem in the wake of global warming) to trace the history of intermeteorological colonization? For these reasons, coming to terms with the imperialized history and symptomology of our own weather may lead us towards better understanding of the fundamental topographical/meteorological irrationality of Canada's existence. From this reappraisal, a new post-free trade, anti-colonial, post-national collective self-consciousness, even patriotism, must surely derive.

But have the evening TV weather reports said anything about the problematic improvement of the nation's climate? Does our favourite weather person tell us: 'Good forecast for you patriots. It will be cold today'? And would it make sense if the weather person did? Will the newspaper's '50 years ago today' column remind us of an earlier golden age of arctic cold, and nudge us into stoic protest against the colonizing intrusion of greater warmth, with its accompanying discourses of pleasure and profit? Or will our comprador bourgeoisie celebrate this climatic change on behalf of its potential fiscal benefits, renegotiating agricultural subsidy and trade agreements with the increasingly impoverished United States, while reiterating familiar platitudes about the manageable price of progress in regard to anticipated problems in more arid zones of the west, and once again ignoring altogether the extra-economic ethics of the nation's destiny? The ongoing construction of temperamental discourse is worth considering. Aside from exposing the foolishness of TV weather people across North America who uncritically celebrate sun in any season, it provides a rarely commented upon illustration of the structural double bind that constitutes Canadianicity, namely, that we are bound together by something constitutionally contradictory at its very core, not just the airwaves, but the air itself, something we love to hate, and nevertheless must hate to lose: our weather. Further, the epistemological and ethical contortions precipitated by the prospect of balmier clime raises specific issues about the social rhetoric and deployment of the body, which mediate and shape our experience of weather; these issues, in my view, uniquely illuminate the historical and contemporary dynamics of Canadian culture as a site of colonization, contradiction, resistance, and fortitude.

But it is not in response to this ecologically induced atmosphere of climatic change and confusion, I would suggest, that Canadians of my acquaintance complain so much more about the weather. Nor is this sensitivity due simply to the ageing process of this same population, which no longer cheers lustily at the invigorating prospect of after school hockey or leisure skating dating in the local park. At first glance, the explanation is simple. It is television. It is not only that TV weather reports offer a simple morality play each day following the news: sun is good, cloud is bad. When was the last time you saw a prairie blizzard on prime-time TV? Of course it never snows in California, people never freeze to death in Florida, and there is never nasty slush in those nameless Ohio or New Hampshire towns that provide the obligingly archetypical setting for soap operas.

Admittedly television is full of such apparently harmless deceptions. Is one idealization the same as any other? From the present vantage point, no. That is, it is not sufficient to critique this particular mediated landscape as *unrealistic*, or purely in pictorial or representational terms, especially since our own visual fictions tend to present an equally idealized pictorial landscape to signify the specificity of our regional horizons. No one believes in realism any more anyway, and the concept has nothing to do with television. Television's effects, in other words, work through and beyond the level of visual symbols; indeed we can see that television has come to represent (its coverage of the weather being exemplary in this respect) a major disciplinary apparatus whose main effect is to supervise the movement, location, ethos, and temperamental tolerance of our physical being while 'naturalizing' this supervision as (in the context of the present subject) an act of nature. Thus we are forced to concede that our shivering intolerance of the cold reveals more than the epistemological effect of spectatorial fantasy, that this unpatriotic misery also exposes the explanatory limitations of thinking about televisual mediation in terms of representation at all, at least as representation is ordinarily conceived. For we really are colder, even if the winters are growing milder, and the result of our maladjusted bodies is an enormous, imperceptible, geological shift of our loyalties, our values, our morals, oh yes unto our very beings. That is the point I want to make about the weather.

UNDER COVER

> The foreman came out to give orders on the ranch – it was
> at the old Bar U. It was 75 degrees below zero. It was so cold,
> d'you see, that the words froze in his mouth – and so he
> broke them off and handed them around so the men could
> get their orders for the day.
>
> (Halpert 1976: 183)

If 'everyone talks about the weather, and no one does anything
about it', as Mark Twain observed a century ago (Ross 1987: 122),
this infantalizing caricature of a quaint pre-industrial folk
humour in the face of implacable destiny represents a paradox
with particular poignancy in our case, for the relationship of
Canadians to weather is very complicated and practically begs for
'clinical' analysis. Weather is a privileged facet of indigenous
experience, which is to say that Canada has never existed as a
cultural or geopolitical entity without it, or independent of its
effects. This weather forms the indifferent frame and cosmic limit
of the social in which we live. Yet weather is also, at the same
time, a site of continuous colonization of representational and
technological practice, which is to say that weather has been the
product of various cultural and disciplinary practices from the
beginning. Thus the most brazenly unruled of all the cyclical
processes of 'Nature' turns out to be shaped differently by our
different imaginations, and now haunts our material symbolic
expressions through inversion, distortion, condensation, and
absence.

Weather has contributed to the sedimentation of our culture in
a dual sense: as a prominently featured part of shared experience
in everyday life, and as part of a hierarchically mediated set of
observational and scientific discourses woven through and across
the everyday. At the intersection of these discourses, we find a
web of complexly patterned descriptions of winter, summer,
temperature, snow, rain, and drought, inside and outside, opportunity and nuisance, efficiency and disruption, tourism and
money, agrarian logic and scenic beauty: ultimately, of the
nature of human pleasure and achievement, and of Nature as an
environment for pleasure and achievement. These discourses
contain and repress the specificity of Canadian experience within
the historical context of continuous colonization: in particular,
the colonization of indigenous cultures by European settlers, and

211

that of Canadian by American culture, especially since the United States expanded its technological prowess during the Cold War to signal its growing knowledge of weather as both a global and a manipulable phenomenon (Berland 1991; Ross 1987: 119). The result of this history is that our weather is constituted by a set of rituals with conflicting expressive and instrumental functions.

How can anyone appreciate cold, or the particular physical and social architecture of a culture shaped by cold, in a colonized public domain (pre)occupied with the programmatic valorization of business and pleasure? This pleasure, it is important to note, is dependent on the overt elimination of displeasure as its complement, which teaches us that displeasure (as dominantly defined) can never be pleasurable, and also the reverse, thus instructing us continuously in an apoliticizing, narcissistic and xenophobic construct of pleasure itself. Living as we do in the shadow of the world's most powerful 'technocracy of sensuality' (Haug 1986: 45), what could an affection for our natural habitus (outside well regulated episodes of Christmas snowmen, touristic landscapes, and winter skiing) reveal other than a pale, spineless toleration for inferior conditions? How can the indomitable, unpredictable and anti-disciplinary excesses of winter precipitation be admitted into a public discourse that is so much ordered and enabled (as satellite views remind us daily) by the frame of technological mastery, without appearing to be caught in a pre-modern, pre-adult condition of perverse glee? Thus weather becomes the subject of constant, highly ritualized, usually humorous conversational exchanges in the face of looming discomfort and unjust catastrophe. Such exchanges signal a mature stance of complicit ideological hedonism and often ironic resignation (it is difficult, though not impossible, to be grace-fully hedonistic – or ironic – when one is tying up one's boots or digging out one's car) and serve as uncontroversial boundary markers for most social encounters. And yet, on the other hand, how is the rising complaint against the heavens' injustices to be admitted into a public discourse of socio-political Otherness organized (as our pre-free trade government assured us) around an anti-hedonist and even stoic collectivist morality in conscious distinction from our southern neighbours? In this context a 'realistic' depiction of wintry weather becomes a metonym for the political will for regional self-determination and social justice, as

212

in historical films about prairie life or pre-war socialism, or the current CBC television drama *Street Legal,* whose urban contemporary leftist lawyers have been shown walking Toronto streets in falling snow. This quandary between the valorization of bodily pleasure and efficient consumerism, on the one hand, and anti-American-imperialism social democratic patriotism, on the other, is a tangible if covert contradiction in the ongoing construction of Canadianicity; as a result of the increasing dispersive advantages of the former discourse, and the virtual collapse of the second in the face of consumer commodities, free trade, and an increasingly sheltered personal visual and topological range (with cable and home video), it is becoming almost impossible to survive a winter free from ritual performances of betrayal. Can we detect a symptomology of sublimated guilt?

The pathology of Canada's relationship with weather is revealed at a glance. In the 'case' of contemporary urban Canadians, we find that we are obsessed with weather. We talk about it continuously, especially when it is cold. And yet, aside from ritual grumbling, we have no evolved creative, poetic, iconographic or epistemological language for it, few cherished myths (though many symbolic condensations, like the Mounties, whose endlessly recycled iconographic signification both references and counteracts the uncivilizing, lawless powers of northern winter hinted at so decorously in the inevitable snowy backdrop), no appropriate artifices or reconstructions with which to reclaim it. One of Canada's major painters, Patterson Ewen, did produce a large and beautiful corpus of work whose weather imagery oscillates between pre- and post-technological systems of representation. But the published critical and catalogue essays addressing this work do not mention the subject of weather once. What can we make of such silences? Our weather occupies a zone of bad conscience, and in the gestures of our public appearances we would much prefer to keep quiet about it. (TV commercials for gas companies do not really count, and even if they did, an intemperate hysteria lurks behind the surface of dependable assurance which talks at you-the-driver through the snow-screened window.)

Only in comedy do we suddenly – almost as a 'return of the repressed', you might say – recognize ourselves under the whiteout of a blizzard. Trudging, half-human figures bundled in wraps, obscured backdrops, a demolished and demonic landscape,

the sound of spinning tyres, the 'snow' on the screen – this is not
grandeur, but uncontrollable absurdity. You probably know the
enraptured, guilty, relieved laugh that erupts upon seeing it
shown like this. Like in the SCTV mock-documentary production *Canadian Conspiracy*, for instance, where Canada is
signalled repetitively – appearing suddenly and violently
between palm tree'd pool side vistas of California and Florida –
by the half invisible Ottawa capital region submerged under still
falling snow. You know this is not entirely a friendly image, that
this white grotesquery has nothing to do with the white magic
that falls from the sky each November and turns us all into
children, amenable and transgressive in equal measure, waiting
for that supreme powerlessness when snow forces everything to
stop and we can stay home without rebuke. You know that your
laughter at this extreme depiction is also not entirely friendly,
though it is not clear whether it is the snow or the sarcasm that
invites your hostility. (Your attitude towards this, as towards the
snow itself, depends on what month it arrives in; we have all been
badly trained to apply concepts of justice to the sky.) This you
prefer not to know, sensing that the issue is important, and
revealing, and you do not have to know, because there is no other
moment that brings the subject into thought.

Understanding the silence which otherwise occupies Canadian
culture in the terrain of weather requires historical, psychoanalytic, semiotic, mythical, and political critique, and demands
that these be deployed within a reflexive analytic mode prepared
to recognize very complex strategies of repression, inversion, and
displacement. Who could otherwise believe that in a mythic
landscape dominated by 'Nature' such capable forces of repression could have taken our weather (and thus our fortitude) from
us? Under such circumstances it is only natural that the indigenous examination of weather (as a discourse, that is, not as a
'natural' phenomenon) threatens to be snowed under by the
heuristic arsenal.

The historical and analytic fragments that follow will help to
clarify our current condition. We begin by returning briefly to
the earliest relevant historical context, when the encounter of
European colonialists with Canadian weather first found
expression.

'AND THUS YOU SEE A STRANGE ABUNDANCE'

Journals of early explorers and missionaries who traversed the north reveal the difficulties of various aspects of their encounters with its strangeness. A Jesuit missionary named Paul le Jeune wrote of 'the great trials that must be endured' by those who 'cross over the seas, in order to seek and to instruct the Savages' (Thwaites 1959: VII, 35). In a passage entitled 'What one must suffer in wintering with the Savages', written in 1634, le Jeune describes the ordeal of navigating between the suffocating smoke and the pitiless cold, between famished dogs and disagreeable foods, compelled all the while to sleep, and drink, and walk plunged to the knees in the snow. This would not have been novel information for his correspondents, as French official circles (by this time thoroughly committed to the establishment of a New France) had already learned of both the severe cold of Canadian winters, and the superiority of Amerindian housing in surviving it (Dickason 1984: 241) and maintained a firm belief in its beneficial effects upon the health.

Perhaps in light of this, le Jeune averts the suspicion of petulance by writing of having given away the mantle off his shoulders, along with some other available comforts, under the evil and covetous gaze of 'the Sorcerer'. This powerful member of the community insisted on playing prophet, 'amusing these people by a thousand absurdities, which he invented, in my opinion, every day. I did not lose any opportunity of convincing him of their nonsense and childishness, exposing the senselessness of his superstitions.' (We do not learn what those superstitions were.) 'Now this was like tearing his soul out of his body; for, as he could no longer hunt, he acted the prophet and magician more than ever before, in order to preserve his credit, and to get the dainty pieces' (Thwaites 1959: 571). Clearly this battle was connected with the just allotment of food, but it was conducted most vigorously, if we are to believe le Jeune's account, on the terrain of language, leaving both protagonists very much exasperated.

The language of the Savages was found 'full of scarcity' on matters of piety, devotion, virtue; on theology, philosophy, mathematics, 'all words which refer to the regulation and government of a city, Province or Empire'; on justice, flowers, punishment, kings, science, and wealth (p. 21). Yet it was quite the reverse in other areas, where richness prevailed: in 'the tongue of our Savages', adjectives changed in accord with the different kinds of substantives, thus, as le Jeune complained, yielding entirely different terms for *tabiscau assini*, 'the stone is cold', *tacabisisiou nouspouagan*, 'my tobacco pipe is cold', *takhisiou khichteman*, 'this tobacco is cold' moving to larger objects *siicatchiou attimou*, 'this dog is cold' and so on: 'and thus you see a strange abundance' which both impressed and depressed the visitors in their attempts to penetrate and influence the Savages.

That Eskimos have many words for snow is a commonplace among school children, having provided all of us with an index of that quaint and child-like adaptability to which we attribute their continuing willingness to inhabit its inhospitable terrain. Yet we understand their prolific descriptive resources in the terms of an objective, functional nominalism more or less parallel to our own, rather than in terms of any fundamentally different spirit of naming. Our terms for snow have a purely quantitative and instrumental purpose, which is to prepare us for how successfully we will be able to carry out the day's business, what the sports conditions are, how far its excesses might go in immobilizing us or relieving us from our duties, in extreme situations threatening to turn us into irresponsible citizens (fun-loving, not showing up for work, unable to drive, unless we are urban cowboys driving snowploughs, and mutually caring in the streets) in its own wilful image. This instrumental and regulative approach emerged more emphatically with the appearance of broadcast weather reports, when high-tech meteorology was introduced on a mass scale as an indispensable resource for the predictive control of weather. As we will see, the weather forecaster's daily display of technical mastery was committed to the aim of protecting business from the effects of weather's more precipitous excesses. In like vein, our own public, essentially disciplinary discourse subjugates the weather by measuring its nuisance value. Therefore words like 'flurry' (do not worry), or 'storm' (cause for alarm). Our snow is either visual backdrop (welcomed only before the New Year) or functional condition; it has no independent life. Other ways of 'naming' snow represent to our culture a childish inability or refusal to subjugate weather in this manner, as though a technology of everyday life without overt mastery of the elements, or a spirit-deity without central authority over them, is no technology, or deity, at all.

216

Francois le Mercier touches on this in 1666–67 in a 'relation' entitled 'Of the false gods and some superstitious customs of the savages of that country'. Here we find one of many instances of that incomprehension with which the white colonizers gazed at their subject 'savages'. A Father Allouez cited at length by le Mercier asserts that

> These people are of gross nature, they recognize no purely spiritual divinity, believing that the Sun is a man, and the Moon his wife; that snow and ice are also a man, who goes away in the spring and comes back in the winter . . .
>
> (Thwaites 1959: L, 289)

This is a snow without separate authorship, without explicated cause, attributed neither to a technologically displayed mass of cold fronts, as we see now in the northern margins of the south, nor to the vengeance of a god playing god, as Americans do in the south, especially after Easter. This 'savage' snow is a snow that tells its own stories.

Our own contemporary narratives offer a conspicuous absence of comparable motifs. This can be attributed, at least in part, to a history of similar encounters between the native cultures and the European colonists, who could neither adopt the languages of the former nor adapt their own to the physical conditions which they encountered. Newly arrived European colonizers of the eighteenth and nineteenth centuries were for the most part unable to describe Canadian winter through the narratives within which they had already invented their presence in the wilderness: Wordsworthian romance, which offered benign landscape, natural beauty, and a luxuriously uncivilized passage of time; and cowboy frontierism, which offered heroic discovery and the occupation of uninhabited space. The encounter between this Romance and the Canadian landscape led to a condition of perceptual and representational repression, as Gaile McGregor (1985) has argued with respect to literature and painting, precipitated by the compelling urge to evoke the landscape, the space, the new natural and social milieu, without being able to confront or accept these in any indigenous terms. The new inhabitants struggled to accommodate their experiences in a language that was both inherited and imposed, a language that could neither articulate the brutality and detachment of this nature, nor celebrate the new ontology of isolation and collective dependency that shaped itself around it. In response to this crisis, McGregor suggests, colonial culture soon eliminated 'naturalistic' reference to nature altogether, and only permitted its return when the representational conventions had been properly tamed by American and European landscape painting and romantic frontier literature.

Yet in other respects, the colonists adapted to the unexpected cold 'with incredible rapidity, transforming the long four or five months of enforced semi-idleness into a season of indoor conviviality, highlighted by traditional religious and secular feasts' (Anderson 1976: 93). Like those aboriginal predecessors whose complexly structured winter/summer polarizations of domestic and social life were noted by Mauss in *Seasonal Variations of the Eskimo* (1979 [orig. 1905]), colonial society quickly found its culture marked by radical seasonal difference, with winters providing a time for collective hibernation and ritual, and summers witnessing the physical dispersion of the community across the working landscape. Among the Europeans, however, a dichotomy between preoccupation and representation made itself evident; this split would achieve fully realized form with the entry of technology into the representational field, by which time, however, such rural rituals were being superseded by the aseasonal technologies of urban life.

SNOW REMOVAL

A tourist inquiring how cold the winter was in Banff, we told him it was so cold last winter that the ice froze in the Upper Hot Springs Swimming Pool. One boy's feet went through the ice, and he got his foot scalded. – Oh, we've lots of stories like that.

(Halpert 1976: 179–80)

The first film crew travelled across Canada on the Canadian Pacific Railway in 1902. Their purpose was to make films to send abroad to encourage emigration. The crew was instructed to show

the premium that western Canada offers for home-making and independence to the man of energy, ambition and small capital; to picture the range cattle, fat and happy, roaming the foothills of the mighty Rockies; to tell the piscatorial enthusiast of cool retreats beside rushing streams where the salmon and trout lurk beneath the rock's over hanging shade . . .

(Berton 1975: 21)

The crew worked under a strict directive from the CPR 'not to take any winter scenes under any conditions' (Morris 1978: 34). Canada was already, they felt, too much thought of as a land of ice and snow. The films were premiered in London in 1903, without any white stuff. This was the first, but not the last injunction to Canadian film makers regarding the production of winterless films.

This doesn't mean that there were no films about Canada with snow in them during the early years of movie history. Quite the opposite was the case! After 1920 Hollywood produced 'Northwoods' movies by the hundreds, and they all had snow in them. 'In the eyes of the movie going public', Berton writes, 'Canada seemed to be covered by a kind of perpetual blanket of white – an unbelievably vast drift that began almost at the border and through which the Big Snow People plodded about like the denizens of Lower Slobbovia' (1975: 25–6). This was obviously a childhood civilization: a landscape in need of conquest, industry and law. Notwithstanding the thrilling and commercially successful adventures of Hollywood's top actors in this rural, log-cabin, woodsy, mythical north (the films, Berton notes, were rarely *made* in Canada, but they *connoted* Canada with pine trees, dishevelled French Canadian villains, Mounties, snow, and uninhabited virgin forests), it takes little imagination to understand why Canadian officials were anxious to counteract the uncivilized aura which had thereby attached itself to their winter, which was, we can safely surmise, uncivilized enough already.

Thus, of course, the Mounties, who fulfilled a crucial narrative function in the entry of this uncivilization into spectatorial drama. The battle for law and order can hardly be fought out in the wilderness without some appropriately iconographic representative of the law (and, conversely, of disorder). Hollywood's Mounties were as violently subjected to the symbolic as was the snow that was their inevitable backdrop, which without doubt has contributed to the humorous respect with which we retain them, in our more ironic modern iconography, in that frozen sphere.

219

Though Hollywood's love affair with the 'Northlands' faded away, the anxiety about snow in Canadian film production did not. Restrictions on later film production derived not so much from the incentive to attract emigrants – though the infamous 1947 Canadian Co-operation Project resulted in the practice of inserting small, more or less arbitrary (and presumably snowless) references to Canadian locations in American films as a means to attract tourists, a trade-off for permission to continue Hollywood's suffocating economic control of film production and distribution within Canada – as from the pressure to produce exportable films. That is the only way to make sense of production processes signalled by headlines like 'Shebib's Ordeal: Faking California in the snow' (*Globe and Mail* 18 November 1972), for instance; Shebib put ice into his actors' mouths to eliminate the steam from their breath. Here, as in subsequent cases, the difficulty posed by winter was not so much how to survive the cold as how to disguise it. The pressure to export anti-indigenous images into an already overgrown California landscape is now fully visible in the film and funding policies of the federal government, which have become more depressingly familiar than a spring freeze.

The landscape of Canadian films, as a result, grows more and more picturesque in accord with the scenic conventions of North American pastoral spectatorship and abstractly regional urban nostalgia. Anglo films, including many contemporary feminist features, tend to forefront the local topography but forfeit its fearfulness. The camera pans across the local landscape with a rough affection (perhaps the wheels bounce, or the sound drifts, but the leaves are gloriously green) that is just this side of post-Wordsworthian pastoral convention, and the seasons are never later than a September blush. What remains of the natural milieu is a technicolour panorama fit for tourists, which we become in the momentary drift of sentimental and ostensibly patriotic pleasure. An exception is Bill Forsyth's *Housekeeping* (1987), filmed in British Columbia, in which a woman's unconventional and enormously endearing inability to distinguish between domestic and natural space is depicted in the always significant context of winter snow and spring floods. But its director is Scottish, and its story is 'set' in the American northwest, so the related recalcitrance of weather and women can be depicted without evident trauma. Quebec film is a different matter, of

course; often enough, as Barrowclough notes in the films of
Lefebvre, landscape, seasons and snow have 'become characters
in themselves and determining factors in either the depiction of
character or event' (Barrowclough 1981: 17). Here snow provides
a cinematic frame in a multiple sense: it appears as the content of
opening and closing shots; as the central feature of a peculiarly
stark, black and white pictorial aesthetic; as the unyielding
framework within which space and time, character and action are
both measured and obscured. Animating this narrative motif, in
other words, once again, is the presence, the naming of snow, not
as synecdoche, as referent for some external and sensually intan-
gible physics, deity or power, but as an autonomous entity with
its own movements and laws, its own effects in the sphere of
character and collective history, its own singularly powerful
poetics.

BODY POLITICS

> Only [in the seventeenth century] when [man] relinquished
> his concept of divine consciousness did he confront the
> choice of either developing his own and accepting all the
> moral responsibilities previously dispensated by divinity, or
> of merging with inconscient nature and enjoying the
> luxurious irresponsibility of being one of its more complex
> phenomena. He resolved this problem by the simple
> expediency of choosing both; the forms of our modern
> culture are an accurate manifestation of this ambivalence.
>
> (Deren 1980: 98)

We are still waiting for that miracle which, following those other
miracles of science that brought us sound floating in space,
electricity, two- or three-dimensional images, and fluoride, will
do something about the weather. This hope is not that dissimilar
(first in inventiveness; second in structures of paradox, delusion,
and vulnerability to conquest) from the hopes which once
attached themselves to national cross country broadcasting; even
in light of the sabotage/betrayal of that enterprise, this desire has
not yet confronted its own paradoxical or regressive character,
other than through the sardonic humour that designs citywide
domes and other devices too close to reality, too far from heaven
for true salvation.

221

In the 1950s, in the climate of Cold War technological prowess previously alluded to, the new technologies of meteorological prediction were the subject of considerable journalistic enthusiasm. *Maclean's*, Canada's national news magazine, started with a gossipy article (Newman 1950) about the daily life of the weatherman. The emergent science of forecasts was headlined as a 'crystal ball for profits' in *Saturday Night*'s business column (Saltzman 1954); the writer, a popular CBC weather forecaster, points out that weather affects agriculture, logging, oil, employment, airplane travel, consumer sales, advertising, storage, pollution reduction, insurance claims and general litigation. 'The point of all this', the writer concludes, 'is that the business man, in casting about for help in the more profitable operation of his activities, should glance weatherwards . . .' (Saltzman 1954: 29–30). A *Financial Post* report (Vol. 51, 30 November 1957) on McGill's 'stormy weather group' traces its scientific adventures in searching for appropriate instrumentation for radar photography and for photographing and transmitting 'constant altitude' photographs of a 200-mile-radius circle. Broadcast, transport and military uses of such photographs are noted. 'Weather', concludes the writer, 'can cause great economic losses to many others who do not know before hand what to expect. It can be a source of great monetary gain to those who can understand and anticipate it.' By this time, and in response to publicity like this, ex-government meteorologists were making a good living selling short-term weather modification and long-range weather forecasts to businessmen.

But as current climatology texts observe, this claim remains empirically questionable: we do not control weather's interventions in the circulation of commodities through prediction (unless we are farmers), but through architecture, as our enclosure in tunnels and malls – Canada has the largest and probably the most per capita in the world – demonstrates. In addition, despite the development of increasingly masterful satellite and aerial based observational technologies, meteorology (which provides the uncontroversial public-service rationale for such technologies) has encountered definite limits in the realistic temporal range of weather forecasts; what we can see from space is not necessarily commensurate with what we can know, or especially, predict, since weather 'systems' still outwit computers. But on the basis of this predictive claim, meteorology joined medicine as 'one of the first scientific disciplines . . . to develop science-based services for the public' (Hare and Thomas 1974: 159). In this manner – via the ostensibly neutral, technologically beautified vehicle of science – weather entered the official landscape of Canadian culture. If, by the late 1950s, it was finally admissible to *show* the weather, this was because the technologies of satellite observation and weather 'system' prediction enabled a rhetoric of management to dominate the subject. Only then could weather be depicted without bringing fear or embarrassment in its wake.

Weather enters official discourse; the children come indoors. Among the Inuit, this was the first change reported as a result of the introduction of television into their community. The children do not play outside any more, they say, and people stop visiting one another.

Or move from the topological to the ontological: like weather reports shielding us from unexpected storms, television shields us from that cognitive insistence on confronting necessity which constitutes the physiological fuel – and, arguably, foundations of an aesthetic – in much frontier or emergent culture. In the metalanguage of most television, credibility is dispersed by excess, and what counts, in an increasingly explicit contract between text and viewer, is the fabulosity of performance. In this domain the only currency is pleasure, and the only pleasant land is green.

This is not vision, not exactly language, something beyond temperament, something which approaches, more fundamentally, an *ethos* of the body. The components of this ethos are decipherable in our contemporary discourses on weather. If pleasure is increasingly the matrix against which experience is assessed, weather is the condition through which we negotiate such experience against the seasonal and cultural vocabulary of a place. Each region has its jokes and prohibitions, its seasonal festivities, its home remedies, its fears and forecasts that have become proverbs over time. These form the ambivalent pleasures of memory and place, of topophilia: the pleasure of the located body. This knowledge has different referents in the city, with television, and daily forecasts, and cars, and supermarkets, and salt in the streets, with time marked by weeks rather than seasons, and the visceral pleasures of beaches and sand at the end of a plane ride.

Beyond this, however, beyond the winter wraps, the clumsy

boots at the door, the mess, the predictable aggravation and pointless suffering, and then the spring, and the unreasonable summer heat, there is something not resolvable, something that cannot be mastered or controlled by any individual male subject battling against the elements, something hinted at when we think of the winter deaths of the homeless, the stranded trains, disintegrating pavements, cancelled flights, cancelled classes, the familiar homilies with their certain knowledge that it rains on weekends and will freeze in February till forever.

In information theory, noise is anything which interferes with the intended communication; it is a rude interruption, a word in a foreign language, uninvited sound, crackle over the wires, dirt on the lens. White noise is noise without meaning, the physical fact which justifies the arbitrary categories through which sound enters culture. Good weather (like good children) is always silent. Like light, it forms the inaudible conduit for other information: the sound of birds through an open window, the sparkle of waves, the sun warming the skin, smooth morning traffic. Bad weather is weather that makes itself audible, that introduces noise to the body's interface with nature and the world, that threatens to demolish the discipline of everyday routine with no reason or need to explain. Bad weather is a transgression of silence and a threat to order. There is nothing in the world like the sound of rain. When you hear a cold wind, even on the radio, your spine tingles.

NOTE

1 An earlier version of this article was published in *Provincial Essays* No. 8: The Post-Colonial Gaze, 1989, Toronto. Thanks to Geoff Miles and Jennifer Oille-Sinclair, editors. It could not have been written without the helpful suggestions and resources offered by a number of people. Thanks to Chris Byford, Michael Dorland, Dennis Murphy, David Tomas, and many students in communication studies at Concordia University.

REFERENCES

Anderson, J. A. (1976) 'The early development of French-Canadian foodways' in E. Fowke (ed.) *Folklore of Canada*, Toronto: McClelland and Stewart.
Barrowclough, S. (1981) 'The films of Jean-Pierre Lefebvre', *Jean-Pierre Lefebvre: the Quebec Connection*, London: BFI.

Berland, J. (1991) 'Reading "weather" as culture'. Unpublished Ms.

Berton, P. (1975) *Hollywood's Canada: the Americanization of our National Image*, Toronto: McClelland and Stewart Ltd.

Deren, M. (1980) 'An anagram of ideas on art, form and film', in Theresa Hak Kyung Cha (ed.) *Cinematographic Apparatus: Selected Writings*, New York: Tanam Press.

Dickason, O. P. (1984) *The Myth of the Savage: And the Beginnings of French Colonialism in the Americas*, Edmonton: University of Alberta Press.

Halpert, H. (1976) 'Tall tales and other yarns from Calgary', in E. Fowke (ed.) *Folklore of Canada*, Toronto: McClelland and Stewart.

Hare, F. K. and Thomas, M. K. (1974) *Climate Canada*, Toronto: Wiley Publishers.

Haug, W. F. (1986) *Critique of Commodity Aesthetics: Appearance, Sexuality and Advertising in Capitalist Society*, Cambridge: Polity Press.

Horne, D. (1986) *The Public Culture: The Triumph of Industrialism*, London: Pluto Press.

McGregor, G. (1985) *The Wacousta Syndrome: Explorations in the Canadian Langscape*, Toronto: University of Toronto Press.

Mauss, M. (1979) [orig. 1905] *Seasonal Variations of the Eskimo: A Study in Social Morphology*. In collaboration with H. Beauchat, English translation, London: Routledge and Kegan Paul.

Morris, P. (1978) *Embattled Shadows: A History of Canadian Cinema 1895–1939*, Montreal: McGill-Queens University Press.

Newman, P. (1950) 'They're selling packaged weather', *Macleans* 69, January 7: 33–6.

Ross, A. (1987) 'The work of nature in the age of electronic emission', *Social Text* 18.

Saltzman, P. (1954) 'Crystal ball for profits: ask the weatherman', *Saturday Night* R. 70, October 23: 29–30.

Thwaites, R. G. (ed). (1959) *The Jesuit Relations and Allied Documents. Travels and Explorations of the Jesuit Missionaries in New France 1610–1791* Vols V, VII, VIII, L, LI, New York: Pageant Book Company.

NAME INDEX

Africa 192
Akwesasne 162
Alberta 156, 163
Alcatraz 162, 162n.5
Allen, Paula Gunn 160
Allor, Martin 21
Althusser, Louis 28, 29, 34, 42, 43, 45-7, 52, 135, 172
America 157, 159, 161, 208
American Indian Movement 162, 162n.5
American Museum of Natural History 163
Ames, Michael 156
Anka, Paul 191
Aqwash, Anna Mae 162
Arnold, Matthew 69
Arscott, C. 75n.5
'Art and Theory/Theory as Art' 100n.5
Atwood, Margaret 129, 161
Augustine, Aurelius 63, 114
Australia 6, 9, 10, 88, 101
Australian Broadcasting Tribunal 82
Australian Cultural Studies 67; Association Newsletter 67n.1

'Back to Batoche' 165
Bailey, P. 73n.4
Banff 155
Barrowclough, S. 221
Barthes, Roland 42, 110, 113-15, 123; *La Chambre claire* 113;

Roland Barthes par lui-meme 113
Baudrillard, Jean 30, 123
Begamudre, Ven 166
Benjamin, Walter 53, 59, 123
Bennett, Tony 9, 10, 13, 15, 68n.3, 76n.7, 88
Berger, John 112
Berland, Jody 11, 16, 100n.5, 193
Berton, Pierre 219
Bhabha, Homi K. 158, 164
Birmingham 2, 3, 28, 101
Birmingham group 30
BMG 182
Borderlines 101
Brazil 184
Breckenridge, C. 79n.8
Britain 2, 6, 26, 186, 187
British Columbia 156, 220
Brown, George Sr. 165

Calgary 156
California 10, 210, 214, 220
Cambodia 136
Canada 6, 9, 10, 12, 15, 16, 88, 91-5, 97-101, 128, 141, 156, 161, 164, 184, 186, 188-90, 192, 193, 208, 209, 211, 213, 218-20, 222
Canada Post 14
Canadian Broadcasting Act of 1968 94
Canadian content 192
Canadian Co-operation Project

226

NAME INDEX

Galbraith, David 98n.3
Ganyiegeh 162, 162n.6
Geertz, Clifford 157
German Democratic Republic 179
Ghost 181
Gitlin, Todd 97
Glasgow 2
Glenbow Museum 156
Goldenberg, Naomi 140
Gordon, Colin 67, 79
Grace, Helen 67, 67n.1
Gramsci, Antonio 28–30, 34, 46,
    48, 49, 56, 57, 62, 68n.2
Grant, B. 191
Grant, George 99, 129
Gray, R. 73n.4
Great Britain 10, 88, 91, 94, 101
Great Exhibition, the 70
Greenwood, Thomas 73, 74
Grenier, Line 174
Grierson, John 94
Griffin, Christine 118
Grossberg, Lawrence 3, 6, 8, 13,
    14, 21n.1, 40n.6, 57n.9, 58,
    89n.2, 105, 157, 158
Guattari, Felix 59, 130

Habermas, Jurgen 186, 188
Hall, Louis 161
Hall, Stuart 2, 21n.1, 22, 27,
    30n.5, 36, 37, 41, 43, 49n.7, 53,
    56, 57, 113, 118, 158; *et al.*,
    Policing the Crisis 48
Harper, Elijah 156, 156n.2
Hebdige, Dick 43, 57n.9, 58, 118;
    'Some sons and their fathers'
    118
Hegel, Georg Wilhelm Friedrich
    129, 130, 133
Heidegger, Martin 130, 133
Henriques, Julien *et al.* 113
Heraclitus, of Ephesus 130
Heron, Liz 115, 116, 116n.6;
    Truth, Dare or Promise 115
Highway, Tomson 5
Hill, Tom 157, 159
Hoggart, Richard 1, 21, 27, 33, 34,
    36-8, 40, 106; *The Uses of
    Literacy* 34, 37, 38

Hollywood 219, 220
Hutcheon, Linda 128

Iaccoca, Lee 113; *Iaccoca* 113
Indian act 162
'Indian Summer of 1990' 167
Innis, Harold 94, 96, 99, 129
Iroquois Confederacy 161
Italy 57

Jackson, Michael, *Thriller* 8, 201
Jardine, Alice 108
Jefferson, T. 43
Johnson, Richard 56

Kahnawake 14
Kanesatake 14, 167
Kant, Immanuel 130
Kennedy, Robert F. 189
Khmer Rouge 136
King, Martin Luther Jr. 189
Kinsella, W.P. 165, 166
Kojève, Alexandre 130, 133
Kroker, Arthur 98, 99; *The
    Canadian Journal of Political
    and Social Thought* 129n.3;
    *The Postmodern Scene:
    Excremental Culture and
    Hyper-Aesthetics* 129
Kroker, Marilouise 98
Kureishi, Hasif 5
Kyoto 129

Labrador 156
Lac du Flambeau 155, 165
Lacan, Jacques 28, 123
Laqueur, T.W. 76n.6
'Lasagna' 167
Learned Societies Conference 98
Leavis, F.R. 37, 69
Leeds 75n.5
Leicester 2
le Jeune, Paul 215, 216
le Mercier, Francois 217
Leppert, R. 176
Levy, Alain 182
Lightfoot, Gordon 189, 190;
    'Black Day in July' 190
Little, Rich 191
Liverpool 171

228

London, UK 219
Loon, Morley 159
Los Angeles 129
Lubicon Nation 156
Lurie, Nancy 164; *Mountain
Wold Woman, Sister of
Crashing Thunder: the
Autobiography of a Winnebago
Indian* 164
Lyotard, Jean-Francois 30, 123

McClary, Susan 174, 176
McGill University 94–6, 100, 222
MacGregor, A. 79n.8
McGregor, Gaile 217, 218
Maclean's 222
McLuhan, Marshall 94, 99, 129
McRobbie, Angela 13, 57n.9, 58,
118
Madonna 181
Manitoba 156, 156n.2
Manitou College 159, 159n.3
Mann, Thomas 42
Many Bears, Chief 163
Marcus, George E. 90, 157
Marcuse, Herbert 133
Marx, Karl 42, 50, 54, 60, 132, 133,
172; *Das Kapital* 54; *Grundrisse*
42; 'Notes on Method' 42
Mauss, Marcel, *Seasonal
Variations of the Eskimo* 218
Meech Lake accord 11, 156n.2,
189
Memmi, Albert 158
Métis, the 165
Miami Vice 181
Middleton, R. 174, 175, 196, 197
Miller, Nancy K. 106n.2
Mills, C. Wright 24
Milwaukee Public Museum 165
Mistassini 159
Mitchell, Joni 189
Mohawk 156, 156n.1, 159, 162,
163
Molino, Jean 178
Momaday, N. Scott 155; *The
Names* 165; *The Way to Rainy
Mountain* 165
Mona Lisa 159

Montreal 10, 14, 94, 98-100, 99n.4,
159
Morris, Meaghan 57n.9, 58,
123n.1, 142n.8
Morriseau, Norval 160
Mounties 16, 213, 219
Museum of Natural History
163n.7

National Deviancy Conferences 2
National Film Board 94
Native Friendship Centre 165
Nattiez, Jean-Jacques 178, 179
Nelson, Cary 89n.2
Nelson, Joyce, *The Perfect
Machine: Television in the
Nuclear Age* 136
Netherlands, the 182, 184
Newark 189
New Brunswick 156
New Criminology 2
New France 215
New Hampshire 210
New Left 25, 25n.3
Newman, John Henry 69
New Right 26
New Sociology of Education 2
New World Perspectives,
Montreal 129n.3
New York City 163, 163n.7
New York state 156n.1
Nietzsche, Friedrich 130, 133
9½ Weeks 181
North America 209
Nowell-Smith, Geoffrey 77
Nureyev, Rudolph 159

Oakes, Richard 162
Office for Multicultural Affairs 82
Ohio 210
Oka 11, 14, 156n.1, 167, 189
Olney, James 111
Olympic Arts Festival 156
Ontario 128, 156, 157, 160
Ontario Institute for Studies in
Education 98, 99n.4
Ottawa 9, 10, 162, 214
Oxford University Socialist

Discussion Group 25n.3

Pankhursts, the 119
Parallelogram 101
Paris Exhibition, the 75
Parkin, Frank 42
People of First Nations 157
Pepsi 181
Phillips 182
Plains Cree 163
Plato 63, 130
Polygram 182
Pope, Carol 191
Poulantzas, Nicos 34, 48
Preston, John 182
Probyn, Elspeth 13–15, 106n.2
Public 101

Quebec 14, 96, 128, 156, 156n.1,
  159n.3, 167, 220

Racket Point 162, 162n.6
Rajchman, John 132
Reagan, Ronald 7; Reaganism
  187; Reaganite 190
Regan, Donald 113
'Re-appropriating Ethnography
  in Cultural Theory' 105n.1
Ritz Carlton Hotel 159
Rivière, Joan 109n.4
Rooney, Ellen 88
Rose, Jacqueline 107
Rosebud 162, 162n.5
Ross, Andrew 25n.2, 58
Rough Trade 191
Rousseau, Jean-Jacques 130
Royal Proclamation of 1763 161
Rutten, Paul 184

Said, Edward 158
Sartre, Jean-Paul 133, 135, 135n.6,
  139
Saskatchewan 166
Saturday Night 222
SCTV, *Canadian Conspiracy* 214
'Shebib's Ordeal: Faking
  California in the snow' 220
Shepherd, John 11, 15, 174
Showalter, Elaine 106–9, 112,

116n.6
Six Nations Reserve 157
Small Legs, Nelson Jr. 162,
  162n.4
Smith, Dorothy 131n.4, 142
Smith, Paul 105–7, 112–15, 119
Smith, Sidonie 110
Social and Political Thought,
  York University 99n.4
Sound Recording Development
  Program 193
South Kensington, London 70
'The Spirit Sings: Artistic
  Traditions of Canada's First
  People' 156, 157
Spivak, Gayatri 116, 158
'Spudwrench' 167
Stanton, Domna 110
'Statement of the Government of
  Canada on Indian Policy' 162
Steedman, Carolyn 107, 115–18
Stimpson, Catherine 108
Strauss, Leo 130
Straw, Will 10, 12, 13, 199, 203
Street Legal 213

Taylor, Ian 187–9
Thatcher, Margaret 6, 7, 26;
  Thatcherism 187; Thatcherite
  190
Thompson, E.P. 1, 27, 118
Thunder, Jim 163, 163n.7
Tokyo Hilton 137, 138
Tomas, David 100n.5
Toronto 98, 99, 128, 129, 213
Trans-Canada railroad 185
Treichler, Paula 89n.2
Trent University, Peterborough,
  Ontario 98
Trigger, Bruce 156, 161, 164
Trudeau, Pierre, Prime Minister
  163
Twain, Mark 211

UK 184
USA 9, 182, 184, 187
United States 3, 6, 7, 10–12, 22, 87,
  88, 94, 96, 97, 99, 101, 162n.5,

SUBJECT INDEX

genocide 136
geography 89
'global village' 125
government 67, 71, 72, 79, 80
governmentality 67, 70, 71, 76-80
gynesis 108
gynocritique 106-12, 114, 115, 119

habitus 212
hegemony 30, 45, 56, 62, 72, 73, 90, 97, 124, 128, 134, 142, 185, 187, 188, 191
heritage 155, 158-61, 163-5
hermeneutics of suspicion 199, 200
hierarchical oppositions 125
history 1, 30, 124, 125, 128, 133, 135, 143, 155, 158, 160, 161, 164, 165, 184, 192, 197, 209, 212; 'official' 116
human presence 138, 139
humanism 28, 29, 41, 43, 45, 49, 94, 95, 111, 124, 125; anti- 28, 29, 43; literary 33, 34; marxist 28, 47; socialist 27
humanities, the 1, 87, 89, 91, 95, 96

icon 195; iconicity 197, 199-202; iconography 213, 219
ideas 140
identity 8-11, 14, 16, 22, 29, 45, 49, 49n.7, 50, 60, 82, 87, 88, 105, 155, 156, 158, 160, 163-5, 167, 171-4, 179, 185-7, 189, 193, 203; geo-cultural 9, 171, 180; identifications 24; national 82
ideology 7, 23, 28-30, 34, 41, 43-5, 47, 54, 59, 63, 72, 73, 113, 114, 134, 135, 137, 139, 142; and art 21; dominant culture 45, 48; dominant 72; interpellation 44, 113, 178; working-class 73
imperialism 134, 208; imperium 126, 128, 131, 133, 136, 137
'Indianness' 159, 160, 163
individualism 126
information theory 224

knowledge 126, 128, 132, 134, 139, 141, 212

labelling theory 43
land claims 15, 158
land rights 164
landscape 210, 212, 214, 217-21, 223; painting 218
language 171, 174, 176-8, 196; of the 'savages' 215
literary: criticism 158; selfhood 107, 110, 111; studies 36, 100; theory 21, 87
literature 71, 107, 171; discipline 90; romantic frontier 218
local 7, 12, 138-40, 158, 180, 181, 188, 193, 201-3
logos 125, 136, 137
lyrical nihilism 127

McLuhanist legacy 97
man 123-5, 127-9, 132, 143
marxism 22, 27, 28, 40, 41, 72, 95, 96, 115; non-reductionist 29
masquerade 109n.4
mastery 127
materialism 23, 27, 28, 30, 53; materialist problematic 29
methodology 36, 39
missionaries 215
modernism 124-6, 128, 134, 137; modernist 127, 128, 133, 135, 137
modernity 8, 32, 41, 48, 57, 62, 124-6, 134, 143, 200; modernization 32
morality 132, 208, 210, 212
multicultural pluralism 187
music 8, 124, 171-203; discipline 90; musical 'essence' 171, 173, 195; popular 15, 16, 98, 174, 175, 177, 179, 181, 182, 194, 203
musicology 4, 174, 176, 179; musicologists 172, 174, 179

narrative 291, 221; master 125
nationalism 95, 190; national imaginary 94; nationhood 10, 88, 90, 94, 171

234

ADU6228